AF833234

Routledge Revivals

Manchester and the Age of the Factory

Manchester and the Age of the Factory (originally published in 1988 and now with a new preface by the authors) focuses on Manchester, the world's first industrial city, and its transformation into 'Cottonopolis'. The book explores the contribution of the factory and the firm to the business structure and political economy of 'Cottonopolis'. The factory is not examined in isolation but in terms of its relation to a range of economic components. A major, and indeed, new emphasis of the work is centred on the relationship between factory and warehouse. These two components are identified as symbolic of two different systems of production, whose political economy at the nodal point of the Industrial Revolution was associated with a struggle over the merits of the mechanised factory as opposed to the manufacturing putting-out system.

To investigate the interdependence of economic components, the authors reconstruct Manchester's business structure for the years 1815 and 1825. The first reconstruction allows for the examination of the city's variegated business structure at a point midway through the classic Industrial Revolution and the ramifications of the empirical findings provide a focus of discussion in the subsequent chapters. The second reconstruction provides a comparative basis for exploring shifting business trends, identifying conflicting business interests and assessing the direct and indirect impact of the factory on the pattern of business development.

For instance, the evolving business relationship between the factory and warehouse after 1815 played a pivotal role in shaping a new political economy, examined at both local and national levels. This transformation prompted cotton firms to develop distinctive business strategies focused on managing the factory's human and physical resources.

Manchester and the Age of the Factory

The Business Structure of Cottonopolis in the Industrial Revolution

Roger Lloyd-Jones and M.J. Lewis

Routledge
Taylor & Francis Group
Routledge Revivals

First published in 1988
by Croom Helm Ltd

This edition first published in 2026 by Routledge
4 Park Square, Milton Park, Abingdon, Oxon, OX14 4RN

and by Routledge
605 Third Avenue, New York, NY 10158

Routledge is an imprint of the Taylor & Francis Group, an informa business

© 1988 Roger Lloyd-Jones and M.J. Lewis

All rights reserved. No part of this book may be reprinted or reproduced or utilised in any form or by any electronic, mechanical, or other means, now known or hereafter invented, including photocopying and recording, or in any information storage or retrieval system, without permission in writing from the publishers.

Publisher's Note
The publisher has gone to great lengths to ensure the quality of this reprint but points out that some imperfections in the original copies may be apparent.

Disclaimer
The publisher has made every effort to trace copyright holders and welcomes correspondence from those they have been unable to contact.

For Product Safety Concerns and Information please contact our EU representative GPSR@taylorandfrancis.com. Taylor & Francis Verlag GmbH, Kaufingerstraße 24, 80331 München, Germany

A Library of Congress record exists under LCCN: 87033286

ISBN: 978-1-041-16994-9 (hbk)
ISBN: 978-1-003-68740-5 (ebk)
ISBN: 978-1-041-16996-3 (pbk)

Book DOI 10.4324/9781003687405

MANCHESTER AND THE AGE OF THE FACTORY

The Business Structure of Cottonopolis in the Industrial Revolution

ROGER LLOYD-JONES and M. J. LEWIS

CROOM HELM
London • New York • Sydney

© 1988 Roger Lloyd-Jones and M. J. Lewis
Croom Helm Ltd, Provident House,
Burrell Row, Beckenham, Kent, BR3 1AT

Croom Helm Australia, 44–50 Waterloo Road,
North Ryde, 2113, New South Wales

Published in the USA by
Croom Helm
in association with Methuen, Inc.
29 West 35th Street
New York, NY 10001

British Library Cataloguing in Publication Data

Lloyd-Jones, Roger
Manchester and the age of the factory =
the business structure of Cottonopolis
in the industrial revolution.
1. Manchester (Greater Manchester)—
Industries—History—19th century
2. Manchester (Greater Manchester)—
Commerce—History—19th century
I. Title II. Lewis, M. J.
338.09427'33 HC258.M2

ISBN 0-7099-4158-7

Library of Congress Cataloging-in-Publication Data

ISBN 0-7099-4158-7

Filmset in English Times by Pat and Anne Murphy, Dorset
Printed and bound in Great Britain by
Biddles Ltd, Guildford and King's Lynn

New Preface

It is nearly 40 years since the publication of *Manchester and the Age of the Factory*, where we argued that the rise of the factory system was the central feature of the dynamic changes associated with the first industrial revolution. The essence of the book was the reconstruction of the business system of 'Cottonopolis' and the rise of Manchester as the first industrial city. Using the townships rate books cross referenced with trade directories, and aided by early database technology, our methodology raised three key issues. First, we conceptualised the factory as a 'property asset' allowing us to identify the 'shared part factory' as a characteristic of Manchester's business system. It was a system of contrast, a pyramid structure, with at the top a small number of giant cotton spinning firms, such as McConnel & Kennedy and A. & G. Murray, and at the bottom a thick layer of small firms that often part rented factory buildings. The small firms experienced a high business turnover demonstrating that the industrial revolution had winners and losers, and it was a precarious environment for new entrepreneurs to risk their capital. Few firms in 1815 survived to 1825, but high mortality rates were counterbalanced by high entry rates, demonstrating that there was no shortage of entrepreneurial endeavour in the volatile business world of early nineteenth century Manchester.

Second, to our surprise, the reconstruction showed that the most predominant business property asset in Manchester in 1815 was not the factory but the warehouse, the former symbolising the new iron, coal, and steam technology of the industrial revolution, while the latter represented the traditional craft methods of hand loom weaving in decentralised rural locations. Manchester cotton merchants operating in warehouses were engaged in the putting out system, placing factory produced cotton yarn to a rapidly growing population of weavers, and thus modern factory methods stimulated the expansion of traditional work processes, at least before the introduction of the power loom from the 1820s. The growth of hand loom weaving, typically studied as part of the phase of proto-industrialisation, may lend weight to those historians who argue that change during the industrial revolution was more gradual than revolutionary. However, in Manchester the growth of the 'modern' factory system acted in tandem with traditional sectors of production, creating a process of combined and uneven development. Think of the later development of the railways, which combined new technologies with the massive demand for horses to feed into the expanding rail network.

Third, in the book we attempted to assess what was at the time a growing consensus amongst economic historians that the dynamic changes we associate with the industrial revolution have been grossly exaggerated. To do this we explored the business relations between the factory and the warehouse, a relationship that not only had economic linkages but demonstrated a political schism between mechanised factory spinning and the traditional non-mechanised sector. This was central to understanding the political economy of 'Cottonopolis' demonstrated by the fractious debate between factory masters and cotton merchants over the virtues of free trade or protectionism. By the 1840s this debate had blossomed into a nation-wide movement for the repeal of the Corn laws, and the introduction of free trade in 1846. During the mid-Victorian decades Manchester symbolised the idea of Britain as the workshop of the world, transferring the influence of the nation well beyond its own shores.

The key aim of the book was to resurrect the dynamic changes associated with the rise of the first industrial nation. Some 40 years on we still contend that Manchester was the centre of the first industrial revolution, its growing factory system was new and dynamic and acted as a critical agent in the economic transformation not only of Lancashire but Britain itself. For those workers who lived through the industrial revolution it was indeed a period of great economic and social change that shaped their lives in ways that no one could have predicted at the time. The cotton industry exemplified the history of capitalism itself, a process of what Joseph Scumpeter called 'creative destruction': the old replacing the new in a constant wave of change. A hand loom weaver may well have looked optimistically to the future in 1820, but industrial change brought with it a more uncertain world. By the end of the decade, the predominately male workforce of weavers was redundant, replaced by a new generation of female factory power loom weavers.

When we collaborated on researching the book in the 1980s, we believed that industry would continue to provide an important role in shaping the future of the British economy. How wrong could we have been. We live today in an economy where working life is predominately shaped by the rhythms of the service economy, and industry, so vital in shaping our national history has faded into memory. Yet the story of 'Cottonopolis' is surely a historical lesson of the importance of industry to economic prosperity. The mechanised steam powered factory was the focal point of rising productivity, so crucial to raising economic growth, industrialisation raised wages and living standards – albeit with massive inequalities – and created an organised working-class movement. The factory was also the fulcrum of technological change, with all the uncertainties it created for the British people, and we may well reflect today in the face of the AI revolution, on the importance of industry to the economic future of the nation.

Contents

Tables and Figures

TABLES

FIGURES

Appendices

Preface

H. A. Simon has observed, 'People . . . find the most interests in situations that are neither completely strange nor entirely known — where there is novelty to be explored, but where similarities and progress remembered from past experience help guide the exploration'. There is much that is known about the nineteenth-century cotton industry but there is much too that remains at the level of novelty. The motivation underpinning this book is to delve into these areas which have been touched upon and which call for a more systematic treatment. The process of inquiry, accumulation and production has been a long one. Indeed for one of the authors the book has been almost two decades in the making. Needless to say a considerable intellectual debt has been accumulated. The two outstanding ones are to Dr Eric Sigsworth, who provided the initial stimulus to pursue the study of economic and business history, and Dr Michael Edwards, who instilled a long-term interest in the cotton industry and whose advice and guidance in the early years provided a major source of encouragement. A productive collaboration for a number of years with A. A. Le Roux was instrumental in focusing attention on the growth and size distribution of cotton firms and triggered a growing interest in the changing forms and patterns of business structure. A subsequent collaboration with the co-author, M. J. Lewis, whose massive labour in accumulating and collating the rateable value data was invaluable, and was the vital element in bringing the work to fruition. Both of us benefited greatly from the advice of John Kirkwood of the Department of Urban and Regional Studies at Sheffield Polytechnic who guided us through the complexities of the computer processing of our data base. Not only was much valuable time saved but a whole new series of possibilities was opened up which smoothed the way to the reconstruction of Manchester's business sytem. Our colleague in the Department of Historical and Critical Studies, Dr B. T. Bradfield, provided us with a lively insight into the politics of Lord Liverpool's governments which formed the basis of our pursuit of a political economy approach to business history. Given the large data source which provides the empirical underpinning of the book we have relied upon the assistance, advice and goodwill of numerous librarians and archivists but none more so than the staff of the archives department at Manchester Central Library. For her assistance in preparing this book for publication there is a special thanks to Pat Peck of Sheffield City Polytechnic who has typed it from its early tentative beginnings to the final draft. A grant from the Pasold Research Fund was especially welcomed and helped finance the numerous trips to Manchester and the Lancashire cotton towns. We would also like to thank Dr S. D. Chapman, the editor of *Textile History*, for his permission to reproduce a part of our article on Manchester business structure which was published in the 1986 edition of that journal. Finally, but not least, we owe a tremendous debt of gratitude to our wives who not only put up with our obsession with Manchester business structure, but provided constructive criticism and support which, in the end, made the project possible.

Dedicated to
Dominic, Belinda and Jessica

1

Introduction

The Industrial Revolution brought in the long term a vast increase in the range of products available to consumers. Factory work with its regular hours of toil, supervisory systems of control and routinised work patterns came to shape the structure of working life. Few historians would deny the cotton factory its symbolic role in the British Industrial Revolution, or Manchester its premier position as 'Cottonopolis'. As Eric Hobsbawm has claimed:

> It was not Birmingham, a city which produced a great deal more in 1780, but essentially in the old ways, which made contemporaries speak of an industrial revolution, but Manchester, a city which produced more in a more obvious revolutionary manner.[1]

Manchester, that is, tends to be directly associated with the idea of an industrial revolution based on machines, steam power and factories. Yet the business structure of the world's first industrial city has received little attention[2] and the structural aspects of the firm and business is a relatively neglected area.[3] It is not the aim of this study therefore to offer another history of the cotton industry; this has been admirably provided by writers such as Edwards,[4] Chapman[5] and Farnie.[6] Neither do we intend to explore the origins of cotton entrepreneurs as in the recent contributions by Honeyman[7] and Crouzet.[8] Rather the aim of this book is to concentrate on business structure, the components that make it up, and their changing patterns and interrelationships. Such an approach tends logically to extend the analysis beyond the study of the factory system in isolation and towards the exploration of business processes and their interconnections. Thus we contend that an understanding of Manchester's business system during a vital stage of the Industrial Revolution requires a detailed analysis of the business relationship between factory and warehouse. It will be argued that before 1820 these two business components represented quite different modes of production and followed different patterns of growth. Indeed the warehouse system may be no less important than the factory system, and the examination of its basic linkages, with other components, will go some way in answering Hartwell's[9] call for a more detailed analysis of the tertiary sector during the Industrial Revolution.

With the focus of attention on the nature and pattern of relationship between business components what is the form of approach to business history that is adopted in this work? As early as 1959 Steigerwalts set an ambitious framework for the study of business history which he defined as 'the application of historical method to the study of the development and role of the business firm in society'.[10] In part this reflects the concern of business history with the individual firm, but the reference to 'society' suggests that business history has a wider connotation 'than company history or business house history'.[11] We may wish to assess the role of the business firm in society by conceptualising it as part of a wider and interconnected business community. As Peter Mathias has claimed, 'one . . . needs to know what is happening to the wood as a whole, as well as the individual trees'.[12] The general direction of this book will be a concern for the 'wood as a whole' rather than the individual trees; although the latter will not be wholly neglected.[13] Neither should the 'wood' be necessarily equated with a specific population of firms, i.e. an industry. To continue the metaphor we are interested in conceptualising the 'wood' as a total business system and exploring the changing relationship between major clusters of 'trees'. The clusters we are primarily concerned with are the factory and the warehouse, and the total system of Manchester's overall business structure as it was evolving during a critical stage of the Industrial Revolution.[14]

Our approach is shaped by the observation of Roy Church that, 'Business history is about business in all its forms, in all its ramifications, economic, social and political'.[15] Thus we explore the proposition that the business relationship between factory and warehouse was not only economic in content but was mediated by a distinctive political economy which had profound implications for the structural coherence of Manchester's business community. The notion of political economy employed is inspired by the view of Gunner Myrdal that,

> Facts do not organise themselves into systematic knowledge, except from a point of view. This point of view amounts to a theory — theory being understood in the only meaning it can have: a logically consistent system of questions to the social reality we are studying.[16]

From the perspective of Manchester's business system the central question posed concerns the form of struggle between the factory and the warehouse over the control and management of economic resources, and the process by which this conflict was heightened in tempo in the first decade and half of the nineteenth century and then accommodated and effectively neutralised by the mid-1820s. The factory was a site for intense debate not only for middle-class radicals and representatives of labour but for business groups operating within the cotton trade itself. The factory was identified at the beginning of the new century as a threat to the very existence of the cotton trade and therefore to the stability of Manchester's overall business sytem. Amongst the most active factory protagonists were some of the most powerful Manchester capitalists of their day.[17]

To establish such a political economy of business, calling as it does for the exploration of general business processes and the form of connection between business enterprises,[18] requires a novel approach to the empirical investigation of business structure. It is only by first of all looking at the 'wood' in its overall context, by a careful and detailed reconstruction of Manchester's business system, that the variegated business structure of Cottonopolis can be adequately revealed. This allows us to locate the place of the factory (and, of course, other business components) in the city's aggregate economy,[19] and sets the minimum condition for exploring business interconnections; this exercise is conducted in Chapter 3 where the totality of Manchester's business units are reconstructed for 1815.[20] Some 17,000 property assets[21] are compiled and are designated to 12 general business categories (which, in turn are divided into 55 sub-categories). The empirical results are startling and call into question both the predominance of the factory in Manchester's business system and the town's status as the nodal point of the Industrial Revolution. The ramifications of these findings provide the focus of discussion in the subsequent chapters. The form and content of the business relationship between factory and warehouse is explored in Chapter 4. The yarn market was the point of mediation between these two components; did the factory, as existing accounts suggest, dominate this market or did warehouse firms exercise a powerful interest, shaping and controlling the course of events? This examination of the relative business power of factory and warehouse provides the basis for exploring the deep schism in the cotton trade (see Chapter 5), which is apparent in the early years of the nineteenth century. What was the basis of the conflict between factory and warehouse and why was the former conceptualised by some of the leading warehouse manufacturers as a threat to the overall stability of the cotton trade? Should the growth of the factory system be restrained, how could this be done and what form of defence did the factory masters adopt in the context of a sustained critique coming from within the trade? The hostility generated between factory and warehouse, and the consequent lack of business unity, poses interesting questions about the former's impact on the structural development of the cotton industry. Was the factory able to impose a particular pattern of growth on the warehouse, was the latter's growth largely determined by the former, and did the factory create an infrastructural system based on the warehouse which may have actually slowed down the diffusion of the power loom, at least before 1820? These questions are examined in Chapter 6, which also suggests the need to reinterpret the technological impact of the factory.

In Waterloo Manchester the dominant characteristic of business structure was the separation of interest between factory and warehouse; after 1815 we examine the extent to which the pattern of the relationship between these two components underwent change. The claim made by writers such as Roland Smith,[22] and frequently taken up in the literature, that Manchester by the 1820s was becoming more a commercial rather than a manufacturing centre is firmly rebuffed. Once again, Manchester's total business structure is reconstructed (Chapter 7), this time for 1825. A comparison with the 1815 figures shows a dramatic shift in the contribution of the factory to the overall structural pattern of Manchester's business system and provides the basis for exploring the types of business strategy pursued by factory and warehouse firms during the turbulent years following Waterloo. Did these developments change the form of relationship between factory and warehouse, is there any evidence to show a convergence between the two, and what implications would such a convergence have for the political economy of the cotton trade? These questions are taken up in Chapter 8 which examines Manchester's evolving business community during the post-Napoleonic period and outlines the growing interconnections between the various business groups. What was the broad shape of the policies the business community advocated and pursued, were these policies consistent with national issues of political economy and what was the implication of a rigid Ricardian stance with regard to trade deregulation? The rapid growth of the factory by 1825 and the growing unification of a business interest poses important questions concerning the impact of the factory for business components other than the warehouse. Did the factory play a key role in the emergence and development of the machine and chemical finishing sectors? In Chapter 9 some 760 machine, foundry, chemical, bleaching, dyeing, printing, etc., firms are examined with particular reference to the structural pattern of their growth. Is there evidence here of a Rostowian linkage effect;[23] if so, how would this relate to issues concerning the unity of interest between the factory and, for example, the strategic machine sector over vital policy matters involving the export of textile machinery? Finally, while the general approach adopted in the subsequent chapters will be to examine the interconnections between business components, and to explore both the economic content and the political economy of the overall business systems in which they operate, we will not forego the opportunity of taking a bird's eye view of the basic unit of business activity, the firm. Chapter 10 offers an approach to the study of the firm which breaks away from standard neo-classical accounts and takes up the challenge of Scott Moss's theory of business strategy.[24] Is there a discernible business strategy which cotton firms followed in the 1820s and 1830s, what implications may such a strategy have had for the management of the firm's physical and human resources and what constraints did the competitive process place on the pattern of firm growth and firm size?

In the early decades of the nineteenth century Manchester was at the very centre of the factory system; industrial capitalism's first city. Yet in the existing literature Manchester, its business structure and its role in the Industrial Revolution, remains at the level of novelty. The business visitor to Manchester could not have failed to be overawed by the giant factories of the Murray Brothers and McConnel and Kennedy, both employing over 1,000 workers each in 1815.[25] Ancoats, the main location of the factory system, seemed to be the centre, indeed the very heart of the bustling business system of Cottonopolis; but away from the smoke stacks, in Cannon Street, High Street, Market Street and the numerous courts and alleys running off these main arteries, it was business of quite a different mode. 'The factory quite rightly was the spectacle that enthralled the visitor to Manchester, those, however, who ignored a visit to the warehouse missed a good deal more than they ever suspected.'[26] In this work we intend to fill the gap in the 'visitors' knowledge. We turn first, as our visitors would have done, to an examination of the factory but explore more closely its relation to the notion of Industrial Revolution to which it is intimately tied. Prior to the detailed reconstruction of Manchester's business system Chapter 2 takes up some of the methodological issues central to the debate over the Industrial Revolution and the factory.

NOTES AND REFERENCES

1. Quoted in R. Lloyd-Jones and M. J. Lewis, 'The Economic Structure of Cottonopolis: Manchester in 1815', *Textile History*, vol. 17, no. 1 (1986).
2. For an examination of Manchester's cotton trade see R. Smith, 'Manchester as a Centre for Manufacturing and Merchanting of Cotton Goods, 1820–1830', *University of Birmingham Historical Journal*, vol. IV (1953–4).
3. For an examination of Manchester's cotton factory structure see R. Lloyd-Jones and A. A. Le Roux, 'The Size of Firms in the Cotton Industry: Manchester 1815–41', *Economic History Review*, vol. XXXIII, no. 1, (1980); and R. Lloyd-Jones and A. A. Le Roux, 'Factory Utilisation and the Firm: the Manchester Cotton Industry c1825–1840', *Textile History*, vol. 15, no. 1 (1984).
4. M. M. Edwards, *The Growth of the British Cotton Trade, 1780 to 1815* (Manchester University Press, Manchester, 1967).
5. S. D. Chapman, *The Cotton Industry in the Industrial Revolution* (Macmillan, London, 1972).
6. D. A. Farnie, *The English Cotton Industry and the World Market*

1815 to 1896 (Clarendon Press, Oxford, 1979).

7. K. Honeyman, *Origins of Enterprise: Business Leadership in the Industrial Revolution* (Manchester University Press, Manchester, 1982).

8. F. Crouzet, *The First Industrialists: The Problem of Origins* (Cambridge University Press, Cambridge, 1985).

9. R. M. Hartwell, *The Industrial Revolution and Economic Growth* (Methuen, London, 1971), p. 205. It should be also noted that the structural unevenness of factory development was not unique to cotton textiles but as Tann has pointed out reproduced itself in a number of industries. J. Tann, *The Development of the Factory* (Cornmarket Press, London, 1970), p. 5.

10. Quoted in A. M. Bourne, 'Business History and Management Education', *Business History*, vol. XXVII, no. 2 (1975), p. 21.

11. G. Holmes and H. Ruff, 'The Perils of Entrepreneurial History', *Business History*, vol. XVII, no. 2 (1975), p. 28.

12. P. Mathias, 'Business History and Management Education', *Business History*, vol. XVII, no. 2 (1975), p. 16.

13. For example, considerable use is made of the business papers of John Heywood and Sons, quilt manufacturers, of Bolton and Manchester. Also attention is focused on such firms as Owen Owens, McConnel and Kennedy, J. Massey and Co, Wm Fairbairn, all of Manchester. Chapter 10 more specifically examines the role of the individual firm, the trees of the forest, and the form of business strategy adopted by factory firms in the competitive conditions of the 1820s and 1830s.

14. The period we are concerned with is 1800 to 1825 with particular attention focused on the years between 1815 and 1825.

15. Roy A. Church, 'Business History in Britain', *Journal of European Economic History*, vol. 5 (1976), p. 218.

16. G. Myrdal, *Against the Stream: Critical Essays in Economics* (Vintage Books, New York, 1975), p. 134.

17. One of the most prominent Manchester businessman of the first decades of the nineteenth century was Nathanial Gould, a large-scale fustian manufacturer. He was a leading opponent of the factory system and his critique of the factory is explored in Chapter 5.

18. This approach is emphasised by Church. Church, 'Business History', p. 218.

19. This point we have stressed in a recent article. See Lloyd-Jones and Lewis, 'Economic Structure', p. 71.

20. 1815 is chosen for it sees the end of the Napoleonic Wars and represents an approximate half-way stage of the classic Industrial Revolution. See Lloyd-Jones and Lewis, 'Economic Structure', p. 71.

21. The notion of property asset is defined in Chapter 2 and applied to Manchester's business system in Chapter 3.

22. Smith, 'Manchester'.

23. By a Rostowian linkage effect we take to mean the impact that investment in one sector or industry has for another sector or industry. Linkages are also examined in Chapter 6.

24. Scott Moss, *An Economic Theory of Business Strategy: An Essay in Dynamics Without Equilibrium* (Martin Robinson, Oxford, 1981).

25. Lloyd-Jones and Le Roux, 'The Size of Firms', Table 1, p. 74.
26. Lloyd-Jones and Lewis, 'Economic Structure', p. 86.

2

The Factory and the Industrial Revolution

The orthodox account of the Industrial Revolution concentrates on the rise of steam power and machinery and the spread of the factory system. In a recent text-book, surveying modern British economic history, Donald McCloskey maintains that 'ingenuity governed the Industrial Revolution'.[1] Symbolic of this growth of 'ingenuity' were the great innovations associated with cotton textiles, the growth of Manchester as 'Cottonopolis' and the forging of the cotton factory with the Industrial Revolution. There is, however, a body of opinion that is more cautious about the notion of an Industrial Revolution based on rapid technological change closely related to the cotton industry. Its sophisticated expression is found in the works of Berg[2] and Samuel,[3] where it is argued that the process of technological change was rather narrow and limited and the changes in technology were not widely diffused until well after the conventional completion date of the Industrial Revolution, at mid-nineteenth century. In particular Samuel has argued that the concentration on cotton and iron has tended to foreclose on the analysis of other sectors of the economy which continued to use non-mechanised and non-factory systems of production late into the nineteenth century.[4] An explicit defence of the factory will be made in Chapter 6; here we intend to explore the relationship between the factory and the notion of an Industrial Revolution, and to spell out our general methodological approach associated with the idea of business structure.

The most sustained attack on the cotton factory, as the engine of industrial change, has been made by Michael Fores,[5] who for good measure also dismisses the notion of an Industrial

Revolution as mythical. Fores' attention is focused on manufacturing industry and the degree to which it was transformed by machine technology, but in his account the cotton industry failed to generate an Industrial Revolution; it did not produce a massive increase in manufacturing in general or advance the more widespread incidence of factory-based activity. But what actually is this Industrial Revolution the cotton factory allegedly failed to generate? There is little doubt that the idea of an Industrial Revolution is one of the central notions of modern economic history;[6] yet it is extremely difficult to pin down. The term, for example, can be used both in a specific sense, the British Industrial Revolution 1760 to 1860, and in a general sense, the Industrial Revolution as a watershed between 'traditional' and 'modern' society. Elaborating these positions, we can offer the following two propositions concerning the meaning of the Industrial Revolution:

(A) We may consider the Industrial Revolution as a series of events associated with technological change, manufacturing production, the rise and development of the factory, etc. These processes in turn are related to an acceleration in manufacturing output that has consequences for the structural basis of the economy. This approach is perhaps best defined by N. F. R. Crafts:

> The Industrial Revolution will be understood as a period of accelerated structural change in the economy, involving a rapid rise in industrial output, in the share of manufacturing in national product and in factory-based activity, based upon major technological innovations.[7]

(B) The Industrial Revolution may be viewed as a conceptual abstraction, as an analytical device which is concerned with the onset of industrialisation and with the idea of a fundamental change or discontinuity in the economic history of societies. In general terms, therefore, the term Industrial Revolution is utilised to inform the beginning of modern economic history with its emphasis upon a quantitatively and qualitatively different pattern and structure of economic growth.

Often these two conceptions will operate alongside each other[8] but there is a need to make a clear analytical distinction between them. Proposition A is an hypothesis which is open to empirical verification. It is central to those who argue over the role of technology and its diffusion in the British economy *c.* 1760–1860. Thus Samuel and Fores have made a case for questioning the revolutionary impact of changes in industry and technology, and this hypothesis will be explored in the subsequent chapters. However, proposition B is not an hypothesis, but a paradigm, and proposition A may be considered as an hypothesis generated from proposition B. Failure to recognise this distinction is at the bottom of much of the debate over the Industrial Revolution; thus Fores questions the revolutionary nature of technological change to cast doubt on the Industrial Revolution as a major discontinuity. But hypotheses constructed to test particular phenomena, associated with the British economy *c.* 1760–1860, need to be distinguished from the conception of the Industrial Revolution as a paradigm. On what grounds does proposition B constitute a paradigm? A proposition of discontinuity, of sharp breaks with previous experience, defines a range of possible hypotheses. For example, the Industrial Revolution as a discontinuity has generated Rostow's[9] Take-Off (set at the aggregate level of the economy), Gerschenkron's[10] 'Great Spurt' (at the disaggregate level) and the big push of balanced/unbalanced growth theory[11] (balanced at the aggregate level, unbalanced at the disaggregate). Furthermore, the notion of discontinuity is at the heart of recent theories of the long-wave where the works of Kondratieff and Schumpeter have been reinterpreted and advanced by Mensch, Mendel, Freeman and van Duijn.[12]

We could further multiply the hypothesis generated by the Industrial Revolution paradigm by invoking Gerschenkron's typologies of industrialisation.[13] It may be noted, too that while proposition A is a hypothesis that is historically specific, primarily related to the British case and the subsequent followers in Europe and North America, the Industrial Revolution as a paradigm allows a portfolio of modes of discontinuity which may or may not be associated with acceleration in manufacturing output. Employing the Industrial Revolution as a paradigm helps clarify other important issues. As Loasby has stated:

> Because a paradigm defines a set, often a very large set, of possible hypotheses, but makes no claims for the validity of

> any particular member of that set, it follows that paradigms, unlike the hypothesis to which they give rise, cannot be validated by experimental or statistical method.[14]

Such questions as 'Was there an Industrial Revolution?' are less than helpful and clearly as historians it is the best term we have.[15] It is the 'best term', for as a paradigm its utility rests upon its ability to produce a wide range of hypotheses which open up the possibility of explanation for a wide range of phenomena. In this work, therefore, we are not questioning the notion of an Industrial Revolution. Indeed, it is the starting point which allows us to focus upon particular questions and hypotheses.

Viewed in this way, our approach to the Industrial Revolution allows flexibility in terms of the choice and utilisation of theoretical frameworks. No apology is made here for an eclectic stance in relation to theory. Use will be made of theories where they are considered to inform the historical analysis, with the important caveat that contemporary theory tends to address itself primarily to contemporary structures.[16] Rigid application of frameworks should be avoided and account taken of the problem of applying theories to an historical context for which they may not have been designed. A range of theories and concepts will be called upon, including that of property assets, business structure and system theory, diffusion theory and business strategy. Let us begin by adopting a system perspective and explore the extent to which this may aid our understanding of business structure; the latter, of course, being a vital, if neglected, element of the British Industrial Revolution.

A SYSTEM APPROACH

The adoption of a system approach is based on the apparently obvious premise that economic systems are interdependent. As McCulloch observed during the early phase of industrialisation: 'Like the different parts of a well-constructed machine, the inhabitants of a civilised country are all mutually dependent on and connected with each other'.[17] More specifically, a structuralist perspective, with its focus upon the diachronic and synchronic properties of system components, will be employed.[18] A system, as opposed to a simple aggregation, may be defined as characterised by relations between its constituent elements; these relations are diachronic (between elements over time) or synchronic (between elements at a point in time).[19] As Kay has pointed out, the couple synchronic/diachronic appear to mirror the couple static and dynamic in conventional economics, but he claims the former pair are 'richer, insofar as they imply the existence of relations between elements'.[20] For example, a series of random events over time affecting, say, the size distribution of a population of firms would be dynamic but not diachronic, because there would be no relationship, adjustment process or causality between events. Similarly, Kay argues that 'a series of independent and unconnected elements at a single point in time would be static but not synchronic'.[21] Adopting a structuralist perspective, let us take Landes' dictum that 'The cotton mill was the symbol of Britain's industrial greatness'[22] and consider the factory system and its basic components. A simple model of the factory system is outlined in Figure 2.1, showing four system components.

Figure 2.1: Factory system model

Components	1	Factory
	2	Firm
	3	Entrepreneur
	4	Market

The synchronic relations between these elements is important in determining the behaviour of the overall system. These relations can be expressed in four ways:

(A) Technical: the technical specifications of factory production, organisational structure, hierarchical controls.

(B) Rights: the relations of ownership and financial control, the role of property rights and the distribution of surplus.

(C) Mediation: sets of decision-making in terms of component objectives, deployment and utilisation of resources.[23]

(D) Reciprocity: exchange relations, identification of system boundaries; sanctions, patterns of relations with other forms of economic activity.[24]

This simple model allows a number of points of departure. Thus if we take relation A we immediately confront a controversy concerning the rise of the factory. To reduce the argument to its basics, one school of thought locates the factory's origins to machine technology, while another school emphasises the role of management control over the labour process. For writers such as David Landes the rise of the factory was associated with the innovation of machine technology and the Industrial Revolution 'required machines which not only replaced hand labour but compelled the concentration of production in factories — in other words, machines whose appetite for energy was too large for domestic sources of power'.[25] Such arguments do not convince Stephen Marglin, who denies that the origins and success of the factory lie in technological superiority.[26] Rather it was the substitution of the capitalist for the worker's control over the work process and the quality of output which allowed the factory to flourish and to eventually dominate other modes of production.[27] We will not elaborate these arguments as we consider them essentially confused. The source of the confusion is twofold: firstly, there is a false separation of the technological (in the sense of machine technology) from the organisational (supervisors, management) when clearly both are required for the successful development of the factory system. That is, rather than attempting to see them as diachronic processes and argue over their causal primacy, they are better conceptualised as basic synchronic properties of a factory system.[28] Secondly, the argument abstracts from the fact that the factory itself was a basic innovation which calls for a close examination of the relationship between the factory and the firm. This can be seen if we consider the factory system model as a whole; then clearly the factory/firm relation is the key to understanding how the system works and signals the direction to follow in the exploration of the linkage between the factory system and the Industrial Revolution. The point is simple enough but nonetheless needs to be stressed with vigour. In the British Industrial Revolution, factories[29] were operated by privately-owned business firms who made the key decisions concerning the type and form of control, decided the response to technological,[30] financial[31] and market[32] constraints, set the pattern of business strategy and resource utilisation and mediated the structure of relationships with other economic components, both factory and non-factory. The factory during the Industrial Revolution cannot be explored independent of the business unit which controlled and operated it.

This relationship can be explored in a variety of ways, as shown in the recent contribution by V. A. C. Gatrell,[33] S. D.

Chapman[34] and R. Lloyd-Jones and A. A. Le Roux.[35] They have provided new insights into the growth and behaviour of cotton factory firms and have raised important issues concerned with size, technology and financial and market processes. One of the benefits of this approach is the recognition of the need to explore the forms of relation between cotton factory firms and other economic components. This is best typified by Chapman's call to examine the ties between factory firms and merchants in the cotton industry.[36] We welcome this line of development and intend to push it further. As a starting point we are taken by Raphael Samuel's challenge that historians of the Industrial Revolution need to 'look at the economy as a whole'[37] rather than concentrate simply on its most novel and striking features. This is not to ignore the factory or relegate it to secondary importance, but to conceptualise it as part of a larger whole. But what 'economy' do we look at and how do we go about reconstructing it?

As our concern is with basic structures and patterns, a holistic approach does not necessarily imply consideration of the aggregate national economy, but, on the contrary, a more feasible proposition may well be to explore the linkages of the factory firm to other economic components by inserting the former into the totality of a local economic system.[38] Manchester provides an ideal site for such an investigation. It is the central nodal point of the Industrial Revolution, and its business structure, as will be shown in Chapter 3, is capable of detailed reconstruction. The method of reconstruction is as follows: a synchronic perspective is adopted by freezing Manchester's business structure[39] in 1815, a year at mid-point of the classic Industrial Revolution.[40] The basic building block, utilised for the reconstruction of Manchester's business system, is the notion of property asset.[41] A property asset is the spacial representation of North and Thomas's[42] concept of property right, and possesses the following characteristics:

(1) It earns a stream of income from a designated function (i.e. an economic activity) which is located within a market context. That is the property asset possesses a market value[43] which in its turn is related to its form of economic activity.

(2) The insertion of the property asset in the market system is based on the assumption that the expected gain from the usage of the asset will exceed the expected cost. That is we agree with

North and Thomas, that if the private cost exceeds the private gain, firms will not be willing to utilise the property asset for its designated economic function.[44]

(3) The utilisation of a property asset is variable, as is its designation. That is over time it may be put to a range of economic functions at varying patterns of capacity usage. Its designation and utilisation, at a given moment of time, is a reflection of its profitable use compared with other potential usages. This has implications for the definition of property assets into specific economic categories as will be outlined below.

(4) The range of economic functions undertaken by the owner/occupier (firm) of the property asset is not necessarily identical to the activity designated to the asset. Thus, for example, a Manchester businessman might combine cotton manufacturing (non-factory based) with cotton factory spinning, or a cotton factory spinner might engage in calico printing, or machine making or dealing in raw cotton or cotton twist and weft. One firm might utilise a number of property assets of the same designation (i.e. more than one factory) or a range of assets of different designations[45] (i.e. factory, foundry, warehouse, etc).

(5) Although a property asset is located within a building it is not necessarily identical to a whole building but allows for the renting of space within a given building. Sub-letting was a widespread practice in Manchester[46] and this was a feature of factory property assets as well as a wide range of other assets. It is a simplification to assume the identification of a factory to a single building. Such simplifications are based on the separation of the factory from the firm,[47] a separation which we have already suggested should be avoided. The phenomenon of the shared-part factory is an important aspect of Manchester's business structure and will be examined in Chapters 3 and 7.

Property assets thus provide a minimum condition for the conduct of economic activity. They may range from a giant six-storey factory to a humble smithy, from the imposing warehouses situated at the terminal of the Bridgewater canal to a bakehouse or slaughterhouse, or from a foundry to a domestic house built for the private renting sector. The notion of property asset, too, may allow us to cut through the problem of how specific economic components may be defined. If we take as our example two of the key components which will be explored in the remainder of the book, factories and warehouses, the distinction between these two rests on the pattern of usage of the asset where the former requires the development and implementation of a centralised power source incorporating a transmission system for the driving of machines.[48] This may be seen clearly from the following advertisement placed in the *Manchester Guardian* in June 1824:

> To be let two capital and well built warehouses with excellent northern lights . . . very suitable for houses in the export trade, in which capacity they have long been occupied. From the strength and size of the buildings they are also well worthy of notice for manufacturing by power, being capable of containing 500 power looms with every facility for putting down an engine.[49]

In other words a property asset may be re-designated from a warehouse to a factory (or vice versa)[50] but it will involve a shift in the pattern of usage and therefore a shift either in the form of control (i.e. from one firm to another) or a change in the decision rules of the existing firm operating the asset. We can thus explore diachronic changes as the pattern of property asset usage changes over time and attempt to locate shifting trends in the structure of Manchester's business system.[51] It may be objected, however, that our definition of the component factory is too restrictive, and tends to exclude establishments 'in which the mechanisations do not form a connected series, nor are dependent on one prime mover'.[52] Tann, in particular, argues that the Ure type definition leads to the exclusion of some of the most remarkable factories of the eighteenth century, and claims a fundamental characteristic of the factory system is the 'concentration of the means of production at the factory site',[53] which may or may not include a prime mover and an interconnected system of machines. Such an interpretation is not without its difficulties. Quite what is meant by the factory site is unclear and if a definition may be criticised for being too restrictive it may also suffer from an excess of openness.[54] Thus if we adopt Tann's definition it is problematic whether we should exclude bakehouses, slaughterhouses, cobblers workshops, smithies, etc. Our interpretation while emphasising the importance of prime movers and interconnected machines by no means excludes the small-scale factory; indeed it easily incorporates the phenomenon of sub-letting, so characteristic of Manchester, which allowed the tiny factory firm to share both space and power. Thus Marx's observation that 'The technical subordination of the workmen to the uniform motion of the instruments of labour . . . is elaborated into a complete system in the factory',[55] applies equally to the giant factory of McConnel and Kennedy, valued at £18,652.00 in 1812, as it does to the pygmy factory of A. Carruthers, valued at £800.00 in the same year.[56]

This approach, with its use of the building block of property asset, is generally informed by a system perspective holding explicit notions of interdependence. A number of subsequent chapters will be concerned with the factory and the production system, but again accepting Samuel's stricture we must avoid the temptation of focusing attention only on one component of the overall system. For example, the analysis of the Industrial Revolution tends to generate a good deal of research effort devoted to technology and production, i.e. the supply side of the economy.[57] At the same time, there are those who express the importance of income, tastes, foreign trade, etc, i.e. the demand side. But, too often, these positions are counterpoised as polar opposites, as independent blades of the Marshallian scissors. Indeed, the sequentiality of demand and supply reflects the contemporary struggle between monetarism (with its emphasis upon the supply side) and Keynesian economics (with its demand side orientation). Yet if we consider the basic structure of a capitalist market economy, supply and demand components are not separate discrete processes, but are part of an interrelated chain. At its simplest level, this chain moves from factory to warehouse to retail and final sale. The outline of the chain may well be simple but it is important nonetheless, and one of the aims of this book is to correct the absence of analysis of the so-called tertiary sector.[58] Productivity gains have been explained at the level of the factory and the foundry to the neglect of the warehouse and the distribution system.[59] In Chapters 3, 4 and 5 we will argue that the warehouse system is a vital component of the cotton industry and the relationship between factory and warehouse is the key to the understanding of the business structure of Manchester. In other words, the Industrial Revolution is concerned with both factory and warehouse systems. We now turn to the reconstruction of Manchester's business system at the close of the Napoleonic Wars.

NOTES AND REFERENCES

1. D. N. McCloskey, 'The Industrial Revolution 1780–1860: A Survey', in R. Floud and D. N. McCloskey (eds), *The Economic History of Britain Since 1700* (2 vols., Cambridge University Press, Cambridge, 1981), vol. 1, p. 108.
2. M. Berg, *The Machinery Question and the Making of Political Economy 1815–1848* (Cambridge University Press, Cambridge, 1980), see especially ch. 2.
3. R. Samuel, 'The Workshop of the World: Steam Power and Hand Technology in Mid-Victorian Britain', *History Workshop*, issue 3, no. 2 (1977), pp. 6–72.
4. Among many examples are the manufacture of boots and shoes which remained predominantly an outwork system until the 1880s. Indeed, it was the boot workers union which demanded factory work in the 1890s. R. Lloyd-Jones, 'The Sociological Context of Trade Union Activity in the East Midland Boot and Shoe Industry in the Late Victorian Era', unpublished MSc thesis, Loughborough University of Technology, 1969, pp. 76–88.
5. M. Fores, 'The Myth of a British Industrial Revolution', *History*, vol. LXVI (1981), pp. 181–98.
6. See, for example, the series of essays in Floud and McCloskey, *Economic History*, vol. 1.
7. N. F. R. Crafts, 'Industrial Revolution in England and France: Some Thoughts on the Question "Why was England First?" ', *Economic History Review*, vol. XXX, no. 3 (1977), p. 321.
8. Fores, for example, utilises proposition A to undermine proposition B.
9. W. W. Rostow, *The Stages of Economic Growth*, 2nd edn, (Cambridge University Press, Cambridge, 1971).
10. A. Gerschenkron, *Economic Backwardness in Historical Perspective* (Harvard University Press, Cambridge, Mass., 1966).
11. A. O. Hirschman, *The Strategy of Economic Development* (Yale University Press, New Haven, 1958).
12. For a review of recent advances see J. Delbeke, 'Recent Long-Wave Theories: A Critical Survey', *Futures*, vol. 13 (1981), pp. 246–57; and J. J. Van Duijn, *The Long-Wave in Economic Life* (George Allen and Unwin, London, 1983), especially chs. 4, 5 and 6.
13. A. Gerschenkron, 'Typologies of Industrialisation', *Second International Conference of Economic History* (1962).
14. B. Loasby, 'Hypothesis and Paradigms in the Theory of the Firm, *Economic Journal*, vol. 81 (1971), p. 865.
15. As Musson points out despite reservations economic historians 'continue to use the term Industrial Revolution'. A. E. Musson, 'The British Industrial Revolution', *History*, vol. 67 (1982), p. 255. In a similar vein, following Sraffa's famous article in the *Economic Journal* in 1926, which seemed to undermine neo-classical perfect competition theory, Hicks' response was that to abandon the assumption of perfect competition 'must have very destructive consequences for economic theory'; quoted in Joan Robinson, *Economic Heresies: Some Old-*

Fashioned Questions in Economic Theory (Macmillan, London, 1971), p. 100.

16. R. Lloyd-Jones and A. A. Le Roux, 'Marshall and the Birth and Death of Firms: The Growth and Size Distribution of Firms in the Early Nineteenth Century Cotton Industry', *Business History*, vol. XXIV, no. 2 (1982), p. 141.

17. Quoted in Berg, *The Machinery Question*, p. 84; also Loasby, 'Hypothesis and Paradigms', p. 863.

18. The structuralist literature is large and the emphasis here will be taken from the work of Kay who has examined the structuralist perspective in relation to the economic system. See Neil M. Kay, *The Evolving Firm: Strategy and Structure in Industrial Organisation* (Macmillan, London, 1982); and Neil M. Kay, *The Innovating Firm* (Macmillan, London, 1979).

19. Kay, *The Evolving Firm*, p. 19.

20. Ibid., pp. 17–18.

21. Ibid., p. 18.

22. D. Landes, *The Unbound Promethius, Technological Change from 1870 to the Present* (Cambridge University Press, Cambridge, 1969), p. 42.

23. The process of decision-making and the role of business strategy will be explored in Chapter 10.

24. Patterns of reciprocity will be a theme running through Chapters 3 to 8.

25. D. S. Landes, *The Unbound Promethius*, p. 81. Landes' position is supported by T. S. Ashton, *The Industrial Revolution, 1766–1830* (Oxford University Press, Oxford, 1948), p. 33; P. Mantaux, *The Industrial Revolution in the Eighteenth Century* (Methuen, London, 1964 edn), p. 39; P. Mathias, *The First Industrial Nation* (Methuen, London, 1969), p. 121; and E. J. Hobsbawm, *Industry and Empire* (Penguin, Harmondsworth, 1969), p. 59. See also an elaboration of his argument in D. S. Landes, 'What Bosses Really Do', *Journal of Economic History*, vol. 46, no. 3 (1986).

26. The notion that technology was not vital to the rise of the factory would tend to lend support for the type of argument developed by M. Fores.

27. S. Marglin, 'What Do Bosses Do', *Review of Radical Political Economy*, vol. 6, no. 2 (1974), p. 62.

28. The basic objective of the factory firm is to survive; to achieve this and thus the possibility of growth, technical and organisational control are basic conditions.

29. It is important to note that the factory system was not entirely confined to England, but there were important centres in Northern Ireland (Belfast), Scotland (Glasgow and Lanarkshire) and North Wales (Holywell).

30. For the importance of technological factors for the factory firm see J. Tann, *The Development of the Factory* (Cornmarket Press, London, 1970).

31. For the role of financial constraints on the growth of cotton firms see S. D. Chapman, 'Financial Restraints on the Growth of Firms in

the Cotton Industry 1790–1850', *Economic History Review*, vol. XXXII, no. 1 (1979), pp. 50–69.

32. Market forces are explored by V. A. C. Gatrell, 'Labour, Power and the Size of Firms in Lancashire Cotton in the Second Quarter of the Nineteenth Century', *Economic History Review*, vol. XXX, no. 1 (1977), pp. 95–139. Also see Chapman, 'Financial Restraints', pp. 54–62.

33. Gatrell, 'Labour, Power', pp. 95–139.

34. Chapman, 'Financial Restraints', pp. 50–69.

35. R. Lloyd-Jones and A. A. Le Roux, 'The Size of Firms in the Cotton Industry: Manchester 1815–41', *Economic History Review*, vol. XXXIII, no. 1 (1980), pp. 72–82; Lloyd-Jones and Le Roux, 'Marshall and the Birth and Death of Firms', pp. 141–55; R. Lloyd-Jones and A. A. Le Roux, 'Factory Utilisation and the Firm: The Manchester Cotton Industry 1825–40', *Textile History*, vol. 15, no. 1 (1984), pp. 119–28.

36. Chapman, 'Financial Restraints', p. 50.

37. Samuel, 'The Workshop of the World', p. 57.

38. It seems to us that the Rostowian linkages may well be examined at the local economic level, which fits more easily with Rostow's sectorial approach. A linkage effect may be defined as the impact that investment in one sector of economic activity has on other sectors of economic activity. For the role of linkage effect and the so-called leading sector in the take-off to sustained growth see W. W. Rostow, *Stages*, pp. 52–8. For a more detailed discussion of linkage effect see Hirschman, *Economic Development*, chs. 2 and 6.

39. As Joan Robinson informs us, 'Everything that happens in an economy happens in a short-period situation; and every decision that is taken, is taken in a short-period situation, for an event occurs or a decision is taken at a particular time, and any particular moment the physical stock of capital is what it is.' Joan Robinson, *The Accumulation of Capital* (Macmillan, London, 1956), p. 180.

40. The dating of the classic Industrial Revolution is usually either 1780–1860 or 1770–1850, giving mid-points at 1820 and 1810, thus 1815 would seem an appropriate compromise.

41. The notion of a property asset is explored in R. Lloyd-Jones and M. J. Lewis, 'The Economic Structure of Cottonopolis: Manchester in 1815', *Textile History*, vol. 17, no. 1 (1986), pp. 71–89.

42. D. C. North and R. T. Thomas, *The Rise of the Western World: A New Economic History* (Cambridge University Press, Cambridge, 1973), ch. 1.

43. The question of value in relation to property assets is discussed in Chapter 3.

44. North and Thomas, *Western World*, p. 3.

45. We will explore the variety of business combinations and the changing pattern of business activities in Chapter 7.

46. Lloyd-Jones and Le Roux, 'The Size of Firms', p. 73. The phenomenon of sub-letting will also be explored in Chapters 3 and 7.

47. Such a separation is apparent in a recent work by Francois Crouzet who claims that 'the unit of ownership — the firm — and the

unit of production — the factory or works were one and the same entity'. F. Crouzet, *The First Industrialists; The Problem of Origins* (Cambridge University Press, Cambridge, 1985), p. 16.

48. This interpretation is close to Andrew Ure's definition of a factory which stresses the importance of mechanised power and an integrated system of production. A. Ure, *The Philosophy of Manufactures: Or an Exposition of the Scientific, Moral and Commercial Economy of the Factory System of Great Britain* (Frank Cass, London, 1967 edn), p. 13.

49. *Manchester Guardian*, 26 June 1825.

50. For an account of the conversion of buildings to alternative uses in the cotton towns see S. D. Chapman, 'Fixed Capital Formation in the British Cotton Industry, 1770–1815', *Economic History Review*, vol. XXIII, no. 2 (1970), pp. 237, 245–6. According to Chapman, the easy availability of 'cheap' buildings for conversion into cotton mills was a crucial factor in reducing the capital costs of entering the industry between 1770 and 1795. Chapman, 'Fixed Capital', p. 252.

51. Chapter 7 will examine in detail the shifting patterns of business activity between 1815 and 1825.

52. Tann, *Factory*, p. 3.

53. Ibid., p. 3.

54. For a recent discussion concerning the controversy over the definition of the factory, see Crouzet, *The First Industrialists*, pp. 8–9, 10–13.

55. K. Marx, *Capital: A Critical Analysis of Capitalist Production* (3 vols, Lawrence and Wishart, London, 1974 edn), vol. 1, p. 399.

56. See Chapter 3, Table 3.1, for a full list of Manchester factory valuations.

57. See, for example, the article by J. Mokyr, 'Demand and Supply in the Industrial Revolution', *Journal of Economic History*, vol. XXXVII, no. 4 (1977), pp. 981–1008.

58. This point is made by R. M. Hartwell, *The Industrial Revolution and Economic Growth* (Methuen, London, 1971), p. 205.

59. A notable exception to this is to be found in the work of M. M. Edwards, *The Growth of the British Cotton Trade 1780–1815* (Manchester University Press, Manchester, 1967)

3

The Business Structure of Manchester in 1815[1]

For those who witnessed the economic changes of the Industrial Revolution, Manchester was recognised as the capital of a new system of production[2] 'and the international emporium for cotton goods'.[3] As Frederick Engels observed, 'in Manchester English manufacture finds at once its starting point and its centre'.[4] Yet Manchester's reputation, as the capital of the Industrial Revolution, has not gone unchallenged. Michael Fores has recently claimed that 'The particular story of cotton manufacture, Manchester commerce, technological change and fairly dramatic events in one . . . county, Lancashire, has been generalised out of all sensible proportion'.[5] Perhaps Manchester's contribution to the process of industrialisation has been exaggerated but before we can accept hypotheses which seek to dismiss its virility as a centre promoting change, we require a greater understanding of the structure and working of the town's economy. In other words, Manchester cannot be easily disentangled from that process of rapid economic change based upon the factory and the machine. It was a recipient of Ashton's 'wave of gadgets which swept over England',[6] though, as Donald McCloskey points out, 'these gadgets came more like a gentle, though unprecedented rain, gathering here and there in puddles'.[7] Undoubtedly Manchester represents the largest and deepest puddle, at the end of the Napoleonic Wars, but how large and how deep?

'The cure for excessive metaphor', McCloskey informs us, 'is counting',[8] and with this we agree. In keeping with our aim of first looking at the 'wood', in its overall context, the total economy of Manchester will be reconstructed based upon a count of all the property assets in the township in 1815.[9] Manchester, as the centre of the Industrial Revolution, suggests a chain of causation linking the town to mechanised factories and the process of technological change. By categorising the variegated business structure of Manchester we can locate the place of the cotton factory, the symbol of the new system of production, in the town's aggregate economy, and explore the interconnections between this and other business components.[10] Its reconstruction will provide new insights into the patterns of economic relationships at a critical point in the transformation of Britain to an industrial economy. But before discussing the place of the factory in the overall economy, and its economic linkages, we turn to the empirical basis of our reconstruction and outline the methodology we have adopted.

MANCHESTER IN 1815: AN ECONOMIC RECONSTRUCTION

The empirical data for the reconstruction is contained in the Manchester Poor Rate Assessment Books,[11] which provide a mine of information on the town's property system: its size, valuation and functions.[12] The systematic usage of this basic data source allows the collation of assets ranging from factories to houses, from bakeshops to smithies, from public houses to warehouses, from foundries to farms, from coal mines to saw pits and so on. Thus the total property structure of Manchester can be reconstructed and an examination made of the distribution of its property assets across different forms of economic activity.

The basic building block of our reconstruction is the notion of property asset which, as we defined in Chapter 2, is the spacial representation of a property right possessing both a function (i.e. an economic activity) and a market value (i.e. open to transactions on the market).[13] Any economic activity in a market context is closely related to the question of value[14] and rateable values (RVs) are taken as a proxy for property asset values.[15] Furthermore, the concept of a property asset allows for the multiple occupancy of individual buildings, and the RV assessment in the rate books distinguishes between single and multiple occupancy. Thus the notion of a rateable unit will be used to define property assets where the latter is not equivalent to a single physical unit.

Let us now employ our basic building block and begin our assessment of Manchester's factory system. The valuation for Manchester factories is based on an independent valuation of 1812, by Messrs Bellhouse, Wallis and Johnson[16] and are shown with their corresponding RVs[17] in Table 3.1. What are the bases of these valuations, why were they undertaken, and do RVs form a reliable proxy for property valuation?

Table 3.1: Valuation of Manchester cotton spinning factories in 1812

Factory (Occupier/Owner)	Valuation 1812 (£)	RV 1815 (£)
E. Robinson	1,131	59
Smith & Townley	4,612	147
B. & W. Sandford	2,268	114
W. Mitchell	10,766	519
B. Gray & Co	4,873	244
J. Pollard	9,564	478
John Kennedy	9,442	499
McConnel and Kennedy	18,652	933
A. & G. Murray	20,455	924
A. Carruthors	810	41
T. Houldsworth	10,575	522
R. Schofield	2,659	195

Source: R. Lloyd-Jones and M. J. Lewis, 'The Economic Structure of Cottonopolis: Manchester in 1815', *Textile History*, vol. 17, no. 1 (1986), pp. 74–5.

Valuation has been defined as 'The art or science of estimating the value for a specific purpose of a particular interest in property at a particular moment in time, taking into account all the features of the property, including the range of alternative investments.'[18] The expression 'specific purpose' refers to the fact that the property asset may be used for a range of different purposes: residential, commercial, industrial, etc. There may well be a variety of reasons for requiring a valuation, covering, for example, valuation for sale, renting, rating, mortgage, replacement, probate, etc.[19] The valuation for factories was part of a general dispute over the assessment of cotton factories in relation to other property assets. In accordance with this dispute, two independent valuations, in 1810[20] and 1812,[21] were commissioned by master cotton spinners to challenge the rating assessment of their mills, in the hope that it would lead to a reduction in the rateable assessment to 'put us on an equal footing with the rest of our townsmen'.[22] The spinners complained that the RVs of their factories were based upon replacement costs, while other assets, especially warehouses, had been valued at their rental earnings.[23] In a memorial sent to the Church Wardens and Overseas,[24] in July 1810, they stated that,

> Factories have been rated upon data . . . different from those which have been adopted by the general assessors in their estimate of all other property. The assessors appointed exclusively for the purpose of assessing factories, have fixed the rate on a percentage of the cost, while the assessors of other properties have been governed by the rental.[25]

In fact, this defensive reaction by the factory masters may have been, in part, a deep-rooted fear that the system of assessment would eventually be based upon an estimate of the profitability of their cotton mills. According to George Lee, a partner in the spinning firm of Phillips and Lee,[26] it was the general practice in Manchester to pay poor rates upon the 'estimated (annual) value of the premises', but recently he had 'heard it discussed' that the poor rate should be in proportion to the profits of the factory.[27] It seems likely, therefore, that the non-factory sector was advocating that the factory assessment should reflect its greater profitability, in relation to other property assets, and that the cotton masters should bear a larger proportion of the poor rate. On a broader level, the dispute concerning the assessment highlights the underlying conflict within Manchester's business community, especially between the factory (representing spinning) and the warehouse (representing manufacturing/weaving), at the end of the Napoleonic Wars. This schism in the trade found its expression in the political debate over the merits of the factory system, in the early nineteenth century, and forms the basis for discussion in Chapter 5.

The spinners' dispute, over the assessment, may cast doubt on the reliability of the RV data as a suitable proxy for property asset valuation, but the weight of evidence suggests otherwise. A positive statistical correlation between RVs and factory employment has been demonstrated for Manchester,[28] and we would expect a similar close correlation between RVs and property valuations. Indeed, this is the case when RVs are correlated against the valuation of twelve Manchester factories in Table 3.1 These figures provide a correlation (r^2) of 0.994 and thus, for the cotton spinning factories, there is a clear case for utilising RVs as a proxy for property asset valuations. Does such a significant correlation hold for other types of property assets? The Manchester firm of Bellhouse, Wallis and Johnson also provides valuation data for 18 warehouses in 1812.[29] The details of these and their corresponding RVs are shown in Table 3.2. The

Table 3.2: Valuation of 18 Manchester warehouses and their RVs in 1812

Warehouse (Owner/Occupier)	Valuation 1812 (£)	RV 1812 (£)
W. Caistor	1,380	90
Gilbert & Co	3,180	200
A. Oldham	4,000	161
W. Cowlishaw	780	45
M. Turner	2,600	220
Wm Boyd/John Lyon	7,500	620
Messrs Brookes & Co	3,180	250
Millington/Peel, Yates & Co		
Peel, Yates & Co	2,880	180
E. Palfreyman	3,030	220
Mather and Lomax	5,700	300
Greenwood	3,300	120
L. W. Whitehead	4,500	170
W. Saunders	3,180	300
Haigh, Marshall & Co	6,000	290
Elliot	4,050	200
J. & W. Bateman	4,150	210
Salter	8,900	410
J. Brookes	1,450	75

Source: Lloyd-Jones and Lewis, 'Economic Structure', p. 75.

data in Table 3.2 gives a correlation (r^2) of 0.933. Therefore, although factories were assessed along different criteria, at least according to the owners, it would appear that the master spinners had little ground for complaint[30] and we can confidently use RVs as a proxy for property asset valuation.[31]

The economic significance of these valuations rests upon the fact 'that the ownership of property is a form of holding money and when we are considering the valuation of property we are concerned with money'.[32] One of the tasks of business historians is to examine what the people who had money actually did with it. A crucial characteristic of a property asset is that it should be a profitable investment to the owner/occupier and consequently of importance is the link between the value of the asset, its potential earnings, and its function or use in the market. Thus the property asset provides a stream of income and its function reflects, at a given moment in time, entrepreneurial judgement about profitable utilisation. At a broader level of economic activity, valuations may be considered as a guide to investment decisions across different property assets. So, for example, the valuation pattern, as represented by the RV proxy, may be utilised to examine the flow of money into Manchester's fixed property asset structure, and interpreted as providing a rough set of signals about investment behaviour at a crucial stage of the Industrial Revolution.

Having established the link between property assets and valuation, and concluded that the RV proxy is a reliable estimator, the next step in the empirical investigation is a reconstruction of Manchester's property asset structure in 1815. There is no intention to construct a fixed capital index for cotton factories or any other asset;[33] the aim is to reconstruct the distribution of fixed capital in property assets across the whole range of the Manchester economy. This was done as follows:

(a) Utilising the rate books, property assets were placed into 12 general functional categories covering production, wholesale, retail, etc. These general categories are listed in Table 3.3, and consist of 5 different sub-categories (see Appendix 1). Such detailed categorisation was possible because of the high quality of property description in the rate books.

(b) The RVs of each property asset (which as we have seen incorporates both separate buildings and rateable units within buildings), was collected and this allowed for aggregation at both the general and sub-category level.

(c) The total number of property assets were counted and placed in their relevant general and sub-categories.

(d) All the names of the property asset occupiers/owners were tabulated, together with street and district location,[34] and property description. This allowed detailed cross-referencing with the Manchester trade and commercial directories.[35]

The distribution of, and the number and valuation of property assets is given in Table 3.4. What is initially striking about the figures in this table is the small proportion that

Table 3.3: Property asset structure, Manchester, 1815, general categories

Category code	Category description
1	Production/general
2	Building trade: construction
3	Food and drink processing
4	Retail/general
5	Retail: drink trade/hostelry
6	Wholesale/distribution
7	Finance/commerce/services
8	Transport services/distribution
9	Residential: housing (private)
10	Public utilities/leisure
11	Extractive industries
12	Land and agriculture

Note: See Appendix 1 for a full description of categories 1 to 12.

Table 3.4: Distribution of Manchester's property assets in 1815

Category code	Total number of property assets assessed	Total RV of assets (£)	% of category value to total RV	% of category value to total RV excluding housing
1	262	18,307	6.15	11.96
2	60	1,662	0.56	1.09
3	53	399	0.13	0.26
4	1,018	26,231	8.81	17.14
5	304	14,966	5.03	9.78
6	1,867	77,650	26.08	50.73
7	141	3,050	1.02	1.99
8	20	5,172	1.74	3.38
9	13,406	144,620	48.58	—
10	48	3,512	1.18	2.29
11	2	280	0.10	0.18
12	49	1,836	0.62	1.20
Total	17,230	297,685	100.00	100.00

Source: Lloyd-Jones and Lewis, 'Economic Structure', p. 77.

category 1 constitutes to total property valuation. This is even more surprising when it is recalled that category 1 includes at least some activities more associated with traditional modes of production rather than those connected with the Industrial Revolution (see Appendix 1). Given this observation, the next step is to assess the place of the cotton factory in the overall fixed property structure of the Manchester economy, and to determine the direction of investment in property assets.

PROPERTY ASSET STRUCTURE AND THE FACTORY IN 1815

To determine the place of the factory in the overall Manchester economy we need to disaggregate category 1 and this is done in Table 3.5, which also excludes the housing sector. For comparative purposes, data for warehouses and public houses are also included in this table. The amount of capital tied up in

Table 3.5: Disaggregated categories: a comparison of cotton factories with other property assets in 1815

Code	Disaggregated category	RV (£)	RV as % of total RV (excluding housing)
1:1	Cotton spinning factories	9,334	6.10
1:2	Metal sector/machines, foundry sector	3,298	2.15
1:3	Chemical sector (dyeing, bleaching, finishing, chemical works, etc)	3,559	2.32
1:4	Rope works	150	0.10
1:5	Unspecified works, workshops, factories	1,966	1.28
6:1	Warehouses	73,627	48.10
5:1	Public houses and inns	13,608	8.89

Note: The figure for category 1 differs from those given in Table 5 of our *Textile History* article, because we have now cross-referenced with the directories unspecified property assets and determined their activity.

Source: Compiled from data in Lloyd-Jones and Lewis, 'Economic Structure', Table 5, p. 78.

cotton factory property assets, shown in Table 3.5, appears astonishingly small in relation to the productive capacity and labour utilisation normally associated with factory production.[36] Certainly, cotton factories are synonymous with rapidly rising output, technological innovation and a large industrial workforce.[37] Indeed, without such developments the very notion of an Industrial Revolution based upon technological change would have been a non-starter. What our analysis allows is for the factory to be placed into the broad spectrum of the overall economic structure of Manchester. In short, it provides some guidelines as to where capitalists were directing their investments at the microeconomic level. For if the changes associated with the Industrial Revolution were about factories, machines and steam power, they were also about the extension of the free market economy: a decentralised economic system based upon individual decision-making. The changes concerned 'that most important and yet most elusive class; the owners of capital'.[38] According to Roland Smith, it was clear where capitalists were directing their capital:

> Manchester, besides being an entrepot for all kinds of cotton goods was also a typical factory town, concentrating in the first quarter of the nineteenth century upon the spinning and weaving of all types of cotton yarn and cloth. At this period roughly one-quarter of the total spindles in cotton production in the whole of the United Kingdom were at work within the town.[39]

But what does a 'typical factory town' mean? Workers may well have flocked to the cotton factories, but capitalists had a far wider spectrum of choice to place their investments. Indeed, the reconstruction shows that property asset investment in the licensed trade, as a proportion of total assets (both including and excluding housing), was higher than for cotton factories. This is quite remarkable, given the observation that in the early nineteenth century Manchester 'spinning mill buildings were mostly imposing structures usually from 4 to 8 stories high'.[40] A town where capitalists directed a higher proportion, albeit marginal, of their capital into the building of public houses than cotton mills, is stretching to almost breaking point the notion of a 'factory town'. More significant than the public house/factory ratio is the overwhelming importance of warehouses in the pattern of real property. Cotton factories were swamped in Manchester's property asset structure by warehouses, who provided 48 per cent of the total valuation, excluding housing.[41]

Of course, we must remember that the RV data excludes machinery and power, but even if we doubled the valuation of cotton factories to take account of this,[42] the sheer economic weight of warehouses in the Manchester economy would remain unchallenged. We would need to multiply the cotton spinning factory RV by a factor of six to achieve parity with the aggregate value of warehouses; Manchester in 1815 was a warehouse town. Recalling our initial metaphor that Manchester represents the 'largest and deepest puddle', the first reading of the data suggests a pattern of change dominated by wholesale, marketing and exchange, rather than production. Certainly, Roland Smith's observation that 'one of the most startling changes in the organisation of the cotton trade in Manchester after 1815 was the emergence of the warehouse system'[43] is historically erroneous. Manchester was 'Cottonopolis' but for wholesale and distribution, well before its alleged emergence as a commercial centre in the 1820s and 1830s.[44]

These empirical findings appear to confirm Fores' proposition that the notion of an Industrial Revolution based upon rapid technological change, centred on factory activity, has been exaggerated. His insistence that terms such as industry and industrialisation require greater precision, and his association of manufacturing with the former and factory activity with the latter,[45] further tends to eclipse the position of Manchester as the citadel of industrial change. Yet such charges are premature; rather more attention should be placed upon the economic relationship between the factory and the warehouse. The examination of this relationship is critical to any understanding of the economic linkages of Manchester's economy. A detailed analysis of the lines of causality between these two business components is the task of later chapters, but let us set the scene by offering some general observations concerning the factory and the warehouse and their linkages with other property assets.

FACTORY AND WAREHOUSE: BASIC PATTERNS 1815

What is characteristic of Manchester in 1815 is the openness of its economic system and the small-scale nature of its business units. It was this openness that the young Richard Cobden was to take advantage of when he established his Manchester business connections in the late 1820s. Recalling this enterprise in later life, Cobden observed that:

> I began business in partnership with two other young men and we only mustered a thousand pounds amongst us, and more than half of it was borrowed. We were literally so ignorant of Manchester houses that we called for a directory at the hotel

> . . . We introduced ourselves to Fort Bros. and Company,[46] a rich house, and we told our tale, honestly concealing nothing. In less than two years from 1830 we owed them forty thousand pounds for goods which they had sent us . . . upon no other security than our characters and knowledge of our business. I frequently talked with them in later times upon the great confidence they showed in men who avowed that they were not possessed of one-hundred pounds each.[47]

The example of Richard Cobden emphasises the opportunities for the small capitalist to set up in business in Manchester.[48] Indeed, the small-scale nature of business enterprise is reflected in the cotton factory system itself. A. E. Musson refers to the 'Lancashire cotton industry' where 'small masters had rooms or floors, together with mechanical power, in a factory building'.[49] At the end of the Napoleonic Wars, the average cotton spinning firm was a pretty small-scale unit, and this is reflected in Manchester's factory sector. The Manchester factory system was dominated by a small number of large-scale firms overlooking a thick undergrowth of very small-scale enterprises. In 1815, two-thirds of Manchester's cotton spinning firms shared part of a factory, while only 27.7 per cent of firms wholly occupied a factory building[50] (this data is shown in Table 3.6). It is a mistake, therefore, to see the factory and the firm as synonymous; a single factory might house up to ten or more separate firms.[51]

In part, the notion of Manchester as 'Cottonopolis' was a product of the impact of the large cotton spinning firms. If we take a large firm as one employing 500 or more workers,[52] then this size of firm employed 44.2 per cent of the factory labour force in 1815, but only accounted for 7.8 per cent of the total number of firms.[53] Two firms alone, McConnel and Kennedy and A. and G. Murray, employed between them 2,235 operatives (19.5 per cent of the total labour force), and no doubt helped to foster the notion of a factory town with its antagonisms between capital and labour. However, these two giants have to be set against the 60 firms who shared factory space, what we may call the shared part factory or SPF firm.[54] The SPF firm was essentially a very small-scale unit, usually renting[55] space and power in a large factory building. The average RV of the 60 firms in this category was only £32.00 while the average RV for firms who wholly occupied a factory was £219.00.[56]

The small-scale nature of enterprise prompted openness as

Table 3.6: Factory occupancy by firms, 1815

Total number of firms	Shared part factory units		Wholly occupied factory firms		Part/occupied part empty[a]	
	No	% of total	No	% of total	No	% of total
90[b]	60	66.6	25	27.7	5	5.7

Notes: a. These were firms who occupied part of a factory building but did not share with other firms, part of the property remaining empty.
b. For a list of these 90 firms see Lloyd-Jones and Le Roux, 'Size of Firms', pp. 81–2.

Source: Compiled from R. Lloyd-Jones and A. A. Le Roux, 'The Size of Firms in the Cotton Industry: Manchester 1815–41', *Economic History Review*, Vol. XXXIII, no. 1 (1980), Table 4, p. 77.

small firms were subject to high exit and entry rates[57] and this provided opportunities for the man of little capital to try his skills at entrepreneurship, usually unsuccessfully.[58] This small-scale pattern of business is also characteristic of the warehouse system. The majority of warehouses were small-scale affairs with an RV of less than £50[59] and this is shown in Table 3.7.

Table 3.7: Distribution of Manchester warehouses by RV, 1815

Size category RV (£)	Number of warehouses units	% of total number of warehouse units
1–50	1,118	71.1
51–100	315	20.0
101–150	94	5.9
151–200	31	1.9
201–250	8	0.4
251–300	3	0.2
301–350	4	0.25
351–400	4	0.25
Total	1,577	100.00

Source: Compiled from the Poor Rate Assessment Book for the Township of Manchester, 1815 (MCL, M9/40/2).

Roland Smith has observed that the size of Manchester warehouses varied according to the capital and requirements of the particular merchant or manufacturer. Many, reflecting the data in Table 3.7, were mere dwellings converted into warehouses on account of their central location, and usually rated at about

£4.00 annually. For example, five houses in Cheapside, Manchester, were between 1815 and 1821 converted to and sold as warehouses.[60] The cost of new fixed capital investment in warehouses may well have been small, and Chapman informs us that 'Even the warehouses built by substantial merchants did not always represent original contributions to capital', because in many cases they could be converted from other property uses.[61] The process of conversion was to continue in later years and offered good prospects of capital gain to the shrewd house buyer, as Richard Cobden was aware when he wrote to his brother, Frederic, in September 1832:

> I have given such a start to Mosley Street, that all the world will be at my heels soon. My next door neighbour, Brookes, of the firm of Cunliffe and Brookes, bankers, has sold his house to be converted into a warehouse. The owner of the house on the other side has given his tenants notice for the same purpose. The architect assures me if I were to put up my house tomorrow, I might have 6,000 guineas for it. So as I gave but 3,000 and all the world is talking of the bargain here, and there being but one criterion of a man's ability — the making of money — I am already thought a clever fellow.[62]

The greed for warehouse space, indicated by the process of conversion, was also typified by the practice of sub-letting.[63] Similar to factories, the multiple occupancy of warehouses was widespread, suggesting the rentier nature of the system. This can be clearly seen in Cannon Street, the centre of Manchester's largest warehouse district,[64] where, in 1815, 57 warehouses were occupied by 106 separate firms[65] (see Table 3.8). Similar to factories, the shared part warehouse firm (SPWH firm), accounting for 75 per cent of the total number of firms in Cannon Street in 1815, was a common feature of the Manchester warehouse system at that time.

The sharing of warehouse space was particularly common amongst the large number of country manufacturers operating in the Manchester market. With the growing demand for warehouse premises, from the 1780s onwards, country manufacturers found it useful to share their warehouses with others in order to spread the burden of high rents. If a manufacturer could not afford to rent a warehouse he might borrow one belonging to a more prosperous trader.[66] Country manufacturers

Table 3.8: Warehouse occupancy in Cannon Street, Manchester, by firms, 1815

Total no of warehouses	Total no of WH units[a]	Total no of firms	Shared part WH units		Wholly occupied WH firms	
			No	% of total firms	No	% of total firms
57	110	106	75	70.75	31	29.25

Note: a. The firms utilising warehouse units is less than the total number of warehouse units because 4 firms occupied 2 warehouse units each.

Source: Compiled from the Rate Book, 1815.

generally travelled to Manchester for the Tuesday or Saturday markets[67] and would usually conduct their business in one of the various large public houses in the town. Altogether, 52 different public houses were utilised by visiting manufacturers in 1815,[68] and J. T. Slugg points out that they would generally put up at some inn, the name of which was given in the directory as well as the address of their place of business.[69] The 1815 Commercial Directory lists some 496 country manufacturers operating in the Manchester market, most of whom had a designated warehouse address plus the name of a public house for meeting. For example, James Dean, a muslin manufacturer from Bolton,[70] rented a small warehouse, rated at £10.00, at 4 Abrahams Court, and was to be contacted at the Windmill Inn, Bridge Street, on Tuesdays and Saturdays.[71] Public houses were extensively used by outside manufacturers as meeting places for the purchase and sale of goods and were an important part of Manchester's marketing/economic structure. Thus the Liverpool merchant, William Duncan, wrote to Samuel Crompton in October 1798: 'Sir, as I intend to be in Manchester on Tuesday should I not meet with you, you will be so good as to call for me at the Star, Deansgate, I shall want all the cambrics you have on hand.'[72] Clearly, apart from their obvious leisure function, supplying a rapidly rising workforce, public houses had a direct economic linkage with warehouses[73] which reinforces the relations of distribution and exchange in the Manchester economy.

In general terms, what the above analysis suggests is that opportunities of becoming a capitalist (albeit a small one) were greater than the stereotype of the cotton lord would lead us to suppose. The small-scale nature of Manchester's capitalists, according to Seed, proliferated from the 1820s[74] but, quite clearly, this was a characteristic of Cottonopolis in 1815, and, no doubt, much earlier. Ironically, Manchester's symbolic role as the centre of the factory system may best be understood in terms of labour rather than capital. Cotton factories were greedy for labour and workers flocked to the mills. Farnie has claimed that the cotton industry 'As an employer of labour . . . expanded its activities most rapidly in the late eighteenth century and . . . reached the peak of its relative importance between 1811 and 1821.'[75] Cotton factories employed a far higher ratio of labour per unit of property asset value than either warehouses or public houses. In 1815, Manchester's 90 cotton spinning firms employed an estimated 11,471 workers, representing approximately 12 per cent of the total population of the town.[76] What was characteristic of the cotton factory was its relatively high labour utilisation and this had an immediate impact on at least one major sector: housing. The housing sector accounted for 48.58 per cent of the total value of property assets in 1815, and its growth may represent an example of a Rostowian lateral linkage effect.[77] The Manchester rating district with the largest number of cotton factories (District 1, Ancoats) had by far the largest number of houses, accounting for 18.6 per cent of the total number of housing units. The second largest district for the concentration of factories (District 4) also had the second largest proportion of housing: 13.2 per cent. Thus the two major districts clustered around them 31.8 per cent of the total housing stock. We can suggest, therefore, that the employment-generating effect of the spinning factories stimulated the demand for housing.[78] Such claims must, of course, remain tentative, but it does suggest an area in which more detailed research could be profitably directed.[79]

The dynamic of the factory, therefore, cannot be simply written off, as will be demonstrated in later chapters.[80] Nevertheless, the reconstruction of Manchester's property asset structure casts considerable doubt on its status as a 'factory town'. What the analysis does show is that in Manchester capitalists, midway through the Industrial Revolution, were building a variegated economy where property asset structure was only lightly spotted with factories, but was literally saturated with warehouses, shops and public houses. At first glance, the case for an heroic interpretation of the factory, and of Manchester as 'Cottonopolis', would appear pretty thin. But the data is open to a variety of interpretations and our reconstruction highlights the need to examine the economic relationship between the factory and the warehouse. This will be the task of subsequent chapters, and we turn first to an analysis of the Manchester yarn market and outline the function of the warehouse firm in Manchester's business system.

NOTES AND REFERENCES

1. The basic empirical findings and the methodological approach we have adopted in the chapter has been examined in a recent edition of *Textile History*. R. Lloyd-Jones and M. J. Lewis, 'The Economic Structure of Cottonopolis: Manchester in 1815', *Textile History*, vol. 17, no. 1 (1986), pp. 71–89.
2. For an excellent description of Manchester in the nineteenth century see A. Prentice, *Historical Sketches and Personal Recollections of Manchester* (Charles Gilpin, London, 1851).
3. S. D. Chapman, *The Cotton Industry in the Industrial Revolution* (Macmillan, London, 1972), p. 48.
4. F. Engels, *The Condition of the English Working Class* (George Allen and Unwin, London, 1892, edn), p. 42.
5. M. Fores, 'The Myth of a British Industrial Revolution', *History*, vol. LXVI (1981), p. 183.
6. T. S. Ashton, *The Industrial Revolution 1760–1830* (Oxford University Press, Oxford, 1968 edn), p. 48.
7. D. N. McCloskey, 'The Industrial Revolution 1780–1860: A Survey', in R. Floud and D. N. McCloskey (eds), *The Economic History of Britain Since 1700* (2 vols, Cambridge University Press, Cambridge, 1981), vol. 1, p. 109.
8. McCloskey, 'The Industrial Revolution', p. 105.
9. The year 1815 falls approximately half-way through the 'classic' Industrial Revolution period and post-dates Rostow's'take-off' (1783–1802) by over a decade. For the dating of the 'take-off' in Britain see W. W. Rostow, *The Stages of Economic Growth* (Cambridge University Press, Cambridge, 1965 edn), p. 38.
10. The reconstruction also forms the basis for later chapters which analyse Manchester's changing economic structure and the conflict of interest between the factory and other business components, notably the warehouse.
11. Manchester Central Library (MCL), Poor Rate Assessment Book for the Township of Manchester, 1815 (MCL, M9/40/2).
12. For a recent statement on the usefulness of rate books in reconstructing the local economy see R. Lloyd-Jones and M. J. Lewis, 'Rate Books: A Technique of Reconstructing the Local Economy', *The Local Historian*, no. 1 (1987).
13. Property assets thus provide a minimum condition for the

conduct of economic activity and play an increasingly important role in those new modes of production associated with the Industrial Revolution. See, for example, the emergence of multi-storied cotton mills in the 1790s, described in F. Crouzet, 'Editor's Introduction', in F. Crouzet (ed.), *Capital Formation in the Industrial Revolution* (Methuen, London, 1972), p. 37. Also see S. D. Chapman, *The Cotton Industry*, p. 68, and J. Tann, *The Development of the Factory* (Cornmarket Press, London, 1970), ch. 8.

14. For an economic interpretation of the system of valuation see A. F. Millington, *An Introduction to Property Valuation* (Estates Gazette, London, 1972).

15. The property asset values for factories, employed here, are closely related to fixed capital but exclude machinery and the prime mover in terms of power source. For example, Nathanial Gould, the Manchester cotton manufacturer, informed the 1816 Select Committee that the poor rate assessment represented 'the rate at which the buildings are assessed and not the machinery in them'. PP, 1816 (397), 111, *Select Committee on the State of Children Employed in the Manufactories of the United Kingdom*, pp. 323–4.

16. A Comparative Statement Relating to the Assessment of Factories, Houses and Shops, Warehouses and Other Property in the Township of Manchester made by Messrs Bellhouse, Wallis and Johnson, July 1812 (MCL, M9/40/1/20). David Bellhouse and Company were listed in the 1815 Directory as Builders, Architects and Surveyors, *Pigot's Manchester Directory*, 1815.

17. The RV data is compiled from the 1815 Rate Book for Manchester.

18. Millington, *Property Valuation*, p. 4.

19. Ibid., p. 37. One obvious reason why cotton factories were valued was for insurance purposes, especially given the high risk of fire in these premises. For a discussion on the use and reliability of insurance valuations see S. D. Chapman, 'Fixed Capital Formation in the British Cotton Industry, 1770–1815', *Economic History Review*, vol. XXIII, no. 2 (1970), pp. 253–6.

20. See G. W. Daniels, 'Valuation of Manchester Cotton Factories in the Early Years of the Nineteenth Century', *Economic Journal*, vol. XXV (1915), pp. 625–6.

21. Messrs Bellhouse, Wallis and Johnson, Assessment, 1812.

22. Master Cotton Spinners Memorial Sent to the Church Wardens and Overseers of the Poor Law in Manchester, 10 July 1810 (MCL, M3/3/7).

23. The rentier nature of Manchester's warehouse system will be discussed in the last section of the chapter.

24. The rate in Manchester was set by the Police Commissioners who empowered District Assessors, under the administration of the Church Wardens and Overseers, to collect the poor rate and assess property. See A. Redford *et al.*, *The History of Local Government in Manchester* (3 vols, Longmans, Green, London, 1939), vol. 1, p.232.

25. Cotton Spinners Memorial, 1810.

26. This firm operated a spinning factory in Salford, employing 911

workers and rated at £700.00 in 1815. PP 1816 (397), 111, p. 325.

27. Ibid., p. 358. This highlights an important characteristic of a property asset, developed in Chapter 2, which is, that its utilisation should reflect, at a given moment in time, its profitable use compared to other potential uses.

28. See R. Lloyd-Jones and A. A. Le Roux, 'The Size of Firms in the Cotton Industry: Manchester 1815–41', *Economic History Review*, vol. XXXIII, no. 1 (1890), pp. 72–82.

29. Messrs Bellhouse, Wallis and Johnson, Assessment 1812.

30. This contention is supported by the conclusion of the 1812 valuers who found no evidence to support the spinners' case that their property was greatly overvalued in relation to other property assets. Messrs Bellhouse, Wallis and Johnson, Valuation 1812.

31. In any case, there is little danger of underestimating the contribution of factories to the overall property asset structure, since if factories were overvalued it would inflate their importance in the overall account.

32. Millington, *Property Valuation*, p. 4.

33. For an excellent account of fixed capital in the cotton industry up to 1815 see M. M. Edwards, *The Growth of the British Cotton Trade 1780–1815* (Manchester University Press, Manchester, 1967), pp. 182–215; and S. D. Chapman, 'Fixed Capital', pp. 235–66. However, in terms of any systematic quantitative analysis, Crouzet has warned that contemporary estimates of fixed capital were no more than 'flights of fancy', Crouzet, 'Editor's Introduction', p. 47.

34. Thus we can compile a geographical distribution for property assets across Manchester's rating districts. Manchester was divided into 14 districts for rating purposes and for a description of these see Lloyd-Jones and Lewis, 'Economic Structure', Appendix B, pp. 85–6.

35. The cross-referencing of large amounts of data was greatly aided by the use of a computer data bank.

36. This becomes more striking if we consider the fact that 'Only in cotton did . . . fixed capital ever become the major component . . . in the typical up-to-date mill of the period 1780–1830 fixed capital represented . . . a little more than half of the capital invested.' S. Pollard, 'Fixed Capital in the Industrial Revolution in Britain', in Crouzet (ed.), *Capital Formation*, pp. 148–9.

37. For a recent re-statement of the productivity impact of the cotton industry see McCloskey, 'The Industrial Revolution', pp. 108–17.

38. J. Seed, 'Unitarianism, Political Economy and the Antinomies of Liberal Culture in Manchester', *Social History*, vol. 7, no. 1 (1982), p. 4.

39. R. Smith, 'Manchester as a Centre for Manufacturing and Merchandising of Cotton Goods 1820–1830', *University of Birmingham Historical Journal*, vol. 4, (1953–4), p. 48.

40. Ibid., p. 42.

41. The total number of warehouse units in 1815 was 1,577, with a total RV of £73,627.00 and, as will be shown in Chapter 4, the economic activity of 1,450 warehouses were positively identified. Warehouses were predominantly engaged in the various cotton trades and textile

finishing, accounting for 70 per cent of the total number of units. See Table 4.1.

42. Such judgements are, of course, only rough and ready compounded by the great variety in the size of cotton firms, the use of second-hand machinery, the hiring of power, etc. However, Chapman shows that 12 factory buildings in 1795 were valued at £26,780 and the machinery and steam engines incorporated in those factories were valued at £24,670. S. D. Chapman, 'Fixed Capital', Appendix D, p. 260. It seems to us that a one-for-one ratio between factory property assets and machinery and power is a reasonable estimate.

43. Smith, 'Manchester', p. 43.

44. By 1815 the central business areas of Manchester in districts 6 and 9 were saturated with warehouses. For the growth of Manchester warehouses *c.* 1807–15, and the distribution of warehouses by district, see Appendix 5.

45. See Fores, 'Myth', pp. 187–8. Fores also associates industrialisation with the process of urban living and non-traditional activities, though he is highly critical of this interpretation. Ibid., p. 188.

46. Fort Bros and Company were calico printers who in 1815 operated a warehouse at 9 Cannon Street Buildings, district 6, rated at £150.00. Manchester Rate Book, 1815 and *Pigot's Commercial Directory*, 1815.

47. J. Morley, *The Life of Richard Cobden* (T. Fisher Unwin, London, 1905 ed.), vol. 1, pp. 16–17.

48. Richard Cobden fits in neatly with Crouzet's notion of the 'self-made man', and he claims that 'this expression had a broader meaning than an individual of working-class origins, and that a substantial proportion of industrialists had been the architects of their own fortunes'. See F. Crouzet, *The First Industrialists: The Problem of Origins* (Cambridge University Press, Cambridge, 1985), pp. 131, 143. Undoubtedly, the openness of Manchester's business system fostered the notion of the small capitalist of independent means.

49. A. E. Musson, *The Growth of British Industry* (B. T. Batsford, London, 1978), p. 14.

50. As outlined earlier, the concept of a property asset allows for the multiple occupancy of individual buildings.

51. For example, one factory in district 4, rated overall at £252.00, housed 12 separate firms with one part empty. Rate Book, 1815.

52. For an explanation of the employment size categories see Lloyd-Jones and Le Roux, 'Size of Firms', pp. 74–5.

53. Ibid., Table 2, 3(a) and 3(b), pp. 75, 76.

54. The changing pattern of factory utilisation and the demise of the SPF firm in the period between 1815 and 1825 will be discussed in Chapter 7.

55. The rentier nature of Manchester's factory system lends support to the spinners' case that the factory assessment should be based upon rental earnings and not replacement cost.

56. Lloyd-Jones and Le Roux, 'Size of Firms', p. 77.

57. For a discussion of entry and exit rates, in Manchester's cotton factory sector, in the first half of the nineteenth century, see Lloyd-

Jones and Le Roux, 'Size of Firms', pp. 72–82, and R. Lloyd-Jones and A. A. Le Roux, 'Marshall and the Birth and Death of Firms: Manchester 1815–33', *Business History*, vol. XXIV, no. 2 (1982), pp. 143–50. The pattern of exit and entry rates, for cotton firms, will be analysed in Chapter 7.

58. Crouzet reminds us that business history tends to be 'biased towards the successful and the big men', forgetting the many small businessmen 'who participated in short-lived partnerships'. Crouzet, *The First Industrialists*, pp. 60–1.

59. The average RV of a warehouse unit in 1815 was £46.70.

60. Smith, 'Manchester', p. 64. For an excellent description of the rapid growth of warehouse building in Manchester in the last quarter of the eighteenth century see J. Ashton, *The Manchester Guide: A Brief Historical Description of the Towns of Manchester and Salford* (Joseph Ashton, Manchester, 1804), p. 272.

61. Chapman, 'Fixed Capital', p. 237. For examples of the conversion of buildings, especially inns and houses, to warehouses, see T. Swindells, *Manchester Streets and Manchester Men* (Morton, Didsbury, Manchester, 1908), especially pp. 78–9, 196–7, 203–4, 206.

62. Quoted in Morley, *Richard Cobden*, p. 22.

63. In fact, the rate books indicate that little space was unutilised in a typical warehouse building, with cellars and rooms being partitioned to house business firms.

64. District 6, centred around Cannon Street, was the heart of Manchester's warehouse system, possessing 663 warehouse units and representing 42 per cent of the total in 1815. This, together with district 9 (possessing 421 warehouse units, 26.7 per cent of the total), formed the centre of Manchester's warehouse business community. See Appendix 2.

65. A single warehouse might accommodate up to 10 or more separate firms. Thus, for example, a warehouse at 13 Cannon Street, rated overall at £182.00, housed 9 separate firms. Of these, 6 were engaged in cotton manufacturing and dealing and 3 in calico printing. Rate Book, 1815, and *Pigot's Commercial Directory*, 1815. The pattern of warehouse property asset utilisation will be discussed in Chapter 7.

66. Edward, *British Cotton Trade*, p. 174.

67. For example, Roberty Heywood, a partner in the firm of John Heywood and Sons, quilting manufacturers, Bolton, was from about 1805 involved in the Manchester end of the business and travelled to the firm's warehouse in Riding's Court 'usually on Saturdays'. See W. E. Brown, *Robert Heywood of Bolton 1786–1868* (S.R. Publishers, Wakefield, 1970), p. 8. In 1815, this firm rented a small warehouse, rated at £10.00, at 3 Ridings Court and was to be contacted at the Windmill Inn. Rate Book, 1815, and *Pigot's Commercial Directory*, 1815.

68. Information compiled from *Pigot's Commercial Directory*, 1815.

69. J. T. Slugg, *Reminiscences of Manchester Fifty Years Ago* (Marshall, Simpkin, London, 1881), pp. 1–2.

70. Seventy Bolton cotton manufacturers are listed in the directory as renting warehouse space. *Pigot's Commercial Directory*, 1815.

71. Rate Book, 1815, and *Pigot's Commercial Directory*, 1815.

72. Irving MSS, Letter from W. Duncan to Samuel Crompton, Oct. 1798.

73. Thus District 6, by far the largest warehouse district in Manchester, also possessed the biggest public houses and inns. The average RV for public houses and inns in district 6 was £73.64, the largest for any Manchester district.

74. Seed, 'Unitarianism', p. 18.

75. D. A. Farnie, *The English Cotton Industry and the World Market 1815–1896* (Clarendon Press, Oxford, 1979), p. 23.

76. The population for 1815 was taken at the mid-point between the 1811 and 1821 census. For the employment estimates see Lloyd-Jones and Le Roux, 'Size of Firms', pp. 73–6. An independent contemporary estimate puts the number of spinning operatives in Manchester in 1811 at 9,000, which fits easily with the 1815 figure of 11,471. See evidence of Thomas Whitelegg, in PP 1816 (398), 111, p. 144.

77. Rostow defines lateral linkages in terms of the ability of the leading sector (cotton) to 'induce around it a whole set of changes which tend to reinforce the industrialising process on a wider front'. These lateral effects are 'symbolised by the acceleration of urbanisation', and obviously the demands for housing by the working population, in the face of expanding industry, present an ideal example of such spreader effects. See W. W. Rostow, 'Leading Sectors and the Take-Off', in W. W. Rostow (ed.), *The Economics of Take-Off into Self-Sustained Growth* (Macmillan, London, 1963).

78. It is quite likely that the vast majority of housing was constructed for private rent and reflected the profitability of this investment in the context of a rapidly rising town population. Manchester's population rose from 75,000 in 1801 to 89,000 in 1811 and 126,000 in 1821, rising by 1.9 per cent per annum in the first decade and 2.9 per cent in the second.

79. For a detailed analysis of housing in the nineteenth century see S. D. Chapman (ed.), *The History of Working Class Housing: A Symposium* (David and Charles, Newton Abbott, 1971). See also *Table of assessments to poor rates in Manchester . . . tables of number of houses and inhabitants*, 1821–31 (M63/7/12 n.d. M.C.L.).

80. See Chapters 6, 7 and 9.

4

From Factory to Warehouse: The Warehouse System and the Yarn Market in Manchester

A competitive market economy requires channels of distribution to direct the flow of goods from producer to consumer. Such a channel may well take a variety of different forms and perform a range of different functions. In a recent text, a warehouse has been defined as providing 'what is required, when it is required, in the condition which it is required, and, to do all these things economically'.[1] The Manchester warehouse system at the end of the Napoleonic Wars is no exception to this and provides an example of a complex chain of distribution linking producer to consumer. But the system was more than a distribution chain; it will be argued that the warehouse was a key nodal point in a mode of production quite different to that of the factory. This immediately raises issues of warehouse growth, structure and function. The latter two categories will be dealt with in the remainder of the chapter while questions of growth will be examined more thoroughly in Chapters 6 and 7.

As a starting point, however, the following contemporary observations by Joseph Ashton conveys the dynamic growth of the warehouse system during the early phase of the Industrial Revolution. Ashton stated in 1804 that,

> The increase in trade has not only contributed much new building . . . in order to manufacture goods, to lodge them when made, and display them for sale, but it has materially altered the appearance of the older parts of town. Thirty years ago, the neighbourhood of St Anne's Square, King Street and St James' Square, were the best situations for warehouses of consequence. High Street and Cannon Street contained

> nothing but dwelling houses, Peel Street and its neighbourhood were . . . quite remote from business. Building after building arose, and dwelling after dwelling metamorphosised into warehouses[2] which have spread into Cannon Street, High Street, Duke Street, Marsden Square and part of Church Street, and the upper end of Market Street.[3]

By 1815 the central business area of Manchester in districts 6 and 9 were saturated with warehouses.[4] These were located not

Table 4.1: Manchester warehouses by type of economic activity, 1815

Economic activity	No wh units	RV of wh units	% of units to total units	% of RV to total RV wh sector
Cotton various (manufacturers, dealers, spinners, etc)	809	39,264	55.8	55.4
Cotton preparations (calenders, dressers, sizers, etc)	31	1,268	2.1	1.8
Calico printers	105	6,883	7.3	9.7
Finishers (bleachers, dry-salterers, dyers)	39	1,810	2.7	2.6
General merchants	53	3,106	3.7	4.4
Textile (non-cotton)	37	2,018	2.6	2.8
Haberdashery	36	1,386	2.5	2.0
Commission dealers, auctioneers, agents (unspecified)	21	803	1.4	1.1
Carriers and packers	36	5,278	2.5	7.4
Provision merchants (food, drink, tobacco)	90	3,173	6.2	4.5
Timber, furniture dealers, coach makers	21	756	1.4	1.1
Metal trades	18	628	1.2	0.9
Miscellaneous	57	1,350	3.9	1.9
Empty	97	3,090	6.7	4.4
Total[a]	1,450	70,813	100.0	100.0

Note: a. The total number of warehouse units assessed in the 1815 rate book was 1,577, with a total RV of £73,627.00. The number of unspecified warehouses were 127, with an RV of £2,814.00, representing 3.8 per cent of the total RV of all warehouse units.

Source: R. Lloyd-Jones and M. J. Lewis, 'The Economic Structure of Cottonopolis: Manchester in 1815', *Textile History*, Vol. 17, no. 1 (1986), p. 79.

only in the principal streets and thoroughfares but in a complex warren of alleys and courts running off the main arteries. Let us now explore the structural properties of this system. By cross referencing the names of warehouse occupiers, listed in the Manchester rate books for 1815,[5] with their corresponding names in the trade directories,[6] it has been possible to identify the main economic activity of 1,450 warehouses. These activities are listed in Table 4.1.

Certainly, warehouses were dominated by the cotton textile sector. If we take the first four categories in Table 4.1, then these represent 67.9 per cent of the total number of warehouse units and 69.5 per cent of the total RV.[7] We will now concern ourselves with the cotton warehouse system. Cotton warehouses, as a key structural component of the Manchester business system, operated along two distribution paths possessing overlapping yet varying economic functions. The first path involves functional relationships of pure exchange, and the second path involves a combination of exchange with fabrication. The basic synchronic patterns of these distribution paths are illustrated in Figure 4.1

Figure 4.1: Warehouses, basic synchronic patterns of distribution

Path	Function
Pure exchange	Storage — Display — Sale/disposal
Exchange and fabrication Combined	Purchase — Putting out/receiving in — Sale/Disposal

The pure exchange path involves the storage of raw cotton, of yarn, of grey cloths, of printed and finished cloths, etc. Warehouses could be used for specialised storage; for example, 32 Manchester firms occupying warehouse units were cotton twist and weft dealers only; or they might store a range of cotton, from the raw state to the finished product. Storage itself involves handling, packaging, sorting and stock control. In terms of the first three functions, Smith has pointed out that for the cotton cloth merchant Manchester warehouses 'provided premises in which cloth from country manufacturers, Manchester manufacturers or even from handloom weavers could be accepted, weighed, sealed and placed ready either for despatch to the finishers or for sale after finishing to retail in the United Kingdom.'[8] The importance of stock control is reflected in the columns of the Manchester newspapers; there are frequent advertisements for book-keeping positions 'in print or manufacturing warehouses'.[9] In addition to storage, and its related functions, warehouses offered a convenient place for the display of goods[10] where patterns[11] could be shown or customers inspect goods prior to public auction. In March 1815 Richard Langston, a cotton dealer operating a warehouse rated at £120.00, at 10 Back Square, Manchester, informed potential buyers of bales of Surat (47 bales in all), to be auctioned at his warehouse, that the cottons 'may be viewed on the morning of the sale . . . in lots to suit purchasers'.[12] Public auction was one of the forms that sale could take in the warehouse system, and ranged over a variety of goods including the sale of textile machinery.[13] Sale also took place by private contract and this, coupled with auctions, meant that 'The most widely adopted method of marketing cottons was by means of the warehouse sale'.[14] The sales themselves, at times, took on a frenzied atmosphere, as the young Samuel Bamford, recalling his time as a warehouse assistant in Manchester in 1808, informs us. On market days, which occurred on Tuesdays, Thursdays and Saturdays, the warehouse was opened at 6 am and at 7 am the sale commenced. The material was carried by Bamford upstairs to the sales room where it was placed on a clean white cloth spread over the floor of the room. Then,

> A scramble . . . commenced amongst the buyers which should get the most pieces; sometimes they met me at the sale door, and tore them off my back . . . and many a good coat have I seen split up, or left with the laps dangling, after a struggle of that sort.[15]

The advantage of warehouse space in the Manchester market was obvious[16] and following a path of pure exchange, a number of different functions were performed which contributed to the development of a complex chain of distribution within the Manchester economy.

Clearly, therefore, the functional relationships of pure exchange, involving no fabrication, allows for a variety of commodity forms and is the normal conception of a warehouse system, firmly locating it within the field of distribution. However, warehouses played a pivotal role in the system of manufacturing and followed the second distribution path which combined exchange with fabrication. Warehouses were utilised by master weavers as part of a putting-out system of manufacture, and were the nodal points of a large-scale system of cotton production.[17] Yarn was put out from the warehouse to be fabricated into cloth and subsequently brought back for finishing and sale. William Cooke, a master weaver, stated in 1803 that contracts were made at the warehouse and 'we always made a bargain when the work goes out and we expect it to be fulfilled'.[18] Indeed, the term warehouse or house was used to describe the manufacturing firm[19] and was the base from which the weaver was paid. As a master weaver stated, 'there are workmen who will, perhaps, take out of the warehouse as much as two guineas for an odd week or two'.[20] The warehouse also operated as a point of quality control in the manufacturing system. As another manufacturer admitted to the 1803 committee, not all masters were experts at judging the quality of a weaver's work but 'if, and when a piece comes before him, (the master) he is not competent to judge, he generally has an experienced workman in the warehouse who knows'.[21] Quite clearly, the warehouse may be identified as a basic component in the manufacturing system and, as Bythell points out, while the master weaver required little fixed capital to start up in business — a collection of loom accessories, a warping mill and winding machinery — he did need a warehouse.[22] According to George Smith, a partner in a Manchester cotton firm, the Manchester master manufacturers at the end of the Napoleonic Wars purchased twist and yarn from the spinners and 'employed handloom weavers to weave into cotton goods,'[23] this system being co-ordinated at the warehouse. It took a more complex form in the hands of the large Manchester merchant manufacturers who, rather than employing handloom weavers directly, engaged agents or putters-out as intermediaries. This can be seen in the activities of Nathanial and George Gould[24] who operated one of the largest warehouses in Manchester at Peel Street, rated in 1815 at £280.00. Their weaving was done about 7 to 12 miles outside of Manchester and was managed by a foreman or putter-out.[25] The material, mainly fustian, was brought back to the Manchester warehouse where it was distributed to fustian cutters directly employed by the Goulds.[26] Smaller manufacturers, on the other hand, directly employed handloom weavers and in Manchester it would appear that weavers worked mainly in cellars.[27] Samuel Stocks, a partner in the firm of S. &. S. Stocks, cotton manufacturers and dealers, Manchester, informed the 1816 Select Committee, inquiring into child factory work, that he employed 20 directly 'under his own eye', that is, in his own warehouse. But, he also employed handloom weavers who worked in their own cellars.[28] Thomas Whitelegg also put-out from his warehouse to handloom weavers and confirmed that many of them worked in their own cellars.[29] This system of work had not changed in any large degree for over half a century. John Kennedy, the Manchester cotton spinner, claimed in 1815 that weaving 'remains nearly the same as it was 50 or 60 years ago'.[30] We can safely assume that Wadsworth and Mann's observations concerning Manchester weaving in the mid-eighteenth century will serve as a useful model for 1815. The two authors note that 'Most of the weavers of Manchester parish probably lived near enough to their employers to carry their piece to the warehouse'.[31]

Warehouses were not only points of exchange and mediation of yarn, cloth prices, wages and quality control but they were also directly integrated within the system of capital-labour relations. In 1755 the Society of Smallware Weavers and Journeymen presented an outline of their organisational structure:

> As there is now in this town (Manchester) many . . . smallware makers, everyone of those who keeps any hands in this Branch, we call a Shop, and each of these Shops appoints a Man to go in the Name and Behalf of the whole Shop; and these Men, when met, which is once a month, form what we call the Trades Society.[32]

Wadsworth and Mann are certain that 'shop' actually refers to the warehouse. They state: the 'shops must mean, as Professor Daniels had suggested, the putting-out warehouse of the master manufacturer'.[33] It would appear, therefore, that the warehouse formed the nucleus for the building of trade union organisations prior to the emergence of the mechanised factory. It is further evidence of their focal position in the business system and prompts the question of what form the relationship between warehouse and factory took. Let us begin by making two basic assumptions; firstly, factories were concerned primarily with cotton spinning[34] and their linkage in the chain of production and distribution would be forged in the yarn market; secondly, the yarn market, in turn, provided the source of input for weaving manufacture which in 1815 was still based predominately on a non-factory system of production. Warehouses, acting as nodal points in the distribution of yarn, are the agency and site of exchange between two different forms of production systems; one factory (based on power mechanisation and satisfying at least one notion of the Industrial Revolution), the other non-factory, warehouse (based on a non-mechanised, non-power mode). Having identified the yarn market as a key link in the factory-warehouse chain, let us explore it in some depth.

THE YARN MARKET

The yarn market is conceptualised as a system possessing the basic synchronic components, representing firm types, outlined in Figure 4.2. At the relational level the exchange of yarn could

Figure 4.2: Yarn market system — basic components (firms)

Firm type
A Spinner (factory)
B Manufacturer (warehouse — non factory)
C Spinner/Manufacturer (combined factory-warehouse)
D Cotton dealer only (warehouse — non-fabrication)
E Manufacturer/dealer (combined warehouse — fabrication — non-fabrication)

occur in two basic ways. Firstly, internally via exchange in a combined spinning and weaving firm (firm type C). Here the commodity crossed factory and non-factory fabrication within the boundary of the same firm. Secondly, exchange occurred externally via sales between firm type A and firm types B, D and E. In Manchester, combined factory and warehouse firms were of little economic significance. Of the 90 firms operating cotton factories in 1815 only 9 firms could be positively identified as combining spinning and manufacturing.[35] Combined spinning and weaving firms were more common in the country districts, but the larger cotton towns such as Bolton and Blackburn followed the Manchester pattern and operated only a small number of business firms of the C type.[36]

A good deal of our information about the structure and workings of the yarn market has been provided by the excellent work of Edwards[37] and Lee.[38] They base their evidence largely on the letter books of the large-scale spinning firm of McConnel and Kennedy.[39] A critical evaluation of this firm's role suggests the need for a reappraisal of Edwards' and Lee's interpretation of the workings of the yarn market. McConnel and Kennedy operated a spinning factory in Ancoats rated at £933.00 in 1815 and employed just over 1,000 operatives. It was the highest rated factory in Manchester and was exceeded in numbers employed only by the factory of A. & G. Murrary, also located in Ancoats.[40] In terms of McConnel and Kennedy's operation in the yarn market Lee informs us that 'McConnel and Kennedy's principal customers were the dealers . . . although they did sell direct to master weavers'. In turn, the dealers 'customers were merchants involved in the export trade or in putting-out to local weavers, often in the merchants' employ'.[41] That is, merchants were manufacturers receiving their yarn from the dealers, and this relationship is illustrated in Figure 4.3. The dotted line

Figure 4.3: Yarn market relationships by firm type

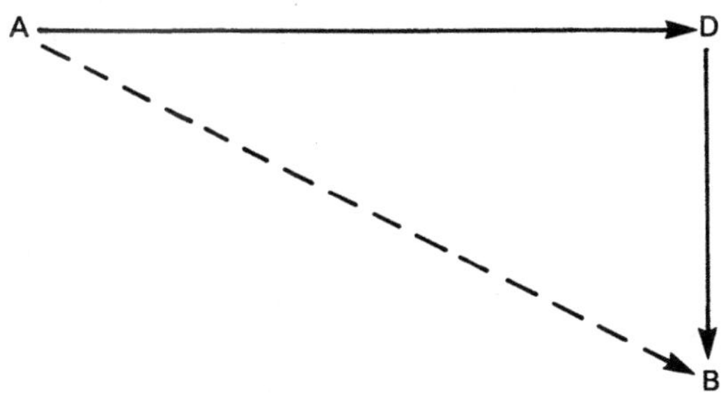

suggests that the more direct route from factory spinner (firm type A) to warehouse manufacturer (firm type B) was in fact less predominant than the more elongated chain (A–D–B) where the yarn was routed through the warehouse cotton dealing firm (firm type D). Edwards points out that McConnel and Kennedy preferred to sell to the large dealers 'who would be responsible for selling yarn to a large number of weavers and other dealers'.[42] For example, in the important Scottish yarn market the firm from 1808 consigned most of its yarn to one dealer only, Robert McGavin, who was responsible for selling yarn for the company in all the Scottish markets.[43] The large spinner clearly wished to avoid dealing directly with small weavers and consequently made use of the services of the cotton dealer. The yarn dealers themselves operated in all the major cotton centres but especially in the central Manchester market 'where they probably rented warehouses or they had a contact there who kept them supplied with yarn'.[44] Given the ascendancy of the A–D–B route, the suggestion from Edwards and Lee is that McConnel and Kennedy and other spinning factory firms dominated their dealers. The power of the factory spinner was transmitted through the A–D–B circuit by the role of commission. Rather than direct sale to their dealers, firms such as McConnel and Kennedy utilised them as agents selling their yarn on a commission basis.[45] The degree to which the commission agent could exercise control over the price of yarn, or influence selling policy, was a function of market conditions and the relative size and resource base of factory firms compared with warehouse dealing firms.[46] According to Edwards, the large spinner 'was often in a position to dominate the yarn market',[47] and held a tight hold on their dealers. For example, McConnel and Kennedy's dealers were 'expected to keep them informed about the state of the market and the level of their stocks; on no account were they allowed to vary the selling price or the amount of credit and discount the firm offered'.[48] In addition to McConnel and Kennedy, the large Manchester spinning factory firms, such as Adam and George Murray, Houldsworth, Benjamin Gray (Ancoats Twist Company), fixed their own prices and laid down selling policy to their dealers. Concluding his analysis of the yarn market, Edwards claims that 'throughout the entire 35 years (1780–1815) the yarn market seems to have been influenced by a few large spinners'.[49] In this conception the factory spinner is the dominant component in the yarn market, and in terms of diachronic relations the factory is instrumental in linking the chain factory-warehouse.

This may be a rather hasty conclusion, and Edwards himself hints at an alternative interpretation. For example, he draws attention to the difficulty of drawing a distinction between manufacturer and merchant[50] and also to the broader problem of differentiating between different components of the yarn market.[51] One of the consequences of this, is that little attention has been paid to type E firms, the combined manufacturing and dealing warehouse.[52] Edwards does provide one or two examples of the cotton manufacturer and dealer operating in the Manchester yarn market[53] but, as we will show below, their importance has been grossly underestimated. More directly,

Edwards accepts that the small factory spinner may have been 'virtually controlled by their yarn dealers' and concedes that at times even the larger spinners were obliged to make concessions with their dealers, or even circumvent them by selling directly to the manufacturer. Thus, during the severe depression of early 1811, McConnel and Kennedy wrote to John How in Belfast:

> Hearing that you have commenced manufacture with some other gentleman . . . we therefore beg leave in the present depressed state of things to hand you a list of prices which we request you will have the goodness to lay before your partners and we hope the extremely low prices will induce them to favour us with a large order.[54]

There appears to be little influence exerted by the spinner in the yarn market in this example. Of course, this is an extreme case and, to be fair to Edwards, the above example is consistent with his claim that relationships between spinner and dealer were a function of relative size and prevailing market conditions. Nevertheless, it is suggestive of the problematic nature of the factory-warehouse relationship and there are two problems with Edwards' overall interpretation. Firstly, even the large factory spinners, operating in a competitive business environment subject to sharp fluctuations, found their influence perhaps a rather transient commodity. Secondly, the reference to the small factory spinner raises the question of just how representative McConnel and Kennedy were of the typical factory firm, and how much weight should we place on their acitivities as an explanation of the workings of the yarn market.

Taking the first point, the large factory spinners found their potentially dominant position threatened by the system of credit operating in the yarn market. The existence of long terms of credit, whilst a necessity for the economic survival of small spinners with limited capital, was at the same time a source of constant insecurity in the trade. According to Lee, the threat of bankruptcy or at least the inability to meet debts hung over even the largest firms.[55] Attempts were made, at various times, to reduce the length of credit from the date of sale of yarn. In 1811, the large Glasgow factory spinner, Henry Houldsworth,[56] backed by other Glasgow and Paisley spinners, proposed the length of credit, from the date of sale of yarn, should be reduced from seven months to five months. He attempted to solicit

McConnel and Kennedy's support and warned them not to allow

> a lot of fellons called agents to hold us by the noses in the way the long credit for too long enabled them to do so, the shorter the credit the nearer you are to the manufacturer, this the agent sees and it's that that alarms him.[57]

According to Houldsworth, therefore, the existence of long-term credit shifted the balance of power in the circuit A–D–B too much in favour of the dealer. Furthermore, it was in the interest of the dealer to circumvent the more direct route between spinner and manufacturer; in other words, the longer the chain is stretched the more power is likely to shift towards the dealer. Clearly, the influence of the large factory spinner, in the operation of the yarn market, is not a straightforward affair and is a site for further investigation.[58] But there is a more immediate question which is concerned with the representative nature of the larger spinner. Is a firm such as McConnel and Kennedy typical of the general body of factory spinners? At least three objections may be made. Firstly, the large Manchester spinners were predominantly fine spinners — McConnel and Kennedy, A & G Murray, Thomas Houldsworth, Benjamin Gray, all come into this category.[59] Yet, as Edwards himself points out, the 'demand for fine yarns from weavers at home and overseas was limited throughout this period because the market for fine quality cloths, although increasing, was not as significant as the demand for cheaper materials'.[60] The main demand was for coarse yarns, below number 80, and as late as 1833 Baines took number 40 as the average count spun in Lancashire cotton factories.[61] A good deal of the discussion of Edwards and Lee refers only to fine yarn rather than the yarn market in general. Furthermore, the market for fine and coarse yarns could swing in opposite directions. In 1816, for example, the market for fine yarn was depressed but coarse numbers were doing well. McConnel and Kennedy wrote to their Swiss agent in September of that year to the effect that 'low numbers are in good demand here but there is little doing above 100'.[62]

Secondly, fluctuations in the markets for yarns were not unrelated to variations in firm size. Fine spinning firms tended to be larger business units than coarse spinners. The former needed to spread their production over a range of quality yarns to meet quite sharp movements in the market, while the latter required less capital to operate in a large and less irregular market.[63] Lloyd-Jones' and Le Roux's analysis of Manchester cotton factories in 1815 has clearly shown the predominance of small-scale units. Categorising firms as small, medium and large, over three-quarters of Manchester cotton firms, operating factories, fall into the small category. This is shown in Table 4.2.

Table 4.2: Size of Manchester cotton firms utilising factories in 1815

Size category	Number of firms	% of total
Small[a]	71	78.9
Medium[b]	12	13.3
Large[c]	7	7.8
Total	90	100.0

Notes: a. Small firms are defined as employing 150 employees or less.
b. Medium firms – employing 151–500 employees.
c. Large firms – employing 501 + employees.

Source: Compiled from data in R. Lloyd-Jones and A. A. Le Roux, 'The Size of Firms in the Cotton Industry: Manchester 1815–41', *Economic History Review,* vol. XXXIII, no. 1 (1980), p. 75.

It is fairly safe to assume that the majority of Manchester factory spinners produced low numbers of the coarse variety and that the fine spinners were the exception rather than the rule, as most factory firms were pretty small fry.

Thirdly, the representation of the large spinner is thus a problem and one which is compounded when the analysis of the yarn market is based upon the activities of McConnel and Kennedy. The firm sold primarily into the Scottish (Glasgow), Irish (Belfast), and Midlands (Nottingham) yarn markets, but very little into the Lancashire (Manchester) market. For example, Lee points out that the Scottish market remained the main outlet for the firm's yarns from the beginning of the nineteenth century until the late 1820s[64] but the Lancashire market, the most obvious market for their yarns, 'does not appear to have been very significant in the growth of McConnel and Kennedy'.[65] Yet, as Edwards points out, while 'Glasgow was an important distributing centre . . . it was always a smaller yarn market than Manchester'.[66] Material relating to the large fine spinning firms and, in particular, McConnel and Kennedy, is of considerable value in assessing the structure of the Scottish fine yarn market, but it is of doubtful value in the analysis of the larger and more important Manchester market. The Manchester market may, in terms of the structural relations of its components, have operated in quite a different way from that suggested by the experience of McConnel and Kennedy. Let us explore this issue.

THE MANCHESTER YARN MARKET

The immediate problem in analysing the Manchester market is the absence of business papers of cotton firms other than those of McConnel and Kennedy. The lack of a detailed empirical base forces us to return to our simple synchronic perspective which will at least allow us to outline the basic components of the Manchester system. We have already demonstrated that the majority of cotton factory spinning firms were small-scale units; what then of the role of the warehouse and the merchants and manufacturers who occupied them? Roland Smith has argued that there was an increase in the number of business firms, engaged in separate merchandising and finishing processes, particularly after 1820.[67] Indeed, he offers a breakdown of business functions for 1815, and this is shown in Table 4.3.

Table 4.3: Merchants and finishers operating in the Manchester market, 1815

Business activity	Number of firms (1815)
Merchants	131
Agents and commission dealers	53
Calico printers	129
Packers	12

Source: Compiled from data in R. Smith, 'Manchester as a Centre for Manufacturing and Merchandising of Cotton Goods, 1820–1830', *University of Birmingham Historical Journal*, vol. IV (1953–4), p. 61.

Table 4.3 grossly underestimates the non-factory sector of the cotton trade in post-Napoleonic Manchester. It has no place for the manufacturer and is coloured by Smith's hypothesis that the rapid expansion of the Manchester warehouse system was post-1820. We have already shown that warehouses, linked into the process of cotton production and distribution, were a dominant form before 1815. To provide an insight into the operations of the yarn market, we have taken the basic components of our simple synchronic system and cross referenced all those individuals operating warehouse units in 1815 against the description of their activities in the Manchester trade directory. The results are shown in Table 4.4.

Table 4.4: Manchester warehouse use by type of firm, 1815

Firm type		Number utilising warehouse units	% to total number of warehouse units
A	Spinner (factory)	5	0.7
B	Manufacturer (non-factory-weaving)	258	36.5
C	Spinner/Manufacturer (combined factory/ non-factory)	9	1.3
D	Cotton dealer (non-factory/non-fabrication)	137	19.4
E	Manufacturer/Dealer (combined fabrication-non-fabrication/non-factory)	298	42.1
Total		705	100.0

Source: Manchester Central Library (MCL), Poor Rate Assessment Book for the Township of Manchester, 1815 (MCL, M9/40/2/78); *Pigot's Trade and Commercial Directory for Manchester*, 1815.

Whilst Table 4.4. shows that specialist cotton dealing firms were important in the Manchester market, what is interesting is the large number of firms who combined dealing with manufacturing. Type E firms are more than twice the weight of type D, in terms of the number of operating units. There is little direct evidence of the activities of these combined manufacturing and dealing firms, though Edwards offers the example of the Blackburn firm of Smaley, Ellison and Walmsley, who manufactured calicos which were sold in the London and Manchester markets. They were also 'keen to sell other men's yarn . . . and . . . installed their representatives in warehouses in order to do this'.[68] Another example is provided by the firm of James Massey and Sons who are listed in the 1815 directory as manufacturers and dealers, agents and commission dealers. This firm operated two warehouse units in Marsden Square, Manchester, rated at £45.00 and £30.00 in 1815.[69] This firm sold yarn and cloth in the Manchester market on a commission basis, up to 1820, and employed 1,200 to 1,400 handloom weavers.[70]

It is not possible to offer any assessment of the balance between manufacturing and dealing within these firms. But we can compare their size with manufacturing only firms (type B), and we might hypothesise that given they were engaged in combined activities we would expect them to be larger than type B firms. Adopting RVs of their warehouse units as a proxy for size, the results are shown in Table 4.5. The warehouse units

Table 4.5: Warehouse units, size of firm types B and E, 1815

RV size category (£)	Firm type E No of warehouse units	Firm type B No of warehouse units
1–25	80	172
26–50	91	43
51–75	43	14
76–100	34	19
101–125	18	6
126–150	17	5
151+	19	4

Source: Compiled from the Manchester Rate Book, 1815.

utilised by type E firms (manufacturers and dealers) were significantly larger than type B firms (manufacturing only); 44 per cent of the former category had warehouse units rated at over £51.00, while the latter had only 18.6 per cent. Also, type E firms tended to use permanent warehouse facilities in Manchester while type B firms only used them on particular market days. Of the 258 type B firms, 154 were identified from the trade directory as operating their warehouses only on one to three days a week, the norm being Tuesdays and Saturdays.[71]

The larger size and permanent warehouse operation of type E units does not necessarily prove that they were actively engaged in the yarn market, but one suspects this was the case. Of the 137 cotton dealers (type D), only 32 dealt exclusively in cotton twist and weft.[72] This suggests there was ample scope for the activities of the manufacturing and dealing firms in the yarn market, a suspicion reinforced by the lack of spinning factory firms utilising separate warehouse units. Furthermore, these type E firms stand comparison, in terms of size, with the cotton factory. In 1815, 48.8 per cent of cotton spinning factories were rated at £50.00 or less (see Table 4.2), which is roughly the same figure for manufacturers and dealers (46.0 per cent). If we exclude the large fine spinners who, as we have seen, operated mostly outside the Manchester market, the case for a factory spinner dominated market is by no means secure. These are tentative observations, but the role of the manufacturing and dealing firm was in all probability an important one. These firms, coupled with the twist and weft dealers, who also operated substantial warehouses in the town, were a force to be reckoned with, and their overall weight in the business structure suggests a key role in the yarn market. Certainly what can be said, is that there is little hard evidence to suppose that the factory spinners dominated the Manchester yarn market. Manufacturing and dealing firms, utilising warehouses, may well have been the predominant component of the system. Once again, Manchester's status as a 'factory town' remains ambiguous.

NOTES AND REFERENCES

1. J. A. Burton, *Effective Warehousing* (Macdonald and Evans, London, 1973), p. 7.
2. As an illustration of such metamorphosis see Manchester newspapers of the period. For example, the *Manchester Mercury*, 4 April 1815, refers to the conversion of a public house into a warehouse.
3. J. Ashton, *The Manchester Guide, A Brief Historical Description of the Towns of Manchester and Salford* (Joseph Ashton, Manchester, 1804), p. 272.
4. For a distribution of Manchester warehouses by district see Appendix 2, which also provides a description of Manchester rating districts.
5. Manchester Central Library (MCL), Poor Rate Assessment Book for the Township of Manchester, 1815 (MCL, M9/40/2/78).
6. *Pigot's Trade and Commercial Directory for Manchester*, 1815.
7. Clearly, districts 6 and 9 were the centres of Manchester's cotton warehouse system, with 55 per cent and 32 per cent, respectively, of all identified cotton warehouses being located in these districts.
8. R. Smith, 'Manchester as a Centre for Manufacturing and Merchandising of Cotton Goods, 1820–1830', *University of Birmingham Historical Journal*, vol. IV (1953–4), p. 63.
9. For example, see the *Manchester Mercury*, 26 January 1815 and 23 May 1815.
10. It would appear that spinning firms rarely used warehouses for this purpose. See Smith, 'Manchester', p. 63. For a list of Manchester firms specialising in cotton twist and weft dealing only, see Appendix 3.
11. M. M. Edwards, *The Growth of the British Cotton Trade 1780–1815* (Manchester University Press, Manchester, 1967), p. 173.
12. *Manchester Mercury*, 14 March 1815.
13. *Manchester Mercury*, 21 February 1815. Sale of textile machinery

at Mr Barrows' warehouse, Queen Street, Manchester, RV £20.00.

14. Edwards, *Cotton Trade*, pp. 163–4.

15. Samuel Bamford, *Early Days* (T. Fisher Unwin, 1849), quoted in Edwards, *Cotton Trade*, p. 174.

16. As Edwards points out, 'The larger manufacturers preferred to have a permanent Manchester warehouse where they could develop regular trading contacts and employ a staff of salesmen'. Edwards, *Cotton Trade*, p. 174.

17. The master weaver in Lancashire was often referred to by the German term 'Verlager', which meant 'an organiser of the domestic system'. The warehouse therefore acted as the co-ordinating centre of a system which employed workers for manufacture. See F. Crouzet, *The First Industrialists, The Problem of Origins* (Cambridge University Press, Cambridge, 1985), pp. 2–3.

18. PP, 1802–1803 (114), III, Part 4, *Evidence Before the Committee on Petitions on the Law Relating to Disputes Between Masters and Workmen in the Cotton Manufacture*, p. 49. For a description of a visit by weavers to a Manchester warehouse, at the turn of the eighteenth century, see Bamford, *Early Days*, p. 117.

19. PP, 1802–1803 (114), III, part 4, p. 76.

20. Ibid., p. 13.

21. Ibid., p. 46.

22. D. Bythell, *The Handloom Weavers: A Study in the English Cotton Industry During the Industrial Revolution* (Cambridge University Press, Cambridge, 1969), p. 32.

23. PP, 1833 (690), IV, *Select Committee on Manufactures, Commerce and Shipping in the United Kingdom*, p. 560.

24. The activities of the Goulds will be examined in detail in Chapter 5.

25. Edwards observes that foremen were sometimes known as 'festers' and represented the large-scale Manchester merchants and manufacturers. Edwards, *Cotton Trade*, p. 9.

26. PP, 1816 (397), III, *Select Committee on the State of Children Employed in the Manufactories of the United Kingdom*, pp. 96–108, 337–9.

27. Bythell points out that cellar work tended to be typical of the large town but not in the country districts. Bythell, *Handloom Weavers*, p. 36.

28. PP, 1816 (397), III, p. 254. The activities of the Stocks will be discussed in Chapters 5 and 8.

29. Ibid., pp. 144, 163.

30. J. Kennedy, 'Observations on the Rise and Progress of the Cotton Trade in Great Britain, Particularly in Lancashire and the Adjoining Counties', *Memoirs of the Literary and Philosophical Society of Manchester*, 2nd series, vol. III (read Nov. 1815), p. 116.

31. A. P. Wadsworth and J. de Lacy Mann, *The Cotton Trade and Industrial Lancashire 1600–1780* (Manchester University Press, Manchester, 1931), p. 327.

32. Ibid., pp. 344–5.

33. Ibid., p. 345.

34. There is little evidence of handloom factories in Manchester. Possibly the firm of Holt and Firth, who operated a factory rated at £65.00 and a warehouse at £40.00 in 1815, may have run a hand-weaving factory. This firm was described in the commercial directory as cotton manufacturers and dealers as well as spinners. Manchester Rate Book, 1815; *Commercial Directory*, 1815.

35. These were the firms of J. and G. Bennett, Wilson and Fairweather, T. and J. Ramsbottom, Chadwick and Clogg, Stubbs and Mayer, R. Bowman, J. Birch and Co., Holt and Firth and Gallimore. All in all 14 firms operating factories also occupied a separate warehouse in 1815 but 5 firms could not be identified as combining spinning with manufacturing.

36. In 1815, Bolton had 11 type C and 114 type B and E firms, and Blackburn 9 type C and 60 type B and E firms. See Bythell, *Handloom Weavers*, p. 29.

37. Edwards, *Cotton Trade*, especially ch. 7.

38. C. H. Lee, *A Cotton Enterprise 1795–1840: A History of McConnel and Kennedy — Fine Cotton Spinners* (Manchester University Press, Manchester 1972), especially chs. 3 and 5.

39. Edwards' evidence is more wide-ranging than Lee's more narrowly-based work; nevertheless, the former's interpretation is heavily influenced by the McConnel and Kennedy papers as a reading of Chapter 7 clearly shows.

40. See R. Lloyd-Jones and A. A. Le Roux, 'The Size of Firms in the Cotton Industry: Manchester 1815–41', *Economic History Review*, vol. XXXIII, no. 1 (1980), Table 1, p. 74.

41. Lee, *McConnel and Kennedy*, p. 26.

42. Edwards, *Cotton Trade*, p. 143.

43. Ibid., p. 143.

44. Ibid., p. 133.

45. See Edwards, *Cotton Trade*, ch. 7, and Lee, *McConnel and Kennedy*, ch. 3.

46. See Edwards, *Cotton Trade*, p. 136.

47. Ibid., p. 136.

48. Ibid., p. 137.

49. Ibid., p. 146.

50. For a recent discussion of the problems of defining merchant and manufacturer see Crouzet, *First Industrialists*, pp. 2–10.

51. Edwards, *Cotton Industry*, p. 133.

52. Ibid., pp. 133–4.

53. Ibid., p. 134.

54. McConnel and Kennedy MSS, Letter to John How, Belfast, 25 February 1811.

55. Lee, *McConnel and Kennedy*, pp. 33–4.

56. Henry Houldsworth was the brother of the large Manchester factory fine spinner Thomas Houldsworth. In 1799, Henry left Manchester for Glasgow and became managing partner in a cotton mill. see Crouzet, *First Industrialists*, pp. 40, 130. This is another example of the Scottish connection amongst the Manchester fine spinners.

57. Quoted in Lee, *McConnel and Kennedy*, p. 33.

58. The problem here, of course, is a lack of business papers of the large-spinners, apart from McConnel and Kennedy.

59. The aggregate RV for these four firms was £2,623.00, which represented 28.1 per cent of the total assessment of the 90 factories in 1815.

60. Edwards, *Cotton Trade*, p. 126.

61. Lee, *McConnel and Kennedy*, p. 25.

62. McConnel and Kennedy MSS, letter to W. Wenger, St Gall, Switzerland 4 Sept. 1816.

63. Edwards, *Cotton Trade*, p. 128.

64. Lee, *McConnel and Kennedy*, p. 43. Also G. W Daniels, 'The Early Records of a Great Manchester Cotton Spinning Firm', *Economic Journal*, vol. XXV (1915), p. 183.

65. Lee, *McConnel and Kennedy*, p. 7.

66. Edwards, *Cotton Trade*, p. 130.

67. Smith, 'Manchester', pp. 61–2. The increase in warehouse activity, *c.* 1815–25, will be explored in detail in Chapter 7.

68. Edwards, *Cotton Trade*, p. 133.

69. *Pigot's Commercial Directory for Manchester*, 1815, and Manchester Rate Book, 1815.

70. This firm eventually moved into calico printing and 'in 1824, they built a large steam-driven spinning mill'. Crouzet, *First Industrialists*, p. 111.

71. See *Pigot's Directory*, 1815.

72. For a list of these firms see Appendix 3.

5

Schisms in the Cotton Trade: The Political Economy of Factory and Warehouse

The political economy of the factory-warehouse relationship, during a key phase of the Industrial Revolution, suggests a loosely structured chain which at times could be on the point of fracture. What is interesting in the period 1800 to 1815[1] is the extent of hostility and conflict between factory spinners and warehouse manufacturers. By political economy we take to mean the attempt by one particular group or section to manage and control the industry's resources for their own particular interests or ends. In short, to make their own interests the whole trade's interests.[2] In the period under discussion this involved a controversy over yarn exportation, the issue of the substitution of an export duty on yarn and piece goods for a duty on raw cotton, and the right of the state to supervise the hours of work of child factory workers. The latter issue raised the question of the health and morality of factory workers as opposed to those working in the putting-out system, and touched upon the question of the operation of the labour process in two different systems of production. We are concerned, in other words, with the struggle over the 'merits' of the factory which was a struggle fought between two different representatives of capital. Let us examine this struggle by first turning to the contentious issue of yarn exportation.

The notion that there was an automatic link between spinning (factory) and weaving (warehouse) is quickly dispelled by the controversy concerning the exportation of yarn. Paradoxically, the warehouse manufacturers claimed that, in fact, a link was being forged, but one between British factory spinners and continental manufacturers. The advantages associated with machine technology were being diffused abroad owing to the selfishness of the factory spinners and this was to the detriment of the British manufacturers. The protests of the warehouse, concerning the exportation of yarn, began in the 1790s and resurfaced at various times over the first two decades of the nineteenth century — in 1800, 1808, 1811, 1816–17.[3] Protests took a variety of forms ranging from disputes in the embryonic Commercial Society of Manchester,[4] to petitions to Parliament, to public meetings in Manchester and other large cotton towns, and to books, pamphlets and letters to the press which 'groaned with . . . papers upon the subject . . . with a degree of rancour and animosity not at all becoming to so respectable and valuable a body of men'.[5] Such protests, claims Smelser, were handled and channelled through peaceful methods and at 'every stage of the agitation against the exportation of twist, appropriate mechanisms of social control operated'.[6] From a functionalist perspective this may well be reassuring, but it smacks of hindsight and its condescending attitude towards the protesting manufacturers fails to recognise the structural importance of the warehouse during this phase of the Industrial Revolution. Certainly, the rapid diffusion of the power-loom from the mid-1820s did reconcile the differences between the factory spinner and the factory manufacturer[7] but this could not be seen in 1800, any more than it was a foregone conclusion in 1815. The rate of diffusion of the power-loom[8] in the first two decades of the nineteenth century was snail pace. As Radcliffe points out, after the initial experiments by Cartwright 'the loom for many years . . . went into disuse'[9] and Bythell informs us that the total number of power-looms in operation 'at the end of the French Wars was still very small'.[10] It was not until the 1820s that it was accepted that the power-loom had come to stay.[11]

There is little doubt that there was a separation of interest between spinners and manufacturers *c.* 1800–20: a clash of interests that could take on an extreme form. Those interests opposed to yarn exportation involved some of the largest and most powerful Manchester manufacturers and merchants of their day. At a public meeting, held in Manchester in April 1800, a committee to organise this opposition was established which Radcliffe informs us was composed of 'the finest houses in the trade'.[12] The members included Nathanial Gould (warehouse 1815 rated at £280.00), Robert Peel (warehouse rated at £250.00), Thomas Potter (warehouse rated at £300.00), L.

Phillips (warehouse rated at £270,00) and Thomas Slater (warehouse rated at £130.00). On 2 April 1800 a further public meeting resolved that the 'exportation of cotton twist is highly injurious to the manufacturers of this country, and unless some means are speedily adopted to restrict the exportation under certain regulations, will ultimately end in the destruction of the cotton manufacture of the kingdom'.[13] Fifteen years later Wm. Radcliffe was writing to the *Manchester Courier*: 'But Sir, there is a schism in the cotton trade . . . The party which forms this schism consists of some large spinners and a few foreign merchants who export yarns'.[14]

Let us explore this schism and lay out the respective cases of the warehouse (manufacturers) and the factory (spinners). The major themes highlighted by the manufacturers may be reduced to five basic propositions. Firstly, the representatives of the warehouse argued that cotton manufacture was an important and growing sector of wealth and employment and its interests were therefore tied to the national interest. Radcliffe, for example, argues that the Manchester and Stockport manufacturers, who had co-operated over the protest against yarn exports,

> found that there was not a village within 30 miles of Manchester, on the Cheshire and Derbyshire side in which some of us were not putting-out cotton warps, and taking in goods, employing all the weavers of woollen and linen goods who were declining those fabrics as the cotton trade increases.[15]

It was an interest, in other words, that was vital to the economy of a whole region.[16] For example, the weavers of Ashton-Under-Lyne petitioned Parliament in 1817 complaining that for a long time they had been,

> in a state of unparalleled distress, owing to the want of employment and the great reductions of their wages, . . . no inconsiderable share of their distress may be attributed to the unrestricted exportation of cotton twist to every part of the Continent of Europe, thereby giving foreign manufacturers . . . the advantages arising from our superior ingenuity and industry.[17]

Secondly, the manufacturers maintained that the 'shuttles' of the UK should consume all the produce of the spindles of the UK. This was based on the notion that yarn was not a manufactured product but a raw material input, crucial to the prosperity of the British manufacturing sector. As Radcliffe claimed, 'I protest against the produce of our spindles going abroad in the raw state'.[18] The manufacturers claim that yarn as a raw material was also necessary if they were to remain consistent with their general acceptance of free trade. It was accepted as legitimate to exchange manufactured goods for imported corn, and thus the 1815 Corn Laws could be attacked on free trade grounds. But how could they resist the exportation of yarn and still attack the Corn Laws? If, of course, yarn was to be coded as a vital raw material input then the objection was lifted and they could safely argue for the exportation of their manufactured goods without fear of contradiction.[19]

Thirdly, it followed that yarn, as a vital input to a key domestic industry, should not be exported abroad as this would only benefit foreign manufacturers. In April 1800, a writer calling himself 'Spectator' claimed that the rapid export of cotton twist had been so great in the last few years 'as to have occasioned the establishment of a great number of new factories, many of which have been built in the last few years'. The exports generated from these factories led the 'continentals quickly to establish new forms of manufacture including dyeing, bleaching, printing and finishing equal to the British manufacturers'. More serious, the 'general patterns of economic conditions were favourable to the expansion of continental manufacturing — necessities of life cheaper, taxes smaller, wages cheaper'. Consequently, 'Spectator' informs us that the constant subject of these manufacturers' conversations was 'the ability to undersell the British manufacturers in consequence of their local advantage'.[20] In more emotive terms, Radcliffe refers to the export of yarn to German manufacturers as 'taking the bread, due to our weavers here, and giving it to the weavers on the continent',[21] and he backs his claim by reference to the Stockport weavers petition of 1804, 'praying for a tax on twist exported or a prohibition altogether' which attracted 11,000 signatures.[22]

Fourthly, it was argued that exportation was leading to an imbalance in favour of spinning which was unhealthy from a national perspective. Radcliffe thus claims that 'spinning only, which, of itself, without manufacture attached to it, never did and nor ever will enrich any nation'.[23] This point is not elaborated as a technical argument but does lead Radcliffe to attack the factory on moral grounds. Thus, finally, it was held by the manufacturers that a high dependency on factory spinning would sap the moral strength of the nation, in particular, the rising generation might be contaminated. Radcliffe, on his high horse, proclaimed

> In a moral point of view, it's very far from being desirable to become mere spinners for the rest of Europe, as every thinking person must lament the depravity that may be traced to these seminaries of vice (factory); the health of the rising generation is certainly very materially injured by the daily, and frequent nocturnal confinement of children to whom exercise and liberal allowance of time for relaxation are absolutely necessary.[24]

These seminaries of vice are then contrasted to the more healthy occupations of weaving, bleaching, dyeing, etc, 'which require manly exertions and are productive of health and independence'.[25] These occupations offer 'treasures unattained by those . . . wretches who work day and night, to the disgrace of their country'.[26] Now, some of those rather emotive claims could be taken as the rantings of an embittered old man, but Radcliffe was not alone in his attack on the factory. As will be shown below, one of the most prominent Manchester manufacturers and merchants, Nathanial Gould, was a bitter opponent of the factory system. Neither was Radcliffe a one-man band. Between 1816 and 1817, a series of petitions from manufacturers and merchants were sent to the Prince Regent, concerning the exportation of yarn; these were signed by a total of 1,054 individuals. The petitioners of 1816–17 complained that the exportation of yarn was driving the manufacturers to 'Utter ruin' and forcing 'our workmen . . . out of employ'.[27] In 1817 two parliamentary papers, concerned with yarn exportation, were published and echoed the great misgivings amongst the manufacturers.[28]

The essence of the manufacturers' case was that a vital resource input — yarn — was being exported abroad against the direct interest of the British manufacturers and the ancillary and finishing trades. This resource was being appropriated by continental manufacturers, which may well provide the factory spinner with a short-term advantage, but, in the long-run, would lead to the ruin of domestic manufacture. This, in turn, would produce a lopsided development with too much emphasis upon 'unhealthy' factory work and an over-dependence on foreign manufacture.

THE SPINNERS' CASE

The factory spinners adopted a less emotive style and presented a more elegant and precise argument. Their defence of yarn export can be reduced to two basic propositions. Firstly, they offered a set of technical arguments which challenged the alleged connection betwen yarn exportation and damage to British manufacturing interests. In a series of letters 'to the inhabitants of Manchester on the exportation of cotton twist', signed by 'Mercator',[29] it was pointed out that three-quarters of the exported yarn was sent to countries who prohibited the importation of cotton goods. These were protected markets where manufacturers, in the absence of British yarn, would simply establish their own spinning factories. Further, 'Mercator' claimed that while the majority of twist exported in 1800 was of the fine variety it was the lower quality piece goods that were depressed while home manufactured muslins and calicoes 'have been in a rising and improving condition'.[30] At a meeting of factory spinners, held at the Bull's Head Inn in Manchester in May 1800, it was claimed that the mechanical devices innovated by the spinners had benefited the manufacturers. Indeed, it was suggested that the latter's superiority, over their foreign rivals, rested upon the mechanical improvements adopted by the spinners and a prohibition on the export of yarn would simply result in foreigners constructing their own spinning factories.[31] The meeting was attended by some of the most influential factory spinners of the period, including Samuel Oldknow, William Strutt, Richard Arkwright Jnr., Samuel Marsland, William Mitchell, George Lee, James McConnell, etc. A committee, including the above names, was set up and 'authorised to appoint delegates to attend in London, to oppose the injurious attempts of piece manufacturers to lay a tax or restrain the exportation of twist'.[32] Clearly the spinners felt threatened by the manufacturers' attempt to cut off yarn exports.

The deep schism in the cotton trade is reflected by the fact that the factory spinners were not content with technical arguments but were prepared to trade bitter criticisms with the manufacturers. In their May meeting they passed a number of hostile resolutions. For example, Resolution Four stated, 'That an attempt on the part of one class of manufacturer to interfere with the trade of another class, and to embrace it with restrictions and duties is unjust, ungenerous and dangerous.'[33] It was unjust, claimed the spinners, 'because the capitals engaged in cotton mills cannot be diverted, as those of the manufacturers of piece goods may be, to other trades';[34] and it was 'highly ungenerous, in as much as it proceeds from the very persons whose trade has been preserved to them by the ingenuity and exertions of the spinners, whose ruin these measures are calculated to accomplish'.[35] In other words, the manufacturers had no right to interfere in the legitimate activities of the factory spinners. The exportation of yarn was 'legal, fair and honourable' (Resolution 5) and the spinners reminded their opponents that it was the right 'of every subject to dispose of the product of his flock and industry where, and in what manner he thinks proper'.[36] Attempts to regulate the trade in the interest of one group was, according to the representatives of the factory, 'illiberal and selfish'. They had a legitimate right to dispose of the resources produced by their own technical and commercial skills, as they saw fit. Any attempt to interfere would deprive them of that rate of return which justified the utilisation of their property assets. The economic use of the property asset, factory, was based upon an acceptable stream of income which the asset earned.[37] Interference would give the cotton trade an 'unnatural direction'.[38] The schism in the trade was a product of the different systems of production where the link between factory and warehouse was still tenuous and open to a number of different outcomes.

So, on the one hand, Radcliffe could write that without protection 'against a growing evil (yarn exportation) the total ruin of the trade was threatened'.[39] On the other hand, it was recognised that protection was only one option; other policies were offered by manufacturers, but the proposals tended to be contradictory, reflecting the pressure imposed upon their system by factory spinning. Thus the Manchester merchant, John Entwistle,[40] predicted the ruin of the trade if the export of twist was to continue, but also counselled that 'spinners would only consent to prohibition if a new system was found which could consume all yarn domestically'.[41] Entwistle acknowledges that if a balance between factory and warehouse is to be reached, this in turn will require some fairly fundamental changes in the manufacturing system. William Radcliffe devoted most of his career to innovating such a 'new system of manufacture' and maintains that 'Cartwright's machine' and improvement innovations[42] would 'solve the evil of surplus yarn going for export'.[43] The trade-off for a prohibition on yarn export was, therefore, the willingness on the behalf of manufacturers to innovate changes in their system of production. Yet even William Radcliffe, who was prepared not only to accept but also to work towards the 'trade-off', could still claim, in 1815, that the quantity spun and the quantity woven at home would be in equilibrium 'if the master cotton spinners would only work reasonable hours, and not treat their hands worse than slaves',[44] and he further refers to the factory spinners employing 'in their mills, the greatest slaves in the world'.[45] The schism opens up again as the emphasis shifts from innovation to the labour process. The factory labour process was to become a focal point of debate during the inquiry into child factory labour and it is important to stress that it was not just operatives and middle-class radicals who objected to factories and their working methods, but also some of the most prominent manufacturers of the day were bitter opponents of the factory system. These objections will be explored later in the chapter but first, let us examine another inter-capitalist dispute which broke out in the cotton trade in 1815. As was mentioned earlier, the issue of yarn exportation broke out at various times between 1800 and 1820. In 1815 it was once more on the agenda of debate, but there was now an added dimension as the representatives of the factory and warehouse clashed over what may be termed the substitution controversy.

THE SUBSTITUTION CONTROVERSY, 1815

Early in 1815 a committee of Manchester factory spinners was established at Manchester to press for the abolition or reduction of the duty on raw cotton. The duty stood at 2d per lb on British ships and 3d per lb on foreign. The committee included prominent spinners, manufacturers and merchants[46] and was authorised to send a delegation to London to lobby for abolition. As the influential businessman and MP Alexander Baring pointed out, the question of import duties on raw cotton was 'one of the most important subjects that could come under the attention of Parliament'.[47] It was the activities of the Manchester delegation, ostensibly representing a united trade, but, in fact, dominated by spinners, which sparked off the controversy.[48] In the course of a discussion between the delegation and the Chancellor of the Exchequer, Vansittart, it was proposed by the Chancellor that the duty on imported raw cotton should be substituted by a duty on the export of yarn and piece goods. This substitution policy was acceptable to the spinners but it touched a raw nerve as far as the manufacturers were concerned. One of the first to voice his objections was Nathanial Gould, 'a prosperous and universally respected Manchester merchant'.[49] Through the vehicle of the *Manchester Mercury*, Gould informed the trade that,

> So long as it remains a question of whether a duty on the exports should be substituted for one on cotton it seems highly necessary that the manufacturers and exporters of piece goods, together with others immediately involved, should have delegates of their own appointed to confer with the chancellor . . . on their behalf.[50]

Gould's initiative was supported by another Manchester manufacturer who complained that 'I am of the opinion our delegates in London . . . are too much engaged in the spinning and export of yarn to be our only negotiators with the chancellor', and 'The present issue [substitution] must . . . oppose the interest of spinners to those of manufacturers'.[51]

These appeals did not fall on deaf ears and within a week of the letter's publication a public meeting was held at which 137 manufacturers and merchants signed a petition objecting to the proposed tax on the export of cotton piece goods.[52] The objectors included the major manufacturers, merchants and calico printers of the town. It was possible to identify 110 out of the 137 as utilising warehouses.[53] Large-scale warehouse operators were predominant among the protestors; of the 110 identified, 45 occupied warehouses rated at £100.00 or more. But there was a place too for the more humble manufacturing firm; for example, among the signatures were Hall and Travis, cotton manufacturers, who occupied a warehouse at Ormrods Court, rated at £9.00, also J. and B. Homsforth, cotton manufacturers and dealers, working out of a warehouse in the High Street rated at £20.00. Table 5.1 gives some indication of the cross-section of support for the manufacturers' case by showing the distribution of protestors by size class of warehouse. Quite clearly, Table 5.1 shows that the issue of duty substitution excited interest across a broad spectrum of the manufacturing interest.

Table 5.1: Protestors against the export tax on piece goods by size of warehouse

1815 Size category RV (£)	Number of warehouse firms
1–50	34
51–100	31
101–150	31
151–200	7
201 +	7

Source: Compiled from data in Appendix 4.

Not surprisingly, the original 'spinners' committee was taken aback by the manufacturers' hostile action and sought to defend their proposals. *Wheelers Manchester Chronicle* carried their reply on its front page.[54] The spinners opened their defence by confirming that their proposals 'in no degree committed' the cotton trade to a specific decision. Then they went on the offensive and put three propositions before the *Chronicle*'s readers. Firstly, they claimed that the existing duty on imported raw cotton was detrimental to the continued progress of the cotton industry. The aim of the industry should be 'The cheapest possible material, and the cheapest possible labour', but 'the duty we complain of, enhances the cost of the one, and accumulates on the prices of the other'. Secondly, it was held that the cotton duty was an unfair tax and 'That while the cotton duty exists, that part of the trade which adds least labour to the material is unfairly taxed. The manufacturers, therefore, as a body, are favoured'. The proposed substitution would, to an extent, rectify an anomaly, and, as the spinners warned the manufacturers: 'No tax was ever exactly proportionate . . . the allied branches of a great trade never benefitted the common cause by a zealous search for minute distinction'. Thirdly, the notion of a common cause was taken further by the spinners when they stressed the danger of disunity in the trade which might be interpreted by the authorities as a lack of real support for the abolition of the cotton duty. They appealed to the manufacturers that,

> Should a great boon be lost through a want of unanimity amongst those for whom it was intended, it would indeed be grievous . . . but more so, if by refusing the relief offered we bring the reality of our suffering into doubt.[55]

The manufacturers were not impressed by the spinners' call for unity. They proposed that a memorial be sent to Vansittart backed by a delegation,[56] and resolute in the knowledge that the manufacturers were opposed to the subsitution policy and supported 'every practical means . . . to prevent its adoption'.[57] In terms of content, the manufacturers' case was composed of a number of different arguments ranging from the familiar theme over yarn exportation to an appeal to a wider political economy. An *ad valorem* tax on exports, it was contended, would favour yarn compared with piece goods and further encourage the development of foreign manufacture. But, more importantly, they advocated a positive policy of support for domestic manufacture. 'It will not surely be denied', claimed the manufacturers,

> that the balance of protection in favour of our manufacturers, which affords such an extensive degree of employment ought to be more sedulously preserved, nor can it be doubted that the export value of the labour thus produced is among the greatest of our local and national advantages.[58]

The question of employment is related to wider issues of political economy, in particular the state interest in internal stability.[59] Taking the broad perspective, the manufacturers easily dismissed the spinners' claim that the objection to substitution was concerned with a 'zealous search for minute distinction'. On the contrary, the substitution policy is defined as contrary to both local and national interests. The identification of these two levels of interest with the manufacturing cause led some protestors to direct their criticisms against the factory system itself. This critique could, at times, be somewhat obtuse, as a manufacturer, signing himself S.B.J., wrote in coded language to the *Manchester Chronicle*:

> If, by any act of concession, the Minister should again be brought to propose a modification of the duties on cotton . . . and not be able to dispense with a substitute, then, if any portion of the labour of this country should be taxed, surely it must be that, which, whilst it is beyond all comparison most injurious in its effect on the health of the population employed in it, at the same time, the decided groundwork for that rivalship, which we are called upon to anticipate and dread; and consequently must be, of all others, the most proper object of taxation.[60]

The implication of the above statement is the identification of the factory as an appropriate object of taxation, not only because it stimulates foreign manufacture, but also because of its impact on the health of the domestic workforce. Taxation, of course, meant the imposition of a constraint on the stream of income earned on the property asset, factory, and contained therefore at least the threat of a slowdown in the rate of growth of the factory system. This theme is taken up by Nathanial Gould, who was more direct in his critique. Gould directed attention to the high failure rate of cotton spinning factories, the long hours of work that factory spinning seemed to require and the high proportion of children that factories employed. He felt he was highlighting a paradox associated with the substitution policy. That is, the measure was calculated 'to increase the number of our spinners and reduce that of all our other artisans in the cotton manufacture', yet the labour of the cotton spinners had, according to Gould, 'turned in so poor an account as the fate of their . . . employees fully manifests'.[61] The policy would aid the expansion of the factory at the expense of manufacture but the factory system itself rested on fragile foundations and was subject to periodic crises. Gould went on to warn:

> Who that reflects on these things can contemplate without concern the consequences of the contemplated measure, (which) is contributing more and more to crowd the rising generation into Spinning Factories; thereby giving a severe check to the looms of this country, and consequently, to all the various branches of the cotton manufacture dependent upon them.[62]

Rather than a growing link between factory and warehouse,

Gould emphasises their separation and extolls the fear that without some form of external constraint the former may well destroy the latter. The cotton trade was not a homogeneous system for Gould but was made up of two separate structures. This allowed him, and other manufacturers, to condemn the factory with a moral indignation directed alone at the spinner. The obverse, of course, tended to be a romanticised view of the putting-out system, which, at times could descend to the level of the absurd. So, Thomas Whitelegg, a Manchester manufacturer, could inform the 1816 Select Committee that the working conditions of a weaver in winter time, working in an unheated and damp cellar with only a 'broken window' for ventilation, was more conducive to good health than operatives working in a heated and well-ventilated factory.[63] Generally speaking, the factory critique was more sophisticated than Whitelegg's observations. The cotton duty controversy allowed this critique to surface, but it reached its apex over the question of factory hours and legislative controls, and it is to this direct attack on the factory system that we now turn.

THE ATTACK ON THE FACTORY

On one level the critique against the factory takes the form of a moral crusade with the language of debate littered with moral references.[64] In a nutshell, the anti-factory party maintained that excessive hours of work were producing a weak and morally inferior population. George Gould, Nathanial's brother,[65] was in no doubt about the negative impact of the factory. He told the 1816 Select Committee that 'I conceive that children who attend factories are so exhausted by the length of their confinement in the week, that they do not come forward, speaking for them generally, for instruction in Sunday School'.[66] This view was reiterated by Nathanial Gould, and he further added that, in his opinion, factory parents were less attentive to the moral character of their children than non-factory parents.[67] The long hours of work and the allegedly inferior moral habits of factory children were taken up by three other Manchester manufacturers before the 1816 Select Committee: Samuel Stocks,[68] Thomas Whitelegg[69] and T. O. Gill.[70] These manufacturers contrasted factory and non-factory work and emphasised the superiority of the latter in terms of operatives' health. Whitelegg claimed that weavers' children . . . look much better . . . than the children in factories'.[71] Samuel Stocks, apart from his manufacturing business, was active in the Manchester Sunday School movement and this, he claimed, gave him,

> an opportunity to compare the health of children who worked in factories with that of those who do not. The fact is so notorious that if I were to see a child that did not look well, I shall ask it, 'Do you work in a Factory?'[72]

There is no doubting the moral concern which individual Manchester manufacturers felt over the factory question, or the passion and personal dedication with which Nathanial Gould pursued the objective of factory reform. According to Samuel Kydd, Gould spent upwards of £20,000.00 to secure the passing of Peel's Bill in 1819.[73] Nevertheless, 'moral' indignation is only one dimension of the factory critique, and it should not foreclose on other deep-seated objections to the factory system. A clue here is the poor quality of the empirical evidence on which the manufacturers built their case of excessive hours, ill health and moral inferiority of factory workers. George Gould presented the Select Committee with details of the hours worked in 22 Manchester factories, but on closer examination he conceded that he had not visited each individual factory and had been provided with the evidence by 'those factory children attending Sunday School who were in a monitorial position'.[74] Indeed, Gould had not visited a factory at all and admitted to the Committee that 'It was not likely that I should, for there are many factories that even a friend cannot get to look at, and during this present discussion of the subject, there would be an indelicacy in endeavouring to go into factories'.[75] Subsequent evidence, by Thomas Whitelegg and Samuel Stocks, juxtaposes claims concerning excessive hours of work and attacks on the moral habits of factory workers, with the admission that their 'acquaintance with them [factories] is not very extensive'. For example, Whitelegg testified: 'I can give very little account of the internal government of the factory, not being permitted to go in',[76] and Stocks admitted 'I am not acquainted with the internal management of any factory'.[77] It could be argued that such a lack of empirical knowledge of the factory was consistent with a general moral criticism, the latter depending, as members of the 1816 Committee put to George Gould, on 'the result of general reasoning of what would be the probable consequences of . . . [factory] employment, rather than from accurate observations of facts'.[78] While such an empirical position is perfectly plausible, it does not exhaust other possible interpretations. It may be that moral indignation acted more as a safety valve, relieving pressure in an unstable situation; and that the moral critique is rooted in a contradiction which led a group of capitalist employers to generate an anti-capitalist crusade. The contradiction of the manufacturers, we contend, is centred in the capitalist labour process. Let us explore this process.

Under capitalist social and production relations, labour power[79] is a commodity which the labourer contracts to sell to the capitalist. The capitalist labour process is not only a general process for the creation of utilities, but also one which specifically allows for the expansion of capital, for the creation of profit.[80] But it must be emphasised that what is bought and sold between worker and capitalist, is not an agreed amount of labour, . . . but the power to labour over an agreed time'.[81] This is a key structural feature of a capitalist system and it sets the capitalist a major challenge. For what he has purchased has infinite potential, but has limited realisation, in so far as it is constrained by the historical experience of the workers, by general social conditions and by the more specific conditions of the work in both its technical and organisational setting. Braverman maintains that when the capitalist purchases fixed capital in the form of buildings, machinery, etc., he can evaluate with more or less precision their place in the labour process. Systems can be devised which estimate total outlay, determine allocation between different units of production and allow for depreciation, etc.[82] But, when the capitalist

> buys labour time the outcome is far from being so definite that it can be reckoned with precision and in advance. This is merely an expression of the fact that the portion of his capital expended on labour power is the variable portion which undergoes an increase in the process of production, for him, the question is how great that increase will be.[83]

The Manchester manufacturers, such as Gould, Stocks and Whitelegg, denied the role of the variability of labour power under the factory system. Their emphasis on excessive hours of work, the physical property of factory work and the resulting fatigue, all suggest a labour process determined by the pace of the machine. The worker, it would appear, had no opportunity to shape the rhythm of work. This view is perhaps best symbolised by the term used for factory workers — the factory 'hand'. For warehouse manufacturers such as Gould, it was the technology of the factory that dictated the pattern of work and there could be no uncertainty of outcome when the factory master purchased labour time. It was this belief that justified state interference. In the absence of legislative control, the machine-driven pace of factory work would reduce the factory population to an immoral, feeble and unhealthy rabble. It is not surprising that Gould was closely acquainted with the leading medical men in Manchester. He informed the 1816 Committee that,

> I had seen Mr Bill,[84] who says, he has long been seriously impressed with a sense of ill-effect of spinning factories, both as to health and morals. He says that these works crowd the infirmary with patients; they promote scrofula . . . ; they also bring consumption, and . . . many die early in life as a consequence of attending them.[85]

The factory hand is indistinguishable from the factory machine; but as the former is flesh and blood it cannot, in the long run, keep up with the latter, and basic human 'morality' demands the exercise of external control. The assumption that power machinery and the factory creates the automatant worker contradicts, of course, a basic structural feature of capitalism,[86] but it was logically consistent with notions of over-production, the excessive exportation of yarn and the frequent crises of the factory system. The factory reduced the worker to an adjunct of the machine and thus the factory domination of labour power can be utilised to explain excessive production, glutted markets and the constant search for external sales. Gould's critique brings together in a logical whole the issues of yarn exportation, the substitution controversy and the question of legislative control. For him, the machine-powered factory threatened the very survival of the manufacturing sector by precepitating short-term crises of over-production resulting in falling profits and prices, rising unemployment and a frantic search for export markets. The factory was the source of instability in the cotton trade; the subordination of the worker to that of the machine threatened the livelihood of all in the trade and in consequence legislative intervention was not only justified, it was a necessity.

This conceptualisation of the factory may be generalised at an economy-wide level by Boyd Hilton's notion of 'naturalness'.[87] Boyd Hilton suggests that the Liverpool government considered the rapid growth of the cotton factory system was to a large extent 'an artificial consequence of war and monetary instability'. The Liverpool government was 'the last to regard the Industrial Revolution as a malignant aberration' and insisted on distinguishing between what it termed 'the real and the false people'.[88] The former were the yeomanry, the latter, of course, the operatives of the factory town. Gould and his supporters, of course, considered the domestic weaver as 'real' and the factory hand as 'false'; thus their moral condemnation is clothed in an anti-capitalist rhetoric which fully accepts the right of the state to control the factory system. They fully recognised that the legal control of child labour inevitably meant the restoration of adult work,[89] but no such limitations or legal controls of working hours is posited for out-workers. Yet the Gould's were capitalist employers too, no less than any factory master. As George Phillips, the parliamentary representative for Lancashire, argued in 1818, the 1816 Select Committee

> went to prove, that persons were employed at an earlier age, and for longer hours, in weaving, than in the cotton factories. On what principle could they interfere with free labour in cotton factories, and not at the same time regulate the age at which children could be employed in weaving, and the number of hours which they should work.[90]

This contradiction Nathanial Gould was forced to confront before the 1816 Select Committee. Gould condemned factory masters for having little knowledge of the conditions experienced by their child workers: 'I am inclined to think that the owners of factories often knew very little of the children employed in the factory'.[91] This was a fatal observation, for he was immediately asked what his knowledge was of his own weavers' working conditions. He was forced to admit that he did not know the extent to which his weavers employed children, of how long they worked or the condition of that work. All he could do was accept that out-work was often 'irregular'.[92] His knowledge of the 'real' worker was no more advanced than the 'false'. Of course, the distinction between 'real' and 'false' workers is a fiction, both factory operatives and handloom weavers sold their potential to work, their labour power to a class of capitalist employers. There is no reason, *a priori*, to assume that factory masters were any more exploitative of their workers than master manufacturers. But the anti-factory group, denying the underlying structure of the capitalist process and invoking a form of technological determinism,[93] called for the legislative control of the factory on the one hand and tended to idealise the operation of out-work on the other.

Like the issues over yarn exportation and cotton duty substitution, the 'factory question' led one interest group to call for the subordination or acceptance of another group to the 'general' interest of the trade. The problem, of course, was that sectional interests were competing to impose their own vision and programme on the general interest.[94] The political economy of cotton, at the end of the Napoleonic Wars, shows clear divisions between factory and warehouse and supports Radcliffe's notion of a schism in the cotton trade. Yet, because the factory became the site for intense debate, and excited so much interest, its impact cannot be ignored. This impact was not to destroy the warehouse, as Gould feared, but to do the very opposite. The case for the defence of the factory will be made in the next chapter.

NOTES AND REFERENCES

1. These are critical years when the Napoleonic Wars have a major impact on the cotton trade. See, for example, G. W. Daniels, 'The Cotton Trade During the Revolutionary and Napoleonic Wars', *Transactions of the Manchester Statistical Society* (1915–16); M. M. Edwards, *The Growth of the British Cotton Trade 1780–1815* (Manchester University Press, Manchester, 1967), Chapters 2, 3 and 4.

2. This interpretation echoes Marx's conception of class ideology, in which one class attempts to raise its particular interest to that of the 'national interest'.

3. See D. A. Farnie, *The English Cotton Industry and the World Market 1815–1896* (Clarendon Press, Oxford, 1979), pp. 88–9; Neil J. Smelser, *Social Change in the Industrial Revolution: An Application of Theory to the Lancashire Cotton Industry 1770–1840* (Routledge and Kegan Paul, London, 1959), pp. 129–36; E. Helm, *Chapters in the History of the Manchester Chamber of Commerce* (Simpkin, Marshall, London, 1897), pp. 18–20; W. Radcliffe, *Origin of the New System of Manufacture* (James Lomax Advertiser Office, Stockport,

1828); *Journal of the House of Commons*, vol. 72, Jan. 1817 to Dec. 1817, p. 304.

4. See Helm, *Chamber of Commerce*, pp. 17–18. William Radcliffe claims that the dispute over exportation led to a split in the commercial society and 'the Chamber . . . became so divided against itself . . . it expired . . . struggling with this very question', Radcliffe, *Origins*, p. 158. Helm is more reticent, he simply refers to poor attendance, warring factions and the suspension of the society in 1802. Helm, *Chamber of Commerce*, pp. 59–60.

5. Quoted in Smelser, *Social Change*, p. 135.

6. Ibid., p. 135.

7. Farnie, *English Cotton Industry*, p. 19. See aslo Chapter 8.

8. A more detailed discussion of the power-loom's diffusion will be taken up in Chapter 6.

9. Radcliffe, *Origins*, p. 53.

10. D. Bythell, *The Handloom Weavers: A Study in the English Cotton Industry During the Industrial Revolution* (Cambridge University Press, Cambridge, 1969), p. 74.

11. Ibid., p. 75. See also M. Berg, 'The Introduction and Diffusion of the Power Loom 1789–1842', Unpublished MA thesis, University of Sussex, 1972.

12. Radcliffe, *Origins*, p. 12.

13. Quoted in Radcliffe, *Origins*, p. 11.

14. *Manchester Courier*, 26 Feb. 1815.

15. Radcliffe, *Origins*, p. 12.

16. The expansion of the manufacturing system is examined in Chapter 6.

17. *Journal of the House of Commons*, vol. 72, Jan. 1817 to Dec. 1817, p. 304.

18. Radcliffe, *Origins*, p. 56.

19. For a discussion of the issue of raw materials and manufacture see M. Berg, *The Machinery Question and the Making of Political Economy* (Cambridge University Press, Cambridge, 1980). The response of the Manchester manufacturers to the Corn Laws will be examined in Chapter 8.

20. Radcliffe, *Origins*, p. 38.

21. Ibid., p. 30.

22. Ibid., p. 50, and Helm, *Chamber of Commerce*, pp. 17–18.

23. Radcliffe, *Origins*, p. 64.

24. Ibid., p. 84.

25. Ibid., p. 85.

26. Ibid., p. 85.

27. Quoted in Smelser, *Social Change*, p. 133.

28. PP, 1817 (141), XIV, *Statement of the Quantity of Yarn Exported from Great Britain*; PP, 1817 (482), XIV, *Copies of all the Memorials Presented to HRH The Prince Regent During the Present and Last Year, on the Exportation of Cotton Yarn*.

29. According to Radcliffe, 'Mercator' was a German merchant, resident in Manchester, named Rupp Rudulp. Radcliffe, *Origins*, p. 160.

30. Mercator, A Letter to the Inhabitants of Manchester on the Exportation of Cotton Twist (Manchester, 1800), p. 5.

31. Radcliffe, *Origins*, p. 163.

32. Ibid., p. 163.

33. Ibid., p. 163.

34. Here the factory spinners are stressing a major difference in the structure of activity between two systems of production.

35. Radcliffe, *Origins*, p. 163.

36. Ibid., p. 163, Resolution Six.

37. For a discussion of the concept of a property asset see Chapter 2.

38. Radcliife, *Origins*, p. 164.

39. Ibid., p. 174.

40. John Entwistle operated a warehouse rated at £20.00 in 1815 in Bow Street, Manchester.

41. Radcliffe, *Origins*, p. 19.

42. Improvement innovations are important elements in Rosenberg's theory of technological change; see N. Rosenberg, *Perspectives on Technology* (Cambridge University Press, Cambridge, 1976), p. 75. The process of technological diffusion will be discussed in Chapter 6.

43. Radcliffe, *Origins*, p. 50.

44. Ibid., p. 180.

45. Ibid., p. 178.

46. For a list of members of the committee see the *Manchester Mercury*, 2 May 1815. A petition for the repeal of the cotton duty was presented before Parliament, from the Manchester spinners, in January 1816. *Journal of the House of Commons*, vol. 70, Nov. 1814 to Jan. 1816, p. 166.

47. *Hansard Parliamentary Debates*, 1st series, vol. 28, 6 July 1814, p. 614. The activities of Alexander Baring are discussed in Chapter 8.

48. We are not really concerned with the outcome of the controversy, more with the content of the opposing arguments. In July 1815, the duty on imported cotton was reduced to 1d per lb.

49. S. Kydd, *The History of the Factory Movement* (Burt Franklyn, N.Y., and reprint of London edn. 1857), p. 61. Gould contributed substantial sums to a wide variety of Manchester charities. See Kydd, *Factory Movement*, pp. 63–4. Gould was a fustian manufacturer and his warehouse was located at 12 Peel Street, and rated at £280.00 in 1815. *Pigot's Commercial Directory*, 1815, and Manchester Rate Book, 1815.

50. *Manchester Mercury*, 2 May 1815.

51. Ibid., 2 May 1815. Letter signed 'A Manufacturer'.

52. Ibid., 9 May 1815.

53. These are listed in Appendix 4.

54. *Wheeler's Manchester Chronicle*, 13 May 1815.

55. Ibid. The large cotton spinning firm of McConnel and Kennedy were in favour of the substitution policy. See McConnel and Kennedy MSS, Letter to R. McGavin, 15 April 1815.

56. This delegation included, among others, Nathanial Gould.

57. Report of a meeting of manufacturers, in *Wheeler's Manchester Chronicle*, 13 May 1815.

58. *Wheeler's Manchester Chronicle*, 8 April 1815.

59. For a broad discussion of these interests see P. J. Cain and A. G. Hopkins, 'The Political Economy of British Overseas Expansion', *Economic History Review*, vol. XXXIII, no. 4 (1980), pp. 463–89.

60. *Wheeler's Manchester Chronicle*, 3 June 1815.

61. *Manchester Mercury*, 2 May 1815.

62. Ibid., 2 May 1815.

63. PP, 1816 (III), *Select Committee on the State of Children Employed in the Manufactories of the United Kingdom*, p. 157.

64. This echoes the 1st Baronet, Sir Robert Peel's, moral stance against the factory system; the 'consequence' of which 'was, that little children of very tender age were employed with grown persons at the machinery, and those poor little creatures, torn from their beds, were compelled to work . . . from early morn to late at night'. *Hansard Parliamentary Debates*, 1st Series, vol. 32, 3 April 1816, p. 884.

65. The firm was called Nathanial and George Gould.

66. PP, 1816 (III), p. 101.

67. Ibid., pp. 325–6.

68. Ibid., p. 252.

69. Ibid., p. 146.

70. Ibid., p. 285.

71. Ibid., p. 147.

72. Ibid., p. 253. For a discussion of the activities of Samuel Stocks see Chapter 8.

73. Kydd, *Factory Movement*, p. 62. There is no doubting Gould's involvement in the factory question. J. T. Ward has claimed that, following the 1816 Select Committee, 'Parliamentary inaction led to an expansion of the Northern campaign among groups of operatives, doctors, anglican priests and humanitarians under a Manchester merchant, Nathanial Gould'. J. T. Ward, 'Introduction', in John Fielden, *The Curse of the Factory System* (Frank Cass, London, 1969), pp. XIII–XIV.

74. PP, 1816 (III), p. 107.

75. Ibid., p. 99.

76. Ibid., p. 153.

77. Ibid., p. 255.

78. Ibid., p. 101.

79. Labour power may be defined as the potential to work.

80. Henry Braverman, *Labour and Monopoly Capital: The Degradation of Work in the Twentieth Century* (Monthly Review Press, N.Y; London, 1874), p. 53.

81. Ibid., p. 54.

82. Such systems would, of course, be primitive in the early days of the Industrial Revolution. For a discussion of these issues see S. Pollard, *The Genesis of Modern Management: A Study of the Industrial Revolution in Great Britain* (Edward Arnold, London, 1965), Ch. 6.

83. Braverman, *Labour and Monopoly Capital*, pp. 57–8. For the question of factory management and supervisory systems see S. Marglin, 'What Do Bosses Do? The Origins and Functions of Hierarchy in Capitalist Production', *Review of Radical Political Economy*, vol. 6,

no. 2 (1974), pp. 60–112.

84. William Simmons was a member of the Royal College of Surgeons, London, and senior surgeon of the Manchester Infirmary; and 'My friend Mr N. Gould has applied to me for information on the present management of the cotton factories, as far as regards the health of the children employed in them'. PP 1816 (III), p. 286.

85. Ibid., p. 328.

86. It denies, of course, that the worker is free and not a slave. Factory workers of the Industrial Revolution owned their labour power and a set of broad historical and social conditions set the context for work.

87. A. Boyd Hilton, *Corn, Cash, Commerce: The Economic Policies of the Tory Governments 1815–30* (Oxford University Press, Oxford, 1977), p. 305.

88. Ibid., p. VII.

89. See evidence of George Gould, PP, 1816 (III), p. 106.

90. *Hansard Parliamentary Debates*, 1st Series, vol. 37, 23 Feb. 1818, p. 583. Phillips was a staunch supporter of the factory cause; see also ibid., vol. 37, pp. 561–2, 444.

91. PP, 1816 (III), p. 329.

92. Ibid., p. 329.

93. That is, the power-machine factory reduces the worker to an automatant.

94. Thus, factory spinners petitioned Parliament, in February 1818, complaining that they 'have heard, with concern, that it is intended to move in the House, the revival of the Committee . . . of 1816 . . . ; that the minutes of evidence taken before the Committee are very voluminous, and contain a mass of vague and inconsistent charges, which it is impossible to distinguish from the truth, without much laborious application or personal inspection of the factories'. *Journal of the House of Commons*, vol. 73, Jan. 1818 to June 1818, p. 71.

6

In Defence of the Factory

In previous chapters we have called into question the direct economic power and influence of the factory. Its role as an agent of economic transformation appears to have been seriously weakened. This, of course, raises questions concerning the factories' linkage to an Industrial Revolution based on a set of technological innovations radically transforming production. The factory and the warehouse did represent two different systems of production; but while the former has attracted considerable attention in the literature[1] the latter has been more or less neglected. The case for redressing the balance between these two key components has been one of the prime tasks of this book. At the same time, the critique of the 'factory' can be taken too far; it can become counter-productive. The dynamic role of the factory is central to our understanding of the Industrial Revolution. For example, we will show there is a pattern of relationship between factory and warehouse which confirms the dominance of the former over the latter. To substantiate this argument, we will draw upon a typology of economic growth and utilise Rosenberg's notion of innovatory diffusion paths.[2] Consequently, one of the themes of this chapter will be the factory's contribution to the process of power-loom diffusion.

PATTERNS OF GROWTH: FACTORY AND WAREHOUSE[3]

The assumption throughout this work has been that the factory represented powered spinning and the warehouse putting-out weaving. The former is concerned with mechanised, centrally-organised power production, the latter with non-mechanised fabrication and dispersed production.[4] They are two different systems of production which generated two different forms of growth. In economic terms, the warehouse provides an example of extensive growth and the factory intensive growth.[5] If we define economic growth as an increase in total output, then it can result from two different processes. Firstly, extensive growth, which refers to expansion by means of an increase in the number of workers and of the existing vintage of machines and equipment. In simple terms, all this means is doing the same sort of things using existing methods on a wider scale — more output via more input. Technically, this is sometimes referred to as capital widening growth. Secondly, intensive growth, which refers to the fact that expansion occurs, not merely by increasing the number of existing inputs, either of workers or machines, but by an increase in output of existing workers. In other words, output per worker, that is productivity, increases. This may arise for a variety of reasons, but in general terms we may regard it as a function of changes in the quality of plant, equipment, techniques, etc., with which workers operate. In its most dramatic form it is concerned with technological innovation which can drastically increase the quantity of output produced with a given amount of labour and capital.[6] In technical terms, this process is referred to as capital deepening.

In a recent work, Keith Smith has stressed the importance of the second type of growth. Its association with rising productivity has attracted the attention of economists and economic historians, and has become the focus for considerable discussion and research.[7] As Smith points out,

> The reason is obvious: rises in output per head are one of the few paths to rising incomes and standards of living and shorter working hours. Since these are among the central objectives of economic activity as such, the importance of intensive growth stands out.[8]

At the same time Smith is quick to inform the reader that both types of growth have run parallel in the economic development of advanced capitalism since the beginning of the Industrial Revolution.[9] This finds support from Maxine Berg, who points out that 'the cotton industry developed through a combination of dispersed and concentrated, factory and putting-out forms of production, employing a complementarity of mechanised and hand technologies.'[10] Indeed, it is the fact that these two types of growth have gone hand in hand that allows us to gauge the impact of the factory. If we now assume that extensive growth in one sector or sub-sector can be stimulated by intensive activity in another sector or sub-sector,[11] there are strong grounds for supposing that the expansion of cotton manufacture was largely a response to the technological achievements of cotton factory spinning.[12] As Raphael Samuel has argued, 'Mechanisation in one department of production was often complemented by an increase of sweating in another . . . the concentration of production in factories by the spread of outwork at home.'[13]

There is little doubt that the expansion of factory spinning, bringing in its wake a vast increase in the volume of yarn and a sharp fall in its price per pound,[14] had a stimulating effect on the manufacturing sub-sector. In this sense factory spinning was acting as a Rostowian leading sector in which the growth 'momentum came essentially from the introduction and diffusion of changes in the cost-supply environment'.[15] However, in the absence of a technically and economically efficient power-loom[16] the intensive growth of factory spinning triggered off, in the manufacturing sub-sector, an ever-growing demand for 'a new labour force of cotton hand weavers'.[17] This parallel development was reinforced by the fact that cotton spinning 'was essentially process centred rather than product centred'.[18] Rapid technological change in the method of production of factory spinning produced a semi-manufactured product which constituted an input for the manufacturing sector. Shapiro provides an index of cotton yarn production rising from 69.4 (*c.* 1790–99) to 238.8 (*c.* 1810–19), an increase of 244 per cent;[19] the scale of increase of this input placed pressure on the productive factors utilised in weaving, and, in particular, called for a rapid increase in the supply of handloom weavers.[20] As early as 1800 William Radcliffe claimed that such was the demand for labour in the manufacturing districts that it was 'impossible to get more weavers than were then employed'.[21] Another contemporary manufacturer, Thomas Ainsworth of Bolton, was convinced that the changes in the manufacturing sector were a consequence of the technological (i.e. intensive) developments in factory spinning. He estimated that approximately two-thirds of the rise of piece good manufacture could be accounted for by the impact of Crompton's mule, and that the innovation alone had given employment to approximately 150,000 handloom weavers by 1811.[22] Ainsworth's estimates were, in all probability, biased, as he was giving evidence in support of Crompton's petition for a parliamentary pension; nevertheless, while precise changes are impossible to calculate, the overriding trend suggests that there was a substantial growth of handloom weavers from the 1790s to the end of the Napoleonic Wars. Chapman, for example, suggests that the number of handloom weavers rose from 75,000 in 1795 to 225,000 in 1811,[23] and Bythell maintains that their numbers went on increasing until the 1820s.[24]

This increase in numbers at the same time increased the organisational complexity of the manufacturing sector and called for a greater degree of control over the enlarged and scattered workforce.[25] According to Edwards, the principal changes in weaving, under the impact of spinning inventions, were 'in the field of organisation and management'. With the spinning sector producing 'a greater volume and variety of yarn it was necessary for the master-weavers to increase their control over the outworkers they employed'. An elaborate system of delegation was erected 'employing festers or foremen, who, on their masters' behalf, put-out yarns, collected finished articles, advanced cash and paid wages'.[26] In some instances manufacturers delegated responsibility for the running of the warehouse to managers. Thus Samuel Oldknow employed a manager in his Stockport warehouse 'who was responsible for the transactions with all the weavers, arranging for the distribution of raw materials . . . and the return of manufactured goods' together with the payment of wages and the auditing of accounts.[27] However, the centre organising manufacturing in the country districts was Manchester; as Bythell points out, 'a great deal of the work done in the countryside was performed on commission for the Manchester capitalists'.[28]

Quite clearly, the expansion of manufacture along extensive lines required an infrastructural system to support it, and at the centre of this system was, of course, the warehouse. Parallel to the rapid expansion of handloom weavers we would expect a substantial increase in the warehouse sector. There is no evidence from the material we have examined of any major improvement in warehouse technique.[29] That is, the system responded extensively by increasing the number of units rather than by an increase in the technical efficiency of existing units.

To test this proposition we will examine the growth of the warehouse system during the latter years of the Napoleonic Wars; years of considerable volatility for the cotton trade.

MANCHESTER'S WAREHOUSE SYSTEM, 1807–1815

The choice of 1807 as a bench-mark year was dictated by the fact that the first comprehensive Manchester rate book appears in that year[30] and consequently allows a comparison with the 1815 data. The trade, too, was affected by the disruption of the Napoleonic Wars; consequently a period hardly conducive to rapid economic growth. The trade throughout 1807 suffered from varying degrees of depression and there was little short-term improvement as most manufacturers complained that 1808 was also a bad year.[31] Stocks of both yarn and cloth increased and conditions remained depressed in the first quarter of 1809. But in the second half of that year, and in 1810, external markets relieved the pressure on stocks and the export figures for 1809 and 1810 'surpassed any previous year'.[32] The speculative nature of much of this trade led to the subsequent problems of 1811 and 1812 when there is growing evidence of idle capacity in the Manchester spinning factories. George Gould claimed that in 1811 and 1812 many of the Manchester factories were working only half-time, especially fine-spinning factories.[33] Although there may be some cause to doubt Gould's objectivity, given his hostility to the factory system,[34] there is no denying the serious problems of these two years. For example, the large Manchester fine-spinners, McConnel and Kennedy, were forced to close their factory for a time in the summer of 1811.[35] But, as Napoleon lost his grip on Europe, trade began to revive and 1813 was a year of progress and posperity.[36] The Manchester fine-spinning operatives, using the pretext of improved trade, 'demanded an increase in wages which was promptly met by the employers'.[37]

However, the prosperity was short-lived, and in 1814 the full effects of the American Wars were being felt; trade in Manchester was described as 'very flat indeed'.[38] This flatness of trade continued into 1815 and in April of that year 'manufacturers were dismissing their weavers and many spinners were working only half-time'.[39] This is the background to the empirical survey of the factory-warehouse systems, *c.* 1807–15.

It is insufficiently stressed that during the vital middle years of the Industrial Revolution Britain was at war, a conflict in which economic warfare became a major plank of strategy and which subjected the cotton industry in particular to sharp fluctuations.[40] Despite these exigencies of trade the Manchester factory system expanded over the period 1807 to 1815. The total RV of the factory sector rose by 26.2 per cent and, given the intensive growth pattern of the system, we would confidently predict a substantial increase of output over property asset valuation.[41] How did the warehouse system respond? Given its extensive growth path substantial expansion would be expected. Table 6.1 shows the growth of the number of warehouse units and the change in the total RV between 1807 and 1815.

Table 6.1: Growth of the Manchester warehouse system, 1807–1815[a]

Year	Number of warehouse units	Total RV (£)
1807	1,182	49,333
1815	1,577	73,627

Note: a. For a breakdown of warehouse growth by rating district, see Appendix 5.

Source: R. Lloyd-Jones and M. J. Lewis, 'The Economic Structure of Cottonopolis: Manchester in 1815', *Textile History*, vol. 17, no. 1 (1986), p. 83.

The number of warehouse units rose by 33.4 per cent and the total RV by 49.2 per cent. The data clearly shows that warehouse growth was not simply a matter of an increase in the multi-occupancy of existing buildings, for the increase in the RV exceeded significantly the growth of rateable units. In the major cotton warehouse districts[42] the trend of growth is shown in Table 6.2. The number of separate warehouses, in district six, the centre of Manchester's warehouse system, rose from 355 in 1807 to 458 in

Table 6.2: Rate of growth of warehouses in the central cotton districts, 1807–1815

Rating	Number of warehouse units			RV (£)		
District	1807	1815	% growth	1807	1815	% growth
5	110	151	37.3	4,692	7,336	56.4
6	501	663	32.3	18,821	29,750	58.1
9	319	421	32.0	15,262	20,402	33.7

Source: Compiled from data in Appendix 5.

1815,[43] a rise of 29 per cent.[44] This further reinforces the point that growth was not simply a matter of an increase in multi-occupancy.[45] Capitalists were directing their investments into warehouses at a rapid rate, and the impact of war was apparently insufficient to dampen their expectations concerning the profitability of the manufacturing sector.[46] The expansion of cotton weaving along an extensive path stimulated the growth of the warehouse system and Manchester clearly reflected this process in its property asset structure.

The case for a factory-induced warehouse growth is overwhelming. The mechanised cotton factory represented a new method and organisation of production and was the agent for the promotion of new products and markets. It provides a classic example of Mensch's notion of a basic innovation. According to Mensch, basic innovations, occurring at the micro-economic level, changed the character of economic development and created new leading sectors which formed the basis for the subsequent surge of economic growth and prosperity.[47] The mechanised factory, fusing with steam power, constitutes an innovatory cluster[48] which creates linkage effects with other sectors and sub-sectors. This position is put clearly by Rostow:

> I would hold that the most fundamental approach [to growth] is to identify the extent to which particular technologies have been absorbed efficiently into the economy, and the sequence in which they were absorbed. This means we must look at the sectors and sub-sectors in which they are absorbed. Technology is not absorbed in GNP. Movement in GNP reflects the process of absorption, as well as other variables.[49]

It has been fashionable in recent years to be dismissive of Rostow's work but this is a stimulating and provocative statement and leaves us in somewhat of a quandary. To put it bluntly: why did the warehouse system expand extensively and not follow the intensive pattern of growth which characterised the factory system? We may well have shown that the factory stimulated the growth of the warehouse system but why didn't it trigger off an intensive expansion in the manufacturing sub-sector? After all, this is where a good deal of the criticism of the supposed dynamic of the factory is directed. This may be a crude reduction of the sceptic's argument but, nevertheless, it lies at the base of the critique. Fores, for example, defining industrialisation[50] 'as the process by which factories come to predominate in working life',[51] claims that,

> Although dark Satanic mills may have been the symbol of modern times for England (or Britain) to the poet, Blake, and to other commentators from Arnold and Toynbee onwards, it seems unlikely that more than 12 per cent of the British workforce — and probably as few as 10 per cent — were employed in factories by the time the 'Revolution' was meant to be over.[52]

Samuel, too, maintains that 'the lateral spread of 'modern' [factory] industry is exaggerated, while its artisan components are ignored, and comparatively little notice is taken of production in the workshop and the home.'[53]

Our focus on the warehouse takes care of the latter part of Samuel's statement; but our contention that the factory, as a basic innovation, stimulated extensive warehouse growth requires us to explain why it did not appear to induce the rapid diffusion of the power-loom. Let us explore this issue and offer a defence of the factory as an agent of dynamic change by restating the question: why did Cartwright's mechanised loom, patented only shortly after Crompton's mule, take over 30 years to achieve rapid diffusion? The factors inhibiting the diffusion of the power-loom have been given detailed empirical treatment by Bythell[54] and Von Tunzleman.[55] We will examine their contribution from the perspective of recent work on the diffusion process. In particular we will concentrate on the work of Nathan Rosenberg, who has laid stress on the need for economic historians to direct their attention 'to the rate at which new technologies have been adopted and embodied in the productive process'.[56] Bythell argues that technical factors inhibited the diffusion of the power-loom until the third and fourth quarter of the nineteenth century:

> the cotton weaving industry was not much affected by technological change until the 1820s, mainly because in the relative primitive state of machine-making, it simply was not possible to produce an efficient machine at a cost which a manufacturer would be prepared to incur in order to enjoy the power-loom's expected advantage.[57]

This view is consistent with the empirical evidence[58] and with the theoretical observations of Rosenberg that the speed with which techniques are innovated from the basic innovation to the subsequent diffusion will depend upon a series of modifications and adaptations.[59] These sub-innovations may be stretched over long periods of time as a technique 'goes through innumerable minor modifications and alterations in design'.[60] Not all adaptations and modifications were successful. John Sutcliffe, the Halifax millwright, stated in 1816 that, 'we see . . . trifling . . . and insignificant improvements . . . make rapid strides for a time; arrest the attention and mislead men of sound judgement, witness the numerous plans that have been designed for steam engines . . . which are vanished like a dream.'[61]

In other words, some 'improvements' went down a blind alley. But even if we assume that 'improvements' did follow an ideal progressive trajectory, there could still be problems. If there is a process of sub-innovation in train, then some entrepreneurs may well delay innovating on the grounds that a machine (let us say a power-loom), of a given vintage may quickly become outmoded. Thus, given a trajectory of improvement, uncertainty concerning the time path of sub-innovations may well adversely affect entrepreneurial expectations. We have already commented in Chapter 3 on the small-scale nature of many of the firms occupying factory space in Manchester. That is, we are dealing with a sector whose industrial structure is characterised by large numbers of small-scale firms operating in a highly competitive environment. Thus, for example, as late as the 1820s, small-scale fine-spinners in Manchester attempted to negate the productivity advantage of the long-spindle mule, which was being increasingly adopted by large fine-spinning masters, not by innovating themselves but by reducing the wages of their spinners operating old vintage machines.[62] Discussion of the innovative impact of the factory should not be divorced from the sub-innovatory process, outlined by Rosenberg, and the response to such processes by entrepreneurs operating small to medium-scale units in an intensive competitive environment.[63] The case for technical barriers inhibiting the power-loom is a powerful one, reinforced by the rapid diffusion of the innovation in the 1820s following solutions to the main technical problems.[64]

Nevertheless, the reference to such factors as industrial structure and firm size should alert us to the importance of economic forces. Von Tunzleman has argued that the diffusion of the power-loom was not just a question of technical factors, but that such factors should be integrated with economic considerations. Diffusion rates, even given technical competence, were affected by the willingness of handloom weavers to absorb lower piece rates;[65] and relative to the handloom the high labour input requirements of the steam loom also acted as a constraint. As late as the 1820s, on the coarse cloths, one operative could not operate more than two power-looms[66] and on the more fancy cloths the 'one loom system persisted', i.e. one worker per loom. Technically, the power-loom might be applied to the fancy cloth, but, according to Von Tunzleman, 'was not yet . . . profitable in them'.[67]

In general terms there is a strong tendency to see the power-loom as a substitute for the handloom; its successful substitution held back because of a combination of technical and economic factors. We have no quarrel with the basic framework of this argument, but we do maintain that more attention should be focused upon the impact of the mechanised factory. The rapid expansion of factory spinning, bringing in its wake a vast increase in the volume of yarn and a sharp fall in its price per pound, afforded manufacturers an opportunity to extend their business activities and their profit horizons. In these circumstances it was perfectly rational to expand via a known method of production rather than innovate a new technique which was not only subject to inevitable teething problems, but also required a radically different organisation of production. That is, the power-loom was a double innovation requiring both power machinery and factory control in a centralised context. As Tann has reminded us, the decision to commence factory production brought with it a new range of problems. The entrepreneur who embarked on factory production needed more than a good deal of knowledge of markets, access to supply of capital, good managerial ability, etc.; he also needed a technical dimension. The 'entrepreneur either had to be prepared to learn the technical process or go into partnership with someone who was technically competent'.[68] The importance of mechanical skills in factory development is also stressed by Honeyman, who claims that in the search for a partner in a factory concern a lack of wealth could be substituted by technical competence.[69] In addition, as Stephen Marglin has pointed out, the shift to the factory system required the development of an effective managerial and supervisory system if the advantages of centralised production were to be fully captured.[70]

Such problems and their requisite decisions needed time, but manufacturers operating under competitive conditions were obliged to make an immediate reponse to the market configuration they faced. Competitive markets may force entrepreneurs into hasty decisions and costly experimentation, as Samuel Crompton found to his cost. In February 1805 Crompton's London agent, William Macalpine, wrote to him:

> One thing I wish to inform you of that what they call the machine loom for weaving calicos and cambrics by little boys and girls seems to be doing great things for the proprietors. I think you should make a point of seeing and making yourself master of them.[71]

Crompton duly followed Macalpine's advice and experimented. But, three years later and subsequent to the innovation of his own machine loom, he found little opportunity for a breakthrough in the market place. By this time Macalpine's enthusiasm had evaporated and he was the bearer of different advice:

> I have reflected fully on the articles you make by your new invented loom — but clearly am of the opinion they are not of that description . . . however cheap they may be rendered as to command the attention of the great buyers and as such can never pay you for the merit of your invention.[72]

That factory spinning created the pressure to innovate there is little doubt; but, as we have argued above, in the absence of a technically efficient machine and the appropriate market configuration the intensive growth of the factory triggered off in the manufacturing sector a process of extensive expansion. The net result was that the expansion of manufacturing along traditional lines raised the threshold for the successful substitution of the power-loom, for it extended the manufacturers' commitment to the handloom.[73] Thus, the putting-out system, where rapid growth was induced by the factory, 'proved hardier than expected'.[74] Indeed, it continued to survive into the Post-Napoleonic period in a growing symbiosis with the factory, a process which we will explore in more detail in Chapter 7.[75]

There was another direction, too, in which the factory stimulated the expansion of the warehouse putting-out system. That is, some of the product innovations,[76] associated with the rapid growth of factory spinning, encouraged the extension of the handloom rather than the substitution of the power-loom. As Von Tunzleman has claimed, the diffusion of machinery and power in the cotton industry cannot be understood if factors of yarn and cloth quality are not taken into account.[77] He also points out that while the period associated with the rapid diffusion of the power-loom (1820s to 1840s) was one of improvement in coarse spinning, in the first two decades of the nineteenth century the major sub-innovation in machine spinning tended to occur in the fine branch. He states:

> At the very beginning of the century the fine spinning branch represented the white heat of technology as then understood. Headed, as it was by several large firms . . . it was frequently in the forefront of applying artificial power to the new textile machinery.[78]

The consequence of these developments was a rapid increase in the output of fine yarn and an improvement in its quality.[79] The upshot of this was an increase in the fancy weaving trade, where the handloom proved a more adaptable technique, and in which the vagaries of fashion called for short production runs and the insistence by buyers of high-quality products. The factory, therefore, pushed the warehouse system along a number of different fronts which created contradictions in the relationships between the two systems. In an important sense the factory helped to expand a set of forces which, in turn, erected extra economic barriers to the diffusion of the power-loom.[80]

Thus it is not surprising, as we have already seen in Chapter 5, that some Manchester manufacturers attacked the factory system, even though it was the underlying mechanism for the warehouse's expansion. As Rosenberg and Frischtak have argued, in the case of substitute innovations (i.e. the power-loom), there may be high 'costs committed to the old'.[81] Abandoning the handloom was not a simple switch of technique, but involved high infrastructural costs as the whole tragic dismantling of the system was to demonstrate in the 1830s and 1840s. As Bythell has claimed, 'Before the 1770s the cotton hand weavers as a body had not existed; by the late 1830s they had effectively vanished. In three generations the process of economic change had first created and then destroyed a new type of labour.'[82]

These processes of economic change were a product of the dynamic impact of the factory. The factory was responsible not only for the creation of a new body of labour,[83] but also for the construction of an infrastructural system required to support the cotton manufacture. The very pace of factory expansion caused swells and bulges in this infrastructure that heightened the threshold of transition and posed some of the major socio-political problems of the 1830s and 1840s. It is a reminder, too, that diffusion paths do not necessarily follow a single trajectory; the fact that the factory stimulated the extensive expansion of the warehouse is no criticism of its revolutionary dynamic, nor grounds for calling into question its central role in the Industrial Revolution. The notion that the factory must carry all before it, before we can accept its revolutionary credentials,[84] is a piece of inverted technical determinism. Having reconstructed the dynamic role of the factory, the next chapter turns to an examination of its growth in post-Waterloo Manchester.

NOTES AND REFERENCES

1. The number of sources would be too long to list for it would necessarily include economic, political and social treatments as well as a host of local and industrial studies.

2. For the main works of Nathan Rosenberg, see N. Rosenberg, *Perspectives on Technology* (Cambridge University Press, Cambridge, 1976); and *Inside the Black Box; Technology and Economics* (Cambridge University Press, Cambridge, 1985).

3. This section draws on the argument advanced by R. Lloyd-Jones and M. J. Lewis, 'The Economic Structure of Cottonopolis: Manchester in 1815', *Textile History*, vol. 17, no. 1 (1986), pp. 71–89.

4. That is, the warehouse operates as a co-ordinating rather than a centralising agency.

5. Intensive and extensive growth are well-known terms used in economics, but for a recent usage see K. Smith, *The British Economic Crisis* (Penguin, Harmondsworth, 1984), p. 38.

6. It is this type of growth which has been directly associated with the spectacular increases in the productivity of the cotton industry during the Industrial Revolution. Thus McCloskey informs us that between 1780 and 1860 technological innovation reduced the cost of producing cloth by one-eighth. In other words, 'a given bundle of cotton, labour and machines in 1860 produced eight times more cotton cloth than it did in 1780'. D. N. McCloskey, 'The Industrial Revolution 1780–1860: A Survey', in R. Floud and D. N. McCloskey, *The Economic History of Britain Since 1700* (2 vols., Cambridge University Press, Cambridge, 1981), p. 110.

7. See, for example, the recent book of edited essays by Joel Mokyr, *The Economics of the Industrial Revolution* (Allen and Unwin, London, 1985), especially 1 to 4, pp. 1–118.

8. Smith, *British Economic Crisis*, p. 38.

9. Ibid., p. 38.

10. M. Berg, *The Age of Manufactures 1700–1820* (Basil Blackwell, Oxford, 1985), p. 217.

11. For the analysis of linkage effects, where the growth and investment pattern of an industry induces growth in another sector, see A. O. Hirschman, *The Strategy and Structure of Economic Development* (Yale University Press, new Haven, 1958), p. 100.

12. Thus, McCloskey claims that the increase in productivity, 'and all of it before 1812–15', was a response to mechanisation in spinning and its preparatory processes, 'rather than the mechanisation of weaving'. D. N. McCloskey, 'Industrial Revolution', p. 110. For estimates of labour productivity in cotton spinning see S. D. Chapman, *The Cotton Industry and the Industrial Revolution* (Macmillan, London, 1972), p. 20.

13. R. Samuel, 'The Workshop of the World: Steam Power and Hand Technology in Mid-Victorian Britain', *History Workshop*, issue 3 (1977), p. 17.

14. For the rapid increase in yarn output and falling prices, see S. Shapiro, *Capital and the Cotton Industry in the Industrial Revolution* (Cornell University Press, Ithaca, NY, 1967), Appendix 13, Table 39, and Appendix 23, Table 51.

15. W. W. Rostow, *The Stages of Economic Growth* (Cambridge University Press, Cambridge, 1865), p. 53.

16. The slow diffusion of the power-loom will be taken up later in this chapter.

17. D. Bythell, *The Handloom Weavers: A Study in the English Cotton Industry During the Industrial Revolution* (Cambridge University Press, Cambridge, 1969), pp. 40–1.

18. D. A. Farnie, *The English Cotton Industry and the World Market 1815–1896* (Clarendon Press, Oxford, 1979), p. 35.

19. Shapiro, *Capital and the Cotton Industry*, Appendix 13, Table 39.

20. See Bythell, *Handloom Weavers*, pp. 40–9.

21. W. Radcliffe, *Origins of the New System of Manufacture* (James Lomax Advertiser Office, Stockport, 1828), p. 12. This is why, in turn, spinners looked to export markets and triggered off the dispute in yarn exportation we examined in Chapter 5.

22. G. W. Daniels, *The Early English Cotton Industry* (Longman, Green, London, 1920), pp. 180, 181.

23. Chapman, *Cotton Industry*, p. 60.

24. Bythell, *Handloom Weavers*, p. 41. See also J. Lyons. 'The Cotton Industry and the Introduction of the Power Loom', Unpublished PhD thesis, University of California at Berkeley, 1977.

25. For example, Thomas Thorpe, a Bolton weaver, told the 1803 Select Committee, investigating disputes in the cotton trade, that the transfer of workers from the linen and woollen trade to cotton hand

weaving had, 'frequently . . . brought forth very bad work, which have occasioned great disputes, and the manufacturers have suffered great loss by it.' PP, 1803 (114), *Select Committee on Settling Disputes in the Cotton Trade*, p. 16.

26. M. M. Edwards, *The Growth of the British Cotton Trade 1780–1815* (Manchester University Press, Manchester, 1967), p. 9. In fact, as Landes has recently claimed, the putting-out system 'offered important cost advantages to the merchant manufacturer. He was able to shift capital expenditure (plant and equipment) to the worker, along with the risk of fluctuation in demand. If orders fell off, the putter-out only had to stop buying. He had no machines to stand idle 'eating up the interest on capital.' D. S. Landes, 'What Do Bosses Really Do?', *Journal of Economic History*, vol. 46, no. 3 (1986), p. 604.

27. G. Unwin, A. Hulme and G. Taylor, *Samuel Oldknow and the Arkwrights* (Longman, Green, London, 1924), pp. 49–50.

28. Bythell, *Handloom Weavers*, p. 16.

29. In this period, there is no evidence to show the application of steam power for lifting or any other function in the warehouse.

30. Manchester Central Library (MCL), Poor Rate Assessment Book for the Township of Manchester, 1807 (MCL, M9/402/2/71).

31. Edwards, *British Cotton Trade*, p. 17.

32. Ibid., p. 18.

33. PP, 1816 (397), 111, *Select Committee on the State of Children Employed in the Manufactories of the United Kingdom*, p. 109.

34. See Chapter 5.

35. Edwards, *British Cotton Trade*, p. 19.

36. C. H. Lee, *A Cotton Enterprise 1795–1840: A History of McConnel and Kennedy, Fine Cotton Spinners* (Manchester University Press, Manchester, 1972), p. 57.

37. Edwards, *British Cotton Trade*, p. 21.

38. Quoted by John Bury, Manchester calico printer. Bury MSS. Letter from Jonas Bury to J. Bury, 1 December 1814.

39. Edwards, *British Cotton Trade*, p. 22.

40. For example, in 1810 the quantity of raw cotton imported was 132.5 million lbs, however, by 1813 it had fallen by over 50 per cent to 51 million lbs. In 1815 it had recovered to 99.3 million lbs. See B. R. Mitchell and P. Deane, *Abstract of British Historical Statistics* (Cambridge University Press, Cambridge, 1962), p. 178.

41. The evidence on yarn output is rather flimsy, given the fluctuations of the period, but Shapiro shows the average volume of yarn production rising by 52.6 per cent between 1800–9 to 1810–19. Shapiro, *Capital and the Cotton Industry*, Appendix 13, Table 39.

42. The concentration of warehouses in districts 5, 6 and 9 is discussed in Chapter 3.

43. The figures exclude New Cannon Street, in district 6, as the 1807 rate book did not provide street numbers and therefore cannot be compared with 1815. The 29 per cent increase probably underestimates the growth trend.

44. See Lloyd-Jones and Lewis, 'Economic Structure', p. 83.

45. The average RV of a warehouse unit rose from £41.6 in 1807 to

£46.7 in 1815. Ibid., p. 89, n. 74. This trend towards larger warehouse size was reversed in the post-war years, particularly after 1820. See Chapter 7.

46. Bythell, for example, has observed, 'But in spite of the unevenness, the growth of the cotton industry during the Napoleonic Wars was so remarkable that it is difficult to imagine that it could have done much better over these 20 years, even if there had been peace and not war.' Bythell, *Handloom Weavers*, p. 51.

47. G. Mensch, *The Stalemate in Technology: Innovations Overcame The Depression* (Ballinger, London, 1979), p. 47. This approach is Schumpeterian, in that it emphasises 'The enormous importance of radical disturbances in the existing equilibrium arising from entrepreneurial innovations in completely new branches of activity.' C. Freeman, *Structural Determinants of Employment and Unemployment* (OECD, Paris, 1979), p. 4.

48. For an examination of the concept of an innovatory cluster see C. Freeman, J. Clarke and L. Soete, *Unemployment and Technical Innovation* (Pinter, London, 1982), ch. 4.

49. Quoted in J. J. van Duijn, *The Long Wave in Economic Life* (George Allen and Unwin, London, 1983), p. 47.

50. Fores also defines industrialisation 'as the process by which non-traditional, modern life has been produced, which is characterised by urban living and more rational guidance for performance at work.' M. Fores, 'The Myth of a British Industrial Revolution', *History*, vol. 66 (1981), p. 188.

51. Ibid., p. 188.

52. Ibid., p. 191.

53. Samuel, 'Workshop of the World', p. 15. This is further emphasised by Maxine Berg, see Berg, *Age of Manufactures*, pp. 193, 229.

54. Bythell, *Handloom Weavers*, especially ch. 4.

55. G. N. Von Tunzleman, *Steam Power and British Industrialisation to 1860* (Clarendon Press, Oxford, 1978).

56. Rosenberg, *Black Box*, p. 19.

57. Bythell, *Handloom Weavers*, p. 82. This point is reinforced by Lyons, who argues that it was only by the 1820s that the power-loom had become quite profitable and continued to be so except in the severe slumps of 1836 and the mid-1840s. J. Lyons, 'Introduction of Power Loom', and 'Vertical Integration in the British Cotton Industry, 1825–1850: A Revision', *Journal of Economic History*, vol. XXXXV, no. 2 (1985), p. 421.

58. See Bythell, *Handloom Weavers*, pp. 76–82.

59. Rosenberg, *Black Box*, pp. 19–29.

60. N. Rosenberg and C. R. Frischtak, 'Technological Innovation and Long Waves', *Cambridge Journal of Economics*, vol. 8 (1984), p. 12.

61. Quoted in J. Tann, *The Development of the Factory* (Cornmarket Press, London, 1970), p. 63.

62. This conflict between large and small fine spinners led to a series of strikes in Manchester between 1829 and 1831. See R. G. Kirby and A. E. Musson, *The Voice of the People. John Doherty, 1798–1854,*

Trade Unionist, Radical and Factory Reformer (Manchester University Press, Manchester, 1975), pp. 153–97; and V. A. C. Gattrell, 'The Commercial Middle Classes', Unpublished PhD Thesis, University of Cambridge, 1972, pp. 323–7. Further discussion of the long mule is taken up in Chapters 7 and 10.

63. The intensity of the competitive system may be gauged from the high exit rate of firms. See R. Lloyd-Jones and A. A. Le Roux, 'Marshall and the Birth and Death of Firms: The Growth and Size Distribution of Firms in the Early 19th Century Cotton Industry', *Business History*, vol. XXIV, no. 2 (1982), pp. 143–6.

64. Bythell, *Handloom Weavers*, pp. 82–3 and Lyons, 'Vertical Integration', p. 423.

65. Von Tunzleman, *Steam Power*, pp. 195–6. See, for example, the evidence of two handloom weavers, working for Jonathan Hitchin, cotton manufacturer, Bolton; PP, 1833 (690), VII, *Select Committee on Manufactures, Commerce and Shipping in the United Kingdom*, pp. 699–714. Lyons also argues that 'employers of handloom weavers . . . reduced wage rates to cope with falling value added'. Lyons, 'Vertical Integration', p. 423.

66. Von Tunzleman, *Steam Power*, p. 193.

67. Ibid., p. 199.

68. Tann, *Development of the Factory*, p. 27. See the 1803 *Select Committee on Weavers Petitions*, where it was noted that the master weavers were generally 'ignorant' of the weaving process. PP, 1803 (114), p. 33.

69. K. Honeyman, *Origins of Enterprise: Business Leadership in the Industrial Revolution* (Manchester University Press, 1981), p. 73. See also F. Crouzet, *The First Industrialists: The Problem of Origins* (Cambridge University Press, Cambridge, 1985), p. 121. This study examines the origins of entrepreneurs in a wide range of industrial activities. See especially chs. 6, 7 and 8.

70. S. Marglin, 'What Do Bosses Do?', *Review of Radical Political Economy*, vol. 6, Summer (1974), p. 62.

71. Irving MSS, W. Macalpine to Samuel Crompton, 18 February 1805.

72. Ibid., W. Macalpine to Samuel Crompton, 26 March 1808.

73. One example of this commitment was sub-innovations of the handloom itself. See Bythell, *Handloom Weavers*, p. 83; and Von Tunzleman, *Steam Power*, p. 200.

74. D. S. Landes, *The Unbound Prometheus: Technological Change and Industrial Development in Western Europe from 1750 to the Present* (Cambridge University Press, Cambridge, 1970), p. 119.

75. For a broader discussion of the putting-out system in the post-war years, see M. Berg, *The Machinery Question and the Making of Political Economy* (Cambridge University Press, Cambridge, 1980), ch. 10; 'The Introduction and Diffusion of the Power Loom, 1789–1842', unpublished MA thesis, University of Sussex, 1972; and *Age of Manufactures*, pp. 198–228, 246–63. See also Lyons, 'Vertical Integration', pp. 419–25.

76. Product innovations are important to Rosenberg, who stresses

the need to consider both process innovation (new methods or technologies of production) and product innovation (new goods and services). Process innovations, 'grounded in theoretical and technical developments have been fundamental in the history of product innovation.' Rosenberg, *Black Box*, pp. 4, 237.

77. Von Tunzleman, *Steam Power*, p. 186.

78. Ibid., p. 184.

79. See PP, 1803 (114), evidence of William Cooke, Bolton manufacturer, p. 50; and Henry Horrocks, also a manufacturer, p. 57.

80. The fine spinning firms remained single-process spinners well into the 1830s/40s, at a time when there was an increase in the number of combine spinning (coarse yarn) and power weaving firms.

81. Rosenberg and Frischtak, 'Technological Innovation', p. 13.

82. Bythell, *Handloom Weavers*, p. 40.

83. And, of course, its subsequent destruction.

84. Such a view is central to Fores' attack on the whole notion of a British Industrial Revolution. See Fores, 'Myth', pp. 181–98.

7

The Growth of Cottonopolis: Manchester's Business System, *c.* 1815–1825

This chapter explores the pattern of changes in Manchester's business structure during the critical years of the post-Napoleonic adjustment, *c.* 1815–25.[1] These years witnessed the rapid development of the factory system and the accelerating diffusion of the power-loom, especially in major manufacturing centres such as Manchester.[2] The business prosperity that 'reached its climax in 1825 has often been referred to as the first truly modern cyclical boom in British economic history'.[3] Yet the years between 1815 and 1825 were punctuated with moments of crisis which posed serious challenges to Manchester's business community.[4] The volatility of these postwar years, with their juxtaposition of growth and high business failure,[5] is reflected in Manchester by the shifting pattern of property asset usage. Both the factory and the warehouse systems will be explored in detail and the changing form of their interconnections assessed. We begin by comparing Manchester's business structure of 1825 with that of 1815; the outline trends that emerge provide the basis for examining the key business components of factory and warehouse.

MANCHESTER'S BUSINESS STRUCTURE, *c.* 1815–1825

As early as 1819 the Prime Minister, Lord Liverpool, acknowledged 'the great increase of our manufacturing population'.[6] Between 1816 and 1825 the Kondratieff index of textile production more than doubled,[7] and between 1822 and 1825, alone, the import of raw cotton rose by approximately 60 per cent.[8] In

January 1823 a sub-committee of the Manchester Chamber of Commerce and Manufacturers,[9] charged with investigating 'the state of trade in Manchester', reported that

> The cotton trade has been carried on to a greater extent (if quantity not value is contemplated) in 1822 than in any former year. Cotton goods have been brought within the reach of a more numerous class of consumer at home and abroad, by the very low price at which they have been afforded and cheap articles have been manufactured to meet the demand. The low price of material — the use of machinery — the low rate of wages of weavers, and some other classes . . . have all contributed.[10]

But this expansion in the market demand for cotton did not create a cosy business environment, or allow for business complacency. The sub-committee also referred to low profits and they warned: 'Profits are reduced on all staple articles, and great attention and skill, as well as quick returns, are requisite to obtain even a small remuneration for capital and risk'.[11]

As we have stressed in earlier chapters, property asset utilisation is a reflection of their profit potential in a market context. Market demand for cottons may well have been buoyant in 1822 with good prospects for 1823 but businessmen would have little trouble in recalling the severe crisis of 1819.[12] Manchester's property asset structure embodied these shifts in business sentiment; let us examine the broad outline of its business structure *c.* 1815–25. This is shown in Table 7.1.

Clearly, there is a marked shift towards production; this category increased by 96.9 per cent between 1815 and 1825, by far the largest increase of any of the categories examined. By 1825 it had outstripped the retail sector and had closed the gap on warehousing and distribution. The latter category actually experienced a marginal fall in its total RV in the first decade after Waterloo. Other sectors experiencing growth were noticeably public utilities and finance, commerce and services. The retail sector and the drink trade remained at more or less the same levels as in 1815. The shift towards production is dramatic and requires further analysis. Table 7.2 disaggregates category 1 and provides comparison with 1815. Data for warehouse and public houses and inns are also included in Table 7.2 following the procedure adopted in Chapter 3. The rapid growth of cotton

Table 7.1: Distribution of Manchester's property assets, 1815 and 1825

Category code[a]	Total RV of assets[b] (£) 1815	% of category value to total RV	Total RV of assets[c] (£) 1825	% of category value to total RV
1	18,307	11.96	36,050	19.9
2	1,662	1.09	2,888	1.59
3	399	0.26	581	0.32
4	26,231	17.14	30,145	16.15
5	14,996	9.78	17,628	9.73
6	77,650	50.73	77,348	42.7
7	3,050	1.99	4,500	2.48
8	5,172	3.38	5,725	3.16
10	3,512	2.29	5,366	2.96
11	280	0.18	218	0.12
12	1,836	1.20	649	0.36
Total	153,065	100.00	181,098	100.00

Notes: a. These are the same codes as used in Tables 3.3 and 3.4
b. The RV of assets are taken from Table 3.4.
c. Category 9 is housing — this data has not been collected for 1825.

Source: Compiled from the 1825 Township of Manchester Rate Book.

Table 7.2: Disaggregated categories: a comparison of cotton factories with other property assets in 1815 and 1825

	1815		1825	
	RV (£)	% of total RV	RV (£)	% of total RV
Cotton factories	9,334	6.10	22,551	12.45
Metal: machine, foundry sector	3,298	2.15	7,298	4.03
Chemical sector (dyeing, bleaching, finishing, etc.)	3,559	2.32	5,432	3.00
Unspecified works, workshops, factories	1,966	1.28	769	0.42
Warehouses	73,627	48.10	77,348	42.7
Public houses and inns	13,608	8.89	17,016	9.39

factories on the one hand (a growth of 141 per cent in RV) and the hiatus in warehouse growth on the other is the dominant trend emerging from Table 7.2.[13] The claim by writers, such as Roland Smith, that by the 1820s Manchester was moving from a manufacturing to a commercial centre[14] simply does not fit the historical evidence. The differing trend of growth between factory and warehouse may well suggest a change in the form of relation between these two business components. At the same time our evidence suggests a growing convergence between the factory and the warehouse by 1825. We turn first to an examination of Manchester's factory system.

THE MANCHESTER FACTORY SYSTEM *c.* 1815–1825

We can discern four main characteristics of factory growth over the period. Firstly, the pattern of factory development reflected the unstable process of growth in the cotton sector. Of the original firms utilising factories in 1815 only 36 survived to 1825;[15] yet the survivor firms, as a group, experienced significant increases in size[16] and the unstable conditions did not prevent a large number of new firms (46) entering factory-based activity.[17] There was a close correspondence between growth and survival. The more than double increase of factory RV *c.* 1815–25 was not accompanied by a proliferation of small firms but by an actual reduction of factory firms from 90 to 82. Consequently, average firm size, as measured by the RV proxy, rose dramatically from RV £103.70 in 1815 to RV £275.00 in 1825.

Secondly, the marked shift in average firm size ran parallel to a change in the pattern of property asset usage by factory firms. The shift was away from multi-occupancy of a factory and towards single occupancy. In 1815 the typical factory firm shared the same factory building either with one firm or in some instances with a number of firms. This unit was defined as the shared part factory or SPF firm.[18] There were 60 of these firms in 1815 but ten years later they had fallen to only eleven. The movement towards single occupancy is shown in Table 7.3. The SPF firm was a very small unit, the average RV of this category in 1815 was only £32.00. Their disappearance may be illustrated by the following example of the occupancy history of a Manchester factory. All factories in Manchester between 1807 and 1841 have been placed in a data bank and we can trace the year-by-year changes in the pattern of factory use.[19] To take the example of factory number 42;[20] in 1815 this factory was occupied by J. Storey (RV £11.00), Bury and Wrigley (RV £32.00), William Marsden (RV £4.00), J. Fitton (RV £25.00), and John Yates (RV £24.00); there was also an empty part, rated at RV £102.00. By 1818 these firms had left the building and the

Table 7.3: Changing factory occupancy by firms: Manchester, 1815–1825

Year	Total no factory firms	Shared part factory firms		Wholly occupied factory firms		Part occupied part empty[a]	
		No	% total	No	% total	No	% total
1815	90	60	66.6	25	27.7	5	5.7
1825	82[b]	11	13.4	57	69.5	14	17.1

Notes: a. These were firms who occupied part of a factory building but did not share with other firms, part of the factory remaining empty.
b. The original table contains 83 firms for 1825 but careful checking shows only 82 for that year. This oversight does not in any material sense affect the shift to single occupied factories.

Source: Lloyd-Jones and Le Roux, *Size of Firms*, Table 4, p. 77.

factory was occupied by Barnes and Swallow, RV £157.00 and an empty part RV £18.60. In 1825 the factory was fully occupied by K. Barnes and rated at RV £236.00.[21]

Thirdly, firm population was volatile. There was a 60 per cent failure rate between 1815 and 1825 and by the latter date 56 per cent of the population consisted of entry firms. The scale of activity of the factory system more than doubled in the first decade of peace but there was no cast-iron guarantee of business success. A business environment of sharp fluctuations in trade was not a healthy context, especially for small-scale firms.[22] The freedom to grow and expand and to shift the pattern of asset utilisation left little room for failure or slowness in adaptation to market pressure. The notion of a 'short, sharp, shock to business'[23] was consistent with the view of the virility of the market and of the right of businessmen to utilise their assets as they saw fit. Indeed, at government level the Liverpool administration welcomed, at least in part, the 'purges' of the capitalist market economy. The received wisdom was that in 'peacetime, any cyclical failure must be the fault of businessmen themselves'.[24] The demise of the SPF firm and its replacement by the larger wholly occupied factory firm was confirmation of the efficient functioning of the capitalist market economy.

Fourthly, this 'Darwinian cold shower of failure'[25] placed a premium on adequate responses to competitive pressures. Factory firms employed a range of adaptations related to technological and organisational changes. This adaptive process followed, not only the expected path of increased integration of spinning and power weaving, but also, rather surprisingly, led to a closer relationship between factory and warehouse. This latter adaptation will be explored later, but for the moment the broad changes in the warehouse system will be examined.

THE MANCHESTER WAREHOUSE SYSTEM *c.* 1815–1825

Warehouses still dominated Manchester's business structure in 1825 although their overwhelming position had been significantly reduced since 1815. They did not display the dynamic growth of the factory sector and they followed quite a different trend of the property asset utilisation. Table 7.4 shows the pattern of growth of the warehouse sector.[26] Over the whole period the number of warehouse units rose by 15.2 per cent while total RV increased by only 5.1 per cent.[27] Average warehouse size fell, an opposite trend to that of factories. The movement towards small-scale warehouse units is shown clearly in Table 7.5, which also compares the proportional size distribution of warehouses in 1825 with that of 1815.

Table 7.4: Growth of the Manchester warehouse system, *c.* 1815–1825

Year	No warehouse units	Total RV (£)	Average size of warehouse unit (£)
1815	1,577	73,627	46.7
1820	1,620	72,324	44.4
1825	1,819	78,368	43.1

Source: Compiled from Poor Rate Assessment Books, 1815 (M.C.L. M9/40/2/78); 1820 (M.C.L. M9/40/2/83); 1825 (M.C.L. M9/40/2/92,93).

Table 7.5: Size distribution of Manchester warehouse units in 1825 and 1815

Size category	No warehouse units (1825)	Percentage of total no of warehouse units	
RV		1825	1815[a]
1–50	1,354	74.48	70.9
51–100	325	17.9	19.91
101–150	97	5.33	5.90
151–200	21	1.15	1.84
201–250	10	0.55	0.44
251+	12	0.59	1.01

Note: a. See Table 3.7.

The number of warehouse units with an RV of less than £50.00 increased by 21.11 per cent between 1815 and 1825. The increasing small-scale nature of warehouses was accompanied by a growing tendency for warehouse firms to operate shared warehouses. As was the case with size, the property asset utilisation pattern of warehouses moves in an opposite direction to that of factories. This can be shown by a detailed survey of Cannon Street, the main thoroughfare of Manchester's central warehouse district. Table 7.6 shows the changing pattern of warehouse occupancy between 1815 and 1825.

Table 7.6: Warehouse occupancy in Cannon Street, Manchester, *c.* 1815–1825

Year	Total no warehouses	Total no warehouse units	Shared part-warehouse units		Wholly occupied warehouse firms	
			No	% total no firms	No	% total no firms
1815	57	110[a]	75	70.75	31	29.25
1825	50	127[b]	106	83.46	19	16.54

Notes: a. The firms utilising warehouses are less than the total number of warehouse units because 4 firms occupied 2 warehouse units each.
b. Two warehouse units were empty.
Source: Compiled from Manchester Rate Books, 1815 and 1825.

Was this shift towards multi-occupancy a sign of growing survival problems for warehouse firms? Survival rates for warehouse firms do not lend themselves to easy calculation; firms tended, as will be shown below, to follow a range of activities. Consequently we have concentrated on the cotton manufacturing and dealing sector and Table 7.7 shows the survival rate of a population of 106 firms operating within the central warehouse district between 1815 and 1825.

Survival rates for warehouse firms were slightly higher than for factory firms. Again we appear to have an opposite trend, although it is far less marked than the trends in multi-occupancy

Table 7.7: Survival and exit: manufacturing and dealing firms occupying warehouses in district 6, Manchester, 1815–1825

Total no firms	No firm exits 1815–1825	No firm survivals 1815–1825	% rate of exit firms 1815–1825
106	56	50	51.9

Source: Compiled from Manchester Rate Books, 1815 and 1825.

and firm size. How are these differences between the factory and the warehouse to be explained? The common element, which these business units shared, was a fluctuating business environment. The period was one of volatile markets which placed a premium on entrepreneurial decision-making;[28] but the factory and the warehouse faced different pressures which called for different methods of adaptation. Factory firms moved away from multi-occupancy because their growth pattern was, to an important extent, determined by technological factors, which required a more efficient utilisation of plant and a growing integration of powered spinning and weaving. That is, their growth process, as was pointed out in Chapter 6, was intensive. Warehouse firms were not directly influenced by technological forces,[29] they developed along an extensive path and adopted a highly flexible response to difficult market conditions.

For the factory firm of 1825 intensive growth, associated with rapid increases in productivity and falling margins,[30] created competitive pressures which effectively meant grow or die. Of the 36 firms which survived from 1815 to 1825, 34 experienced a rise in RV; the total RV of this category rose by 94 per cent from £7,198.00 in 1815 to £13,995.00 in 1825. The major technological development of this period was a sub-innovatory process which increased the number of spindles per mule; a device generally known as the 'large wheel mule'.[31] The increased number of spindles per mule had an important impact on output per spinner[32] and the 'large wheel' began to make rapid progress in Manchester in the early and mid-1820s. For example, the *Manchester Courier* carried the following advertisement in January 1825: 'Mule spinners . . . sober steady men who can cope well, may meet with constant employment upon large wheels . . . and at good prices.'[33] Unfortunately, this method of adaptation created acute problems for the small firm, and in particular for the SPF firm. The difficulty was that the 'economies flowing from increased productivity could not be fully captured by the renting firm, for rent in Manchester was in proportion to the power and the room'.[34] McConnel and Kennedy informed an entrepreneur wishing to rent factory space that the cost of renting premises in Manchester was between 4s 6d (22.50 np) and 5s (25.00 np) per spindle. As early as 1815 that would have cost McConnel and Kennedy £20,000.00 per annum if they had operated in the rented sector.[35] The factory was an intensive method of production and the firms which could not readily innovate technical developments very quickly went to the wall. The competitive process worked against the SPF firms as they faced the challenge of the 'large wheel' mule and it is important to note that 'of the 40 new firms which entered the Manchester cotton factory industry between 1822 and 1825, 27 were units which occupied the whole of a building and 7 occupied a substantial part, the rest of the building remaining empty'.[36]

Technological developments in spinning was not the only factor encouraging an increase in firm size and a shift in the utilisation of plant. Changes in the organisation of the factory firm from a single process unit, exclusively concerned with spinning, towards an integrated unit combining spinning and weaving was well in train in Manchester by the middle of the 1820s. In the summer of 1824 the *Manchester Guardian* advertised 'Land to be sold for building upon . . . near Ancoats Street and Oldham Road, one of the best situations for spinning and power-loom weaving'.[37] The same newspaper, two months later, commented on 'The great number of power looms brought into operation during the last twelve months' and pointed out that this development '. . . has furnished profitable employment to workpeople . . .'[38] One estimate puts the number of power-looms in Manchester and district in 1825 at 30,000 and points out that 'at the close of the year 1814 there was not one in use'.[39] The figure of 30,000 is, of course, a gross exaggeration. As late as 1836 a parliamentary estimate puts the number of power-looms in Manchester (including Hulme, Salford and Braughton) at approximately 15,600;[40] although Bythell claims that there were gaps in the returns and the real totals were probably larger.[41] We can safely assume that the number of power-looms in Manchester were rising rapidly in the 1820s. Some firms operated as single-process power-loom producers, but there is sound evidence to suggest a trend towards combined spinning and power-loom weaving. The following advertisements in the Manchester newspapers of 1825 are suggestive of this trend:

> Wanted, a Person to superintend a Spinning Concern, where there are mules and throstles. An individual having a knowledge of power-loom weaving will be preferred.[42] To Cotton Spinners and Power Loom Weavers — wanted a partner who can command from £4,000.00 to £6,000.00, to commence spinning and power loom weaving. This mill is a new one,

with a 30 h.p. steam engine by Boulton and Watt, also the mill gearing is complete and ready for immediate work.[43]

George Smith, a partner in the Manchester spinning and manufacturing firm of James Massey, referring to the 1820s, claimed that a squeeze on spinning margins may have stimulated entrepreneurs to move into power weaving.[44] In the course of his evidence before the Select Committee on Manufactures of 1833, Smith was asked: 'Are the two branches of the business . . . the spinning and the power-loom weaving united or not?' Smith replied: 'They are beginning to be united, many who are spinners only have added the power-loom of late years, and I think these have derived a small amount of profit.'[45] Manchester was at the centre of power-loom diffusion, and the emergence of the integrated spinning and powered weaving unit began to make its appearance in the town, especially during the boom of 1823 to 1825. As we shall see below there was another form of integration, between spinning and weaving, which involved the convergence of the factory and the warehouse, but before we explore this process let us turn to a brief examination of the warehouse firm.

As was outlined earlier, warehouse firms increased their rate of multi-occupancy and experienced a fall in average firm size. These firms did not face direct pressure from technological innovation until the rapid diffusion of the power-loom in the mid-1820s; and indeed they benefited from improved factory spinning technology via falling yarn prices. Between 1815 and 1823 the index of real prices for number 40 yarn (the average count spun in this period) fell from 27 to 18.[46] Falling input prices, and the absence of a technological base of production, meant they could be highly flexible in their use of property assets and could respond rapidly to shifting market conditions. For example, the acute distress in the cotton trade in 1819 was followed by a marked increase in empty warehouse space. The proportion of empty warehouse units to the total number of units nearly doubled, rising from 6.7 per cent in 1815 to 13.13 per cent in 1820.[47] The result was a moderation in warehouse rents clearly reflected in newspaper advertisements of the period. A typical one ran in 1820: 'To let Two Warehouses, in central and eligible situations in High Street and Nicholls Croft . . . The rents of each are moderate.'[48] The turning point in the fortunes of the cotton trade from 1820 meant that small firms could utilise cheap warehouse space without any of the constraints experienced by the small factory firms. There were little or no barriers to entry and firms proliferated along an extensive path. This allowed an individual with little capital and without an aversion to risk-taking to enter the business community. Small capital could float on the boom from 1822,[49] encouraged by cheap yarn inputs and low rents. Within this structure there was an array of different combinations of manufacturing and cotton dealing activities as warehouse firms avoided too narrow specialisation and sought to diversify their activities. An example was the Manchester firm of Owen Owens who operated a warehouse in Carpenter's Lane rated at £30.00 in 1825. The firm manufactured white shirtings, cambrics and ginghams, umbrellas, and traded in hat trimmings.[50] They also sold 'good quality cotton such as printed calicos and cambrics to New York and Philadelphia'.[51] In 1821–2 market pressures led to further diversification into woollens and worsteds.[52] According to B. W. Clapp, the Owens' constantly urged the need for quick turnover and short credits.[53] He further points out that 'under the domestic system of manufacture it was simple enough to withdraw from an unprofitable trade by working off old stocks of materials, and giving out no more work'.[54]

Clapp shows that the manufacturing side of the business fluctuated sharply over the period 1815 to 1825. Table 7.8 gives a rough idea of the manufacturing activity by tabulating the firm's weekly wage bill.

The business objective of this firm is perhaps best summed up in the comment Owens wrote to his partner, Thomas Owen, in

Table 7.8: Owen Owens and Son: weekly wage bill, 1816–1830

Year	Weekly wage bill
Summer 1816	£20–£40[a]
Summer 1817	£50–70
Spring–August 1818	£100
Summer 1820	£50–60
' 1821	£70
Autumn 1824–1830	No more than £12[b]

Notes: a. Clapp estimates that of this sum only two or three pounds was earned by the non-industrial staff; the two clerks and the packer employed in the warehouse. Clapp, *John Owens*, p. 17.
b. This reflects the firm's move after 1823, out of manufacturing and switching into merchanting and foreign trade.

Philadelphia: 'We are convinced that the trade can never be done to advantage unless conducted with the utmost economy and every vigilance to keep the capital in constant activity.'[55] Adaptability was the golden rule and we would expect warehouse firms to be engaged in a wide range of business activities. Such a pattern does emerge from a survey of cotton manufacturing and dealing firms who operated warehouses in Manchester in 1825. Roland Smith has described these firms as follows:

> Manufacturers and dealers were partly merchants and partly manufacturers . . . they bought yarn from spinners, paid for them to be woven into cloth, and then marketed the finished goods themselves in the retail market. There was an immense difference in the size of these undertakings . . . and since most of their capital was not so much in building or machinery but in stocks of cloth in process of production, they could readily transfer their resources from manufacturing to merchanting, or vice versa.[56]

It is not possible to demonstrate the shifting balance between manufacturing and merchanting, but we can show that warehouse firms, apart from combining dealing with manufacturing, were also engaging in a wide range of other activities. From those firms described as manufacturers and dealers, in Pigot's 1825 Directory, 21 different forms of combination were detected in addition to the dealing and manufacturing activities. These are listed in Table 7.9, with the number of firms in each category plus the RV of their warehouses. The table also shows those firms who were manufacturers and dealers only.

Overall there were 114 cotton manufacturing and dealing firms, occupying 126 warehouse units, and 153 other firms combining a variety of activities with manufacturing and dealing and occupying 185 warehouse units. These latter firms could vary enormously in size. Thus John Brotherton, a cotton manufacturer and dealer and silk and cotton manufacturer, occupied a warehouse at 5 Back Sugar Lane, rated at £8.00, while Henry Tootal and Co, combining the same activities, occupied two warehouses, one in Cannon Street, the other in Fountain Street, rated at £120.00 and £140.00, respectively.[57] Benjamin Binyon, just a few doors away from Tootal's Cannon Street warehouse,[58] combined cotton manufacturing and dealing with fustian manufacturing and calico printing, but in a warehouse rated at only

Table 7.9: Manufacturing and dealing firms occupying warehouses and their range of business activities, Manchester, 1825

Description of business activity	Number of firms	Total RV of warehouse unit occupied £
1 Manufacturing and dealing only	114	5,627
2 M and D[a] plus calico printing	46	3,560
3 M and D, fustian manufacturer	20	1,041
4 M and D, muslin manufacturer	10	577
5 M and D plus manufacture of check	7	462
6 M and D plus silk and cotton manufacture	7	727
7 M and D plus fustian and calico printing	7	602
8 M and D plus silk and cotton manufacture and calico printing	4	285
9 M and D plus Scotch warehouse and calico printing	3	420
10 M and D plus fustian manufacture, merchants and calico printers	1	115
11 M and D plus cotton twist and weft dealers and calico printers	1	40
12 M and D plus muslin manufacturers and calico printers	1	125
13 M and D and cotton dealers	7	924
14 M and D plus cotton twist and weft dealers	7	406
15 M and D plus fustian manufacturers, plus cotton twist and weft dealers	1	45
16 M and D and Scotch warehouse	1	35
17 M and D plus flannel, baize, counterpane and shawl manufacturer	6	504
18 M and D plus small ware manufacturer	1	180
19 M and D plus umbrella and hat lining manufacturers	1	30
20 M and D and Manchester factory operators	16	1,276
21 M and D and outside (Manchester) spinners	6	463
Total	267	17,084

Note: a. M and D = Manufacturers and dealers.

Sources: *Pigot's Directory*, 1825 and Township of Manchester Rate Book, 1825.

£20.00. In turn, Binyon's warehouse was dwarfed by that of Francis Marris, Son and Co, also combining manufacturing with dealing and calico printing, who occupied a warehouse at 37 Cannon Street, rated at £165.00.[59] This range of firm size and combination of activities was also a feature of the manufacturing only sector. Firms might concentrate on fustian manufacture only or combine it with calico printing, or muslin manufacture, or silk and cotton manufacture. Newbury, Hoyle and Co combined their fustian manufacture with silk and cotton production, in two warehouses in Brown Street, rated jointly at £175.00,[60] whereas Nathanial Shelnerdine, also in the fustian business, combined this activity with smallware manufacture in a warehouse in Market Street rated at £20.00.

The rich variety of activities undertaken by warehouse firms is illustrative of their adaptability in the face of competitive pressures. Some idea of the nature of these pressures can be gauged from the records of the manufacturing firm of John Heywood and Sons,[61] who occupied a warehouse in Manchester in the period 1815 to 1825.[62] The firm was founded in Little Bolton in 1803[63] and manufactured fancy quiltings, india jeans, dimitys, webs, etc. The firm quickly established a Manchester warehouse, which was attended by the founder's son, Robert, who visited the Manchester market weekly, travelling to the warehouse usually on Saturdays.[64] A variety of different buyers came to the warehouse in Ridings Court to inspect the firm's range of goods. Peter Jeffries of London wrote to John Heywood in August 1813: 'I will thank [you] . . . to send off on receipt of this, goods I looked at when at your business warehouse in Manchester.'[65]

An examination of the firm's business letters[66] suggests that in order to survive and prosper the firm was required to respond rapidly to orders, to monitor carefully the quality of their products and to keep their prices as low as possible. These factors frequently combined together to put considerable pressure on the firm. Messrs Decan, Son and Ellis of London wrote to John Heywood in the summer of 1811 requesting an order of quiltings to be supplied at the 'utmost haste' and warned Heywood that the prospective buyer 'has been offered cheaper goods since he saw yours, if we do not give him a decisive answer in a day or two he shall immediately close with another house'.[67] The ability to switch quickly into a different line of product was important, as was the ability to supply a range of patterns as the vagaries of fashion dictated.[68] Richard Prior, acknowledging receipt of 30 pieces of web sent to London, 'which our friend approves of', also warned Heywood that the buyer 'wishes to have only 15 pieces of that particular pattern, and 15 of a pattern about as half as wide again'.[69] In the haste to make up orders, and respond to rapid market shifts, the quality of the product could suffer, but agents and buyers were quick to respond to any deterioration in standards. John Gore, writing from London, complained to John Heywood:

> I am sorry to have occasion to complain of the execution of the last order — the quiltings are not so good as Mr Hudson[70] has generally looked at for the money. I do not like them so stiff. With respect to the Indias 4s . . . one piece I shall be . . . returning being so badly made. I hope in future you will be more particular as I cannot make use of bad goods.[71]

Sculthorpe, Brown and Co, of London, also complained about the quality of Heywood's quiltings and informed Heywood: 'If we take them all to account we must have 5 per cent from [the] invoice.'[72] The stress on quality was matched by an equal insistence on the necessity to keep prices as low as possible. Sculthorpe, Brown and Co impressed upon Heywood the need to carefully watch these two factors in respect of their order for 40 pieces of diamond quiltings: 'You must see that they are in good condition and charge as low as if we were present to pick them ourselves.'[73] Similarly, John Gore, requiring 20 pieces of small diamonds, told Heywood that 'you know the sort I like best and if I approve of them you shall have a large order, therefore it will be to your advantage to look them out well and charge the very lowest prices'.[74] Gore, again insisting on the need for quality and low prices, warned Heywood that 'in such times as these if this is not done it will be impossible to do so much business together'.[75]

The stress on speed of delivery, quality of product and low price in a market which shifted with the whims of fashion no doubt placed a major constraint on the size of the firm. A small firm, based on warehouse (putting-out) production, could quickly respond to market movements and still allow for strict control over the quality, cost and level of output. Reference has already been made to Owen Owens' tactic of switching the balance of their merchanting and manufacturing activities, and the Heywoods too were quick to adjust both the level and the composition of their output, as market forces dictated. Richard Heywood, writing to Richard Marsden in Gibraltar, thanked the latter for his market information: 'Your first letter has been of considerable service in directing our manufacture for immediately I stopt many looms of indias and turned others to quilts, accounts of which have been answered better.'[76] R. and J. Gore advised the Heywoods in April 1821 'not to take on weavers for quiltings under 2s 8d as they are not much wanted for the next three months but your stout quiltings to cost us 2s 11d to 3s 0d or 3s 1d you need not be afraid of making regularly, these we use ourselves.'[77] The capacity to quickly switch the product mix was a major advantage of the warehouse firm; as too was the ability to temporarily cease production during severe market contractions.

Charles Darbyshire, who had become a partner in the firm in 1822, wrote to Robert in June 1826:

> with respect to trade . . . generally it remains in status quo, if anything it is now rather worse . . . This is all very discouraging it has determined me upon . . . what I had previously thought of doing namely stopping the weavers and turning off everyone that I have any complaint of.[78]

In contrast to the firms' flexible response to market forces, on the manufacturing side there was little or no innovatory change and 'the business remained entirely conservative until the end in 1854'.[79] It operated handlooms throughout the period, putting out material through the warehouse. This did not hold back the firms' prosperity; in fact the Heywoods accumulated more capital than they were prepared to sink in their warehouse business. They embarked on a series of investments which included not only loans and mortgages, of the normal risk-averting type, but also ones directed towards productive activities outside the sphere of the firm's direct business commitments. It was at this point that a connection with the factory system was made, a connection also made by Owen Owens and Son. In 1824 John Heywood lent £5,100.00 to Henry and Edmund Ashworth, cotton factory spinners, who operated New Eagley Mill at Turton, four miles north-west of Bolton.[80] Rhodes Boyson informs us that 'The £5,000.00 from John Heywood was raised by a mortgage on the mill and was covered by an assurance policy'. 'The interest on this loan was at 4½ per cent, the rate paid on all non-family loans, and the money was used to cover most of the cost of the re-equipment of New Eagley Mill between 1825 and 1828'.[81] The loan was eventually paid off in 1839[82] and undoubtedly the Heywoods' investment contributed to the success of the Ashworths' factory enterprise.[83] Rhodes Boyson claims that 'the Ashworths did relatively well with their profits from 1826 to 1830 when profit margins were falling . . . This indicates that the enlarged New Eagley Mill was running smoothly by the later 1820s'.[84] Like the Heywoods the Manchester firm of Owen Owens and Son also supplied capital to the factory system. In 1825 John Owens formed a partnership with Samuel Faulkner and Co, a firm of Manchester fine spinners, who were erecting a mill in Ancoats.[85] Owens sunk 'altogether nearly £10,000 for his sleeping partnership' and subscribed the bulk of the money 'in 1825 and 1826 with some further calls in the next two years'.[86] Clapp maintains that the factory 'was probably commissioned in 1828, the last year in which it was a substantial drain on the firms' own resources'[87]; but the Manchester rate books list a factory occupied by Owens and Faulkner in 1827.[88] Owens was not guaranteed a fixed income, unlike the 4½ per cent received by the Heywoods, but he 'took his chance of whatever profit there might be'.[89] The partners began to get a return on their capital in 1829, and table 7.10 shows the income earned from Owen's investment and the rateable value of the factory *c.* 1827–43.[90]

The expansion of the factory in the mid-1830s reflects the

Table 7.10: John Owens' and Samuel Faulkner's factory businesses, Manchester, 1827–1843

Year	Name of firm	Income from S. Faulkner & Co	RV of factory[b] (£)
1827	Owens and Faulkner	–	235 empty part 65
1828	Owens and Faulkner	–	230 empty part 44
1829	S. Faulkner & Co	616	287 empty part 109
1830	S. Faulkner & Co	311	
1831	S. Faulkner & Co	1,281	306 empty part 34
1832	S. Faulkner & Co	2,128	340
1833	S. Faulkner & Co	1,080	
1834	S. Faulkner & Co	321	416 empty part 125
1835	S. Faulkner & Co	400	
1836	S. Faulkner & Co	1,000	546
1837	S. Faulkner & Co	3,063	370
1838	S. Faulkner & Co	550	369
1839	S. Faulkner & Co	1,774	375
1840	S. Faulkner & Co	–	386
1841	S. Faulkner & Co	1,919	–
1842	S. Faulkner & Co	1,400	316
1843	S. Faulkner & Co	700	–

Sources: a. Clapp, *John Owens*, p. 45.
b. Computer data file, Sheffield City Polytechnic, Premise No. 62.

prosperity of that period and is mirrored in John Owens' income for 1837.[91] Clapp points out that:

> Between 1825 and 1828 investment in the mill was the principal sign that Owen Owens and Son was a progressive and growing concern; from 1830 to the end of John Owens' connection with the mill it was a source of capital from which the firm's commercial and financial enterprises could draw nourishment.[92]

That firms such as the Heywoods' and the Owens' were prepared to utilise the capital accumulated in their warehouse business in ventures outside their traditional area of activity may well suggest a trend towards the convergence of the warehouse and the factory by the mid-1820s.[93] In 1815, of the 90 factory firms operating in Manchester, only 14 (15.5 per cent) utilised both factories and warehouses. By 1825, however, 38 firms occupied both types of property asset, representing 46.3 per cent of the total population of 82 factory firms. The trend towards the integration of spinning and weaving in individual enterprises had accelerated markedly in Manchester between 1815 and 1825. This trend, however, did not exclusively follow the expected trajectory of combining spinning with power-loom weaving; there was also a parallel development which saw factory spinning and warehouse manufacturing (putting-out) increasingly joined together. (A list of these firms is given in Appendix 6.) Is there any pattern associated with these firms which is suggestive of the underlying causes of this unlikely convergence? Four different categories of 'converged' firm are shown in Table 7.11, along with their corresponding RVs.

Excluding for the moment category four, there does seem a stronger tendency for warehouse firms to move into the factory sector by acquisition rather than factory firms moving into warehouses. When this latter type of move did occur it involved only relatively small warehouses as can be seen from Table 7.11. Only two firms in category 1 occupied warehouses of any significant size: Thomas Walker, who utilised a warehouse rated at £90.00 in Blue Boar Court, and R. Schofield,[94] whose warehouse in Hankinson's Court was valued at £50.00. Conversely, just over one-third of converged firms in 1825 had originated from warehouse-only units. As might be expected these firms operated more modest sized factories than the other categories

Table 7.11: Combined factory and warehouse firms, Manchester, 1825

Type of firm	Number of firms	Total RV of factory (£)	Total RV of warehouse (£)	Combined RV of factory and warehouse (£)	Factory: warehouse RV ratio
Factory-only firms in 1815, who combined via warehouse acquisition by 1825	6	1,600	188	1,788	8.5
Warehouse-only firms in 1815 who combined via factory acquisition by 1825	13	2,205	963	3,168	2.3
Combined factory and warehouse firms in 1815 who survived to 1825	6	2,263	544	2,807	4.2
New firms entering over the period who combined both factory and warehouse in 1825	13	2,589	638	3,227	4.1
Total	38	8,657	2,333	10,990	3.7

Source: Compiled from Manchester Rate Book for 1825 and *Pigot's Directory* for 1815 and 1825.

and they had the lowest factory:warehouse ratio. An example of this type of firm was J. Massey and Co who utilised two warehouses in 1815 rated at £45.00 and £30.00 and in 1825 occupied a warehouse in Marsden Square rated at £100.00 and a factory rated at £218.00. In 1815, J. Massey and Co were described as agents and commission dealers[95] while by 1825 they were engaged in cotton manufacturing, cotton twist and weft dealing and cotton factory spinning.[96] Some insight into the activities of this firm is provided by one of the partners in the concern, George Smith, who gave evidence before the Select Committee on Commerce, Manufacturers and Shipping in 1833. Smith testified before the Committee that 'We are extensively engaged in handloom calico manfacture' and claimed they employed, in the early 1830s, some 1,300 to 1,400 weavers operating handlooms.[97] The Committee were clearly interested in the process of convergence in the cotton trade, and Smith was asked to comment whether: 'A great many of those engaged in the cotton trade have generally added to the business that they originally engaged in?' Smith acknowledged that this was the 'case with us, we were merely agents prior to 1819, in 1820 we added manufacturing to our business, and in 1826 we added spinning to it'.[98] The mill was erected in 1824 and 1825 and Smith pointed out that 'In 1823 and 1824 the circumstances of the trade brought a great deal of capital into it'.[99] While the buoyancy of market conditions in the early 1820s may have triggered the decision to enter the factory sector there were other underlying factors at work. Smith informed the Committee:

> While spinning was a good trade, those who spun their own material constantly undersold the manufacturer who had to buy his own yarns. This trade is now taken up by the spinners generally; either the spinner has become a manufacturer in addition to spinning, or the manufacturer has become a spinner in addition to a manufacturer.[100]

Smith also maintained that more than half of those handloom calico manufacturers 'who had not added spinning to their business, have failed during the time I have been at Manchester'.[101] According to Smith, convergence was a strategy of survival for the manufacturer, but this did not necessarily entail the abandonment of the warehouse for the power-loom weaving shed. As Smith informed the Select Committee: 'I am not engaged in the mill, my department is in the warehouse'.[102] Between 1825 and 1833 J. Massey and Co extended the manufacturing side of the business and, according to Smith, the firm was employing more handloom weavers at the latter date than they were in the mid-1820s.[103]

Apart from the evidence presented by George Smith, a range of other factors encouraged the convergence of factory and warehouse, especially for the new firms entering the industry (category 4, Table 7.11) in the early 1820s. For those firms erecting factories in Manchester, *c.* 1822–5,[104] the addition of a warehouse premise may have looked an attractive proposition.[105] Yarn could be supplied to a manufacturing side of the business which involved little fixed capital; warehouse space in Manchester was plentiful, sub-letting was plentiful, sub-letting was a general practice and rents were low. Labour costs too were low, handloom weavers were in elastic supply, and wages were falling.[106] In addition, the hand trade was highly adaptive to changing market conditions and weavers could be quickly laid off. There is another factor which may well have increased the attractiveness of the hand manufacturing side of the cotton trade, a factor which has been relatively neglected, though nonetheless important, and that is the availability of managerial expertise in the warehouse trade.[107] The combined firm placed a greater premium on management control than the single-process unit, and the existence in the Manchester market in particular of a pool of expertise in the manufacturing trade, was a distinct advantage for firms considering merging their factory spinning with hand manufacturing. A firm contemplating such a move could turn to one of the town's newspapers and find 'A person who has knowledge of goods in general, likewise of the cutting, dyeing and finishing of fustians, is wishful to engage with any respectable house as Putter-Out'.[108] Another member of the warehouse trade advertised to 'Manufacturers . . . Situation wanted as Putter-Out by a person who has for several years had the management of a respectable plain and fancy muslin manufactory'.[109] Others claimed an all-round knowledge of the cotton trade which they considered fitted them for a number of possible functions. One such individual, putting aside any claims to modesty, offered his multi-talents as follows:

> A middle-aged man, who has a thorough knowledge of the spinning and manufacturing business, wants a situation . . . would be glad to engage with either a spinner as Manager, Manufacturer as Putter-Out, cotton dealer as salesman or Merchant as clerk, being perfectly familiar in the Manchester market with both buyers and sellers.[110]

Others were more restrained in advertising their talents, typified by a putter-out with 20 years' experience in the cotton trade, and who was putting-out to 300 weavers in the Warrington district; he simply wanted 'a situation to make fustians either on salary or commission'.[111]

The expansion of the infrastructure of the warehouse system, which was examined in Chapter 6, provided skilled managerial personnel, in addition to a cheap and plentiful workforce, and must have added to the attractiveness of workhouse manufacturing in the 1820s. The combined firm in Manchester was not necessarily a pure technological thoroughbred, integrating mechanised spinning with power-loom weaving, but also took a managerial form with the convergence of the activities of the factory and the warehouse in one business unit. Such a merging of these activities is interesting, not only from a technical-economic perspective,[112] but clearly has important implications for the political economy of Manchester. The schism in the cotton trade that was explored in Chapter 5 was a product of the separation of interest between factory and warehouse. Were these interests increasingly reconciled in the years after Waterloo? The examination of the structural development of Manchester's business system, *c.* 1815–25 takes us logically to an exploration of Manchester's business community and the extent to which it had achieved internal coherence by 1825. These issues are discussed in Chapter 8.

NOTES AND REFERENCES

1. For a detailed description of the cyclical pattern between 1815 and 1825 see A. D. Gayer, W. W. Rostow and A. J. Schwartz, *The Growth and Fluctuation of the British Economy*, 2nd edn (2 vols., Harvester Press, Hassocks, nr. Brighton, 1975), vol. 1, pp. 140–210.
2. It was in Manchester and in neighbouring areas such as Stockport, Stalybridge, Hyde and Middleton that the great expansion of power-looms took place in the 1820s. See D. Bythell, *The Handloom Weavers: A Study in the English Cotton Industry During the Industrial Revolution* (Cambridge University Press, Cambridge, 1969), p. 91.
3. Gayer *et al.*, *Fluctuations*, vol. 1, p. 171.
4. For example, 1819 was a year of severe unemployment and reduced money wages and these problems spilt over into political protest. 'The Movement had its centre in Manchester and reached its climax with the meeting at St Peter's Field on the 16th of August.' Gayer *et al.*, *Fluctuations*, vol. 1, p. 169.
5. For the high level of failure of cotton factory firms, *c.* 1815–33, see R. Lloyd-Jones and A. A. Le Roux, 'Marshall and the Birth and Death of Firms: The Growth and Size Distribution of Firms in the Early Nineteenth-Century Cotton Industry', *Business History*, vol. XXIV, no. 2 (1982), pp. 141–55.
6. A. Boyd-Hilton, *Corn, Cash, Commerce. The Economic Policies of the Tory Governments 1815–1830* (Oxford University Press, Oxford, 1977), p. 179.
7. Gayer *et al.*, *Fluctuations*, vol. 1, pp. 156, 200.

8. Ibid., p. 183.

9. This sub-committee included Messrs Frazer, Garnett, Peel and Bradshaw. Proceedings of the Manchester Chamber of Commerce and Manufacturers 30 Jan. 1823 (Manchester Central Library M8/2/1), hereafter P.M.C.C.M.

10. P.M.C.C.M., 30 Jan. 1823.

11. Ibid. See also A. Redford, 'Some Problems of the Manchester Merchants after the Napoleonic Wars', *Transactions of the Manchester Statistical Society* (1930/31).

12. The sub-committee claimed that 'between 1818–22 . . . the . . . manufacturers have suffered unparalleled loss, by the depreciation in the value of their stock and the reduction of their capital.' P.M.C.C.M., 30 Jan. 1823.

13. The metal and chemical sectors, which also show significant increases in growth, will be explored in detail in Chapter 9.

14. R. Smith, 'Manchester as a Centre for Manufacturing and Merchanting of Cotton Goods, 1820–30', *University of Birmingham Historical Journal*, vol. IV (1953–4).

15. The survival and exit figures were calculated from the Manchester Poor Rate Assessment Books for 1815 and 1825 (1815, M.C.L., M9/40/2/79) and (1825, vols. 1 and 2, M9/40/2/92,93).

16. The size of firm is measured by the RV proxy. Not only did already large survivor firms from 1815 increase in size but the small fry who survived from 1815 also experienced a significant increase in RV. Exactly half the survivor firms of 1815 had an RV of less than £100.00, by 1825 12 now had an RV of over £100.00 and 5 over £200.00.

17. Forty-six firms made up the 1825 population, in addition to the 36 survivor firms. These figures exclude those firms who entered after 1815 but left the industry before 1825.

18. The SPF firm was also referred to in Chapter 3 and is examined by R. Lloyd-Jones and A. A. Le Roux, 'The Size of Firms in the Cotton Industry: Manchester 1815–1841', *Economic History Review*, vol. XXXIII, no. 1 (1980), p. 77.

19. For an analysis of factory utilisation in the post-1825 period see R. Lloyd-Jones and A. A. Le Roux, 'Factory Utilisation and the Firm: Manchester 1825–1841', *Textile History*, vol 15, no. 1 (1984).

20. All Manchester factories placed in the data bank have been given a premise number.

21. R. Barnes also occupied a warehouse in 1815 located in McDonald's Lane, district 6, rated at £16.00. The firm was described in *Pigot's Directory* as cotton spinners and swandown pillow manufacturers.

22. Chapman has argued that 'it was far less easy for the small man to cushion himself against financial crisis or sudden contradictions in the market'. Quoted in Lloyd-Jones and Le Roux, 'Size of Firms', p. 77.

23. Boyd Hilton, *Corn*, p. 228.

24. Ibid., p. 227.

25. Ibid., p. 229.

26. See Appendix 5 for a detailed survey of warehouse growth between 1807 and 1825.

27. Growth, both in terms of number of units and RV is markedly slower after 1815 than before.

28. See Lloyd-Jones and Le Roux, 'Size of Firms', p. 77, and Gayer *et al.*, *Fluctuations*, vol. 1, pp. 170–2.

29. The indirect effect of factory technology was considerable as was shown in Chapter 6. For the description of work in Manchester warehouses see G. Anderson, *Victorian Clerks* (Manchester University Press, Manchester, 1976), pp. 9–10.

30. If we take the differences between the price of raw cotton and the price of cotton twist as a rough indicator of spinning profit margins, those fell from 13.07d (£0.05.45) between July and December 1816 to 10.2 d (£0.04.23) between January and June 1821. The fall between 1816 and 1821 was 21.3 per cent and between 1816 and 1832 it was 58.9 per cent. Gayer *et al.*, *Fluctuations*, vol. 1, p. 155.

31. For the development of the increased spindle mule and other sub-innovatory processes see Lloyd-Jones and Le Roux, 'Size of Firms', pp. 77–8. Also see Chapters 9 and 10.

32. Spinners' wages were far higher than other classes of cotton operatives and the increase in output associated with the 'large wheel' triggered off disputes over piece rate payments. For a detailed treatment of these disputes and the role of the spinners union see R. G. Kirby and A. E. Musson, *The Voice of the People. John Doherty, 1798–1854 Trade Unionist, Radical and Factory Reformer* (Manchester University Press, Manchester, 1975), Chapters 2, 3 and 4. See also the discussion in Chapter 10.

33. *Manchester Courier*, 1 Jan. 1825.

34. Lloyd-Jones and Le Roux, 'Size of Firms', p. 78.

35. Ibid., p. 78.

36. Ibid., p. 78.

37. *Manchester Guardian*, 10 July 1824.

38. *Manchester Guardian*, 25 Sept. 1824.

39. Estimate reported in the *Manchester Courier*, 26 March 1825.

40. P.P., 1836 (24), XLV, *A Return of the Number of Powerlooms Used in Factories . . .*, pp. 2–3.

41. Bythell, *Handloom Weavers*, p. 88.

42. *Wheeler's Manchester Chronicle*, 15 Jan. 1825.

43. *Wheeler's Manchester Chronicle*, 2 April 1825. The factory was situated in Manchester on the banks of the Ashton canal.

44. P.P., 1833 (690), VI, *Report of the Select Committee on the Present State of Manufacturers, Commerce and Shipping in the United Kingdom*, p. 554.

45. Ibid., Q. 9167.

46. S. Shapiro, *Capital and the Cotton Industry in the Industrial Revolution* (Cornell University Press, Ithaca, New York, 1967), p. 198.

47. Figures calculated from the Poor Rate Assessment Books for Manchester, 1815 and 1820.

48. *Wheeler's Manchester Chronicle*, 25 March 1825.

49. Clapp refers to the tone of business improving in 1823 and 1824; 'By the spring of 1823 the consumption of raw cotton was increasing with unprecedented rapidity and manufacturers were getting higher

prices'. B. W. Clapp, *John Owens, Manchester Merchant* (Manchester University Press, Manchester, 1965), p. 46.

50. Clapp, *John Owens*, p. 24.

51. Ibid., p. 35.

52. Ibid., p. 36.

53. Ibid., p. 23.

54. Ibid., p. 20.

55. Ibid., p. 23.

56. R. Smith, *Manchester's Changing Role in the Lancashire Cotton Trade, 1820–30, and its concomitant effects*, unpublished BA thesis, University of Birmingham, 1950, p. 30.

57. Manchester Poor Rate Assessment Book for 1825.

58. Binyon was located at no. 40 Cannon Street.

59. Francis Marris also operated a Scotch warehouse at no. 36 Cannon Street rated at £25.00. The other activities of Francis Marris will be discussed in Chapter 8.

60. Newbury and Hoyle's warehouses were rated at £160.00 and £16.00; both were situated in Brown Street.

61. The John Heywood papers are located in Bolton Reference Library. See Heywood Papers (Z.H.E,/1–30). Also see W. E. Brown, *Robert Heywood of Bolton 1786–1868* (S.R. Publishers, Wakefield, 1970). This work is primarily concerned with the political and socio-cultural activities of Robert Heywood, the founder's son, and has only little to say about the firm's business activities.

62. The warehouse was situated in Ridings Court.

63. John Heywood was a taker-in for Thomas Naylor, a fustian and later a quilting manufacturer. On Naylor's death in 1803 John Heywood set up in business with his son, Robert, in Mount Pleasant, Little Bolton. Brown, *Robert Heywood*, p. 6.

64. Brown, *Robert Heywood*, p. 8.

65. P. Jeffries to John Heywood, 12 Aug. 1813 (Heywood Papers Z.H.E./9/14).

66. The business letters primarily fall within the period 1805 to 1821. The letters after 1821 tend to deal with personal, family and political (local and national) issues.

67. Decan, Son and Ellis, London, to John Heywood, 25 July 1811 (Z.H.E/7/7).

68. The shift in fashion could be immediately affected by a Royal death. John Gore wrote to John Heywood in November 1817: 'In consequence of the lamented death of the Princess Charlotte — all fancy trade will for the present be at a stand and quiltings will not be wanted so early in the spring'. John Gore, London, to John Heywood, 8 Nov. 1817 (Z.H.E/13/52). For a recent detailed discussion of fashion see B. Lemire, 'Developing Consumerism and the Ready-Made Clothing Trade in Britain, 1750–1800', *Textile History*, vol. 15, no. 1 (1984), pp. 21–44.

69. Richard Prior, London, to John Heywood, 4 Jan. 1816 (Z.H.E/12/1).

70. Hudson was located at Chester, and acted for some of the London houses, frequently visiting Heywood's warehouse in Manchester.

71. John Gore, London, to John Heywood, 9 April 1817 (Z.H.E/13/13).

72. Sculthorpe, Brown and Co., London, to John Heywood, 27 April 1816 (Z.H.E/12/10).

73. Sculthorpe, Brown and Co., London, to John Heywood, 4 April 1816 (Z.H.E/12/8).

74. John Gore, London, to John Heywood, 12 Sept. 1816 (Z.H.E/12/16).

75. John Gore, London, to John Heywood, 28 Sept, 1816 (Z.H.E/12/18).

76. Richard Heywood, Bolton, to Richard Marsden, Dec. 1811 (Z.H.E/7/13).

77. R. and J. Gore, London, to John Heywood, 18 April 1821 (Z.H.E/17/20).

78. Derbyshire however admitted to Heywood that 'it is rarely that I have any complaint of the weaving . . . the pieces are generally stout and very well wove'. C. Derbyshire, Bolton, to Robert Heywood, Milan, 6 June 1826 (Z.H.E/22/16). It is interesting to note that during the severe trading conditions of 1826 Robert Heywood was apparently content to holiday in Italy leaving the firm's affairs in the hands of his relatively new partner.

79. Brown, *Robert Heywood*, p. 8.

80. Heywood bought his yarn from the Ashworths. Brown, *Robert Heywood*, p. 8.

81. Rhodes Boyson, *The Ashworths Cotton Enterprise: The Rise and Fall of a Family Firm, 1818–1880* (Oxford University Press, Oxford, 1970), p. 19.

82. Ibid., p. 33.

83. The Heywoods also invested in a bleaching concern in Salford run by the Slaters which 'eventually Robert Heywood had to foreclose on'. Brown, *Robert Heywood*, p. 8.

84. Boyson, *Ashworths*, p. 17.

85. Clapp suggests that friendship ties may have been an important factor in encouraging the Owens' investment in the new factory: 'George Faulkner, a life-long friend of John Owens and the first chairman of Owens College, was associated with the firm'. Clapp, *John Owens*, p. 44.

86. Clapp, *John Owens*, p. 44.

87. Ibid., p. 44.

88. The factory is listed as Premise no. 62 in the computer data bank at Sheffield City Polytechnic. The name of the firm changed to S. Faulkner in 1829.

89. Clapp, *John Owens*, p. 44.

90. John Owens 'withdrew from the partnership, apparently in 1844, recovering his original capital of £10,000.00', Clapp, *John Owens*, p. 45.

91. The fall in RV of the factory in 1837 reflects re-rating of property downwards associated with the depression of that year.

92. Clapp, *John Owens*, p. 45.

93. The integration between factory spinning and handloom

manufacture has been explored by Lyons. He suggests that by the 1820s the share of this type of firm in factory employment was probably high. Certainly our evidence for Manchester suggests a trend towards the convergence of factory and warehouse after 1815. J. S. Lyons, 'Vertical Integration in the British Cotton Industry, 1826–1850: A Revision', *Journal of Economic History*, vol. 45, no. 2 (1985), p. 421.

94. In 1825 Thomas Walker was described simply as a spinner and R. Schofield as spinner and cotton manufacturer (nankeen and velvet) and dealers. *Pigot's Directory*, 1825.

95. *Pigot's Directory*, 1815.

96. *Pigot's Directory*, 1825.

97. Smith also claimed they operated no power looms. P.P., 1833 (690), VI., p. 548.

98. P.P., 1833 (690), VI., p. 600.

99. Smith maintained that the factory was filled with the best machinery 'according to the best of our judgement'. Upwards of £20,000.00 were advanced for the factory and the machinery. P.P., 1833 (690), VI., p. 549.

100. P.P., 1833 (690), VI, p. 559.

101. Ibid., p. 559.

102. Ibid., p. 550.

103. Ibid., p. 602.

104. J. L. Bradbury, a Manchester calico printer, giving evidence before the Select Committee on Artisans and Machinery in 1824, claimed that 'a great many cotton factories were being erected in Manchester'. P.P., 1824 (51), V, p. 546.

105. Of the 46 new entrants in the 1825 population 28.3 per cent of firms occupied a warehouse in addition to their factory.

106. A meeting of weavers in Manchester in October 1824, apart from complaining of falling wages and the need to combine to prevent further wage cuts, also warned those present that 'It will be necessary to adopt some official means, to prevent such an influx of strange hands into the trade. We would seriously impress upon the minds of the different delegates this important measure'. *Manchester Guardian*, 2 Oct. 1824.

107. From a more general perspective Sigworth has suggested that an important factor affecting business performance 'is the dependence of manufacturing industry on efficiency in distribution . . .', which, of course, includes warehousing. Quoted in B .W. E. Alford, 'Entrepreneurship, Business Performance and Industrial Development', *Business History*, vol. 19 (1977), pp. 125–6.

108. *Wheeler's Manchester Chronicle*, 15 Jan. 1825.

109. Ibid., 19 Feb. 1825.

110. Ibid., 5 March 1825.

111. Ibid., 19 March 1825. See also *Manchester Guardian*, 23 Oct. 1824, for an advertisement for a 'Putter-out . . . who can command a set of out-door weavers'.

112. It is the technical-economic perspective which Lyons concentrates upon in his analysis. However, he has little to say about Manchester, a point made by Herman Freudenberger in his discussion of

Lyons' article in the same issue of the *Journal of Economic History*. Lyons, 'Vertical Integration', pp. 422–5. Our intention, developed in Chapter 8, is that the clear trend in convergence shown by the Manchester data between 1815 and 1825 requires a political economy approach to assess its implication for Manchester business structure.

8

The Business Community and Political Economy in Manchester, *c.* 1815–1825

Changes in local economic structure associated with the rapid expansion of the factory and the growing integration of spinning and manufacturing were inevitably linked to the evolving political economy of Manchester in the post-Waterloo period. At the same time local structures should not be treated in isolation at the cost of discounting national economic developments. We will examine some of these dominant national issues[1] and examine their relationship to the local political economy of Manchester. In doing so we hope to shed light on the development of Manchester's business community as it sought to advance the claims of manufacturing industry in the overall pattern of the nation's economic priorities.

The first decade following Waterloo generated heated debate concerning the stability, structure and management of the economy. Policy issues centred on the 'correct' balance between agriculture and manufacturing and the pace and extent of reform of the currency and the protective system.[2] Clearly, there is a close relationship between the form of economic management and the level of economic stability. The theoretical underpinning of the government's overall stance to economic management in the early years of peace was provided by Ricardian political economy. This position was sketched out by Ricardo in his *Principles*:

> The commencement of war after a long peace, or of peace after a long war, generally produces distress in trade. It changes in a great degree the nature of the employment to which respective capitals of countries were before devoted;

> and during the interval while they are settling in the situations which new circumstances have made the most beneficial, much fixed capital is unemployed . . . and labourers are without full employment. The distress which proceeds from a revulsion of trade is often mistaken for that which accompanies a diminution of the national capital and a retrograde state of society . . . When, however, such distress immediately accompanies a change from war to peace, our knowledge of the existence of such a case will make it reasonable to believe that the funds for the maintenance of labour have rather been diverted from their usual channel than materially impaired, and that, after temporary suffering, the nation will again advance in prosperity.[3]

Put in crude terms, the government had no need to pursue panic measures of economic management and should rather aid the underlying processes which were leading to recovery. As we shall see later, there were other interpretations of Ricardo's political economy that the Liverpool government chose to ignore, but they were more than content to accept the notion of spontaneous recovery. As the Prime Minister, Lord Liverpool, stated, 'our manufacturers must wait with patience until the supply and the demand adjust themselves to each other'.[4] If the government was to act it would be in the area of a 'passive administration of dear money, deflation, and the winnowing out of inefficient or otherwise unsound producers'.[5] On the whole Manchester's business community did not object to this overall strategy. We have already referred to the evidence of Thomas Walker, the factory spinner, who acknowledged the acute distress of 1819 in Manchester, yet emphasised what he believed to be its temporary nature. At the beginning of 1820 the *Manchester Mercury* was reporting rising cotton prices, and in 1821 Thomas Wallace, the Vice-President of the Board of Trade, claimed in the House of Commons that great improvements in the cotton trade 'had recently taken place'.[6] It would appear that Ricardian faith in spontaneous recovery had been justified and in other controversial areas too Manchester businessmen endorsed national objectives. The government's decision to return to gold was not accompanied by unanimous commercial support for a policy of currency deflation. Thomas Attwood, of Birmingham, argued that 'all the economic instability of the post-war generation arose from the error of restricting the expanding trade of a growing population within the inelastic bounds of a gold currency'.[7] Such a view found little sympathy in Manchester. G. W. Wood,[8] a cotton manufacturer and dealer and treasurer of the Manchester Chamber of Commerce and Manufacturers, reflected, according to Arthur Redford, the public opinion of the town when he declared that 'we want a regulating medium and there is nothing like gold for that purpose. No circumstances can depreciate its value. Nothing can impair our confidence in it'.[9] That Manchester business welcomed the return to a metallic currency is witnessed by their hostility to any issue of local banknotes. In 1821, three Manchester banks, Jones, Lloyd and Co, Heywood Brothers and Co, and Dainty, Ryle and Co, announced their intention of issuing local notes 'from the impossibility of providing a sufficient quantity of cash to meet the weekly payments required by the manufacturing interests in this district'.[10] The decision of those banks did not win universal approval and a public meeting was called to debate the issue which was held in Manchester on 23 August 1821. It was attended by some of the largest factory and warehouse businessmen in the town, including spinners, manufacturers, cotton dealers, calico printers, etc.[11] The temper of the meeting ran strongly against the idea of local notes and only Thomas Sharp,[12] a textile machine maker, spoke in favour of a local issue. Archibald Prentice informs us that the following declaration 'was very numerously signed':

> We the undersigned, being deeply impressed with the inconvenience and danger to be apprehended from the circulation of local notes in this great commercial town, do hereby declare it to be our intention not to receive any such notes in payment after the 31st inst, except in cases of extreme necessity, in all which cases we pledge ourselves not to circulate such notes.[13]

Underlying this declaration is a search for stability, which the government's currency reform appeared to offer the Manchester business community. Spontaneity of market forces, associated with stable financial management, was an ideal which linked Manchester business to the political economy of the Liverpool government. But Manchester was not simply a mirror image of Whitehall, history rarely provides such neat causal relations. There were tensions and strains within Manchester's political economy which created contradictory and sometimes hostile stances to national policy.[14] A variety of forces were at work here, but two were critically important. One was Peterloo, the other the rapidly changing business structure of Manchester itself. Peterloo gave Manchester an unwanted notoriety and threatened to fragment that relationship between the economic and political which was crucial to the stable development of a capitalist market economy. Within weeks of the massacre at St Peter's Field there were petitions to Parliament protesting against the outrages at Manchester. Between 8 and 13 December 1819 there were petitions from Liverpool, Westmorland, Westminster, Rochester and Southwark 'condemning the events at Manchester and the actions of the government'.[15] For example, the Westmorland petition stated that, 'the Petitioners have seen, with astonishment and deep regret, the late most alarming proceedings at Manchester. May it therefore please the house, to institute a strict inquiry into all the late proceedings at Manchester'.[16] Manchester symbolised as a centre of social unrest was hardly conducive to a healthy business environment; but more seriously, Peterloo connected social unrest to economic distress and the combination of the two threatened to undermine economic stability. The relationship between unrest, distress and stability was put clearly by Alexander Baring,[17] MP, who, according to Barry Gordon, was more 'the representative voice in parliament for the businessman of his day than David Ricardo'.[18] Like Ricardo, Baring acknowledged that the transition from war to peace had given rise to uncertainty among businessmen, but in the aftermath of Peterloo expectations had been further depressed by 'the want of tranquility and security in the manufacturing districts themselves'.[19] Speaking in the House of Commons, on 8 May 1820, Baring maintained that 'The fundamental requisite for [economic] recovery . . . was the establishment of domestic tranquility so that those with capital could employ it without apprehension'.[20] He argued that the lack of tranquillity was a function of economic distress associated with 'the desire and policy of men engaged in trade . . . to screw down the price of labour as low as possible'.[21] Manchester businessmen disassociated themselves from Baring's prescription of a minimum wage[22] but they did recognise that Peterloo had changed the political content of economic distress,[23] paradoxically on the eve of the upturn in Manchester's economy which, as we have seen, can be traced back to 1820. The business community's response was in part institutional, a process aided by structural changes in Manchester's economy. Out of Peterloo came a desire on the behalf of Manchester businessmen to forge a more united front which was typified by the formation of the Manchester Chamber of Commerce and Manufacturers in 1820. Prior to the formation of the Chamber 'collective action among Manchester merchants and manufacturers still depended upon the calling of public meetings'[24] and, as we saw in Chapter 5, bitter disputes between factory and warehouse divided the business interest and prevented the establishment of a continuous central business organisation to promote the objectives of the business community. Peterloo may have been the catalyst, but the underlying structural changes in the town's economy, associated with the converging interest of factory and warehouse, eased the path to business unity. Nathanial Gould's savage critique of the factory faded rapidly in post-Peterloo Manchester; the rapid growth of the factory system, the increase in the size of the factory firm, and the process of combination of spinning and weaving provided fertile grounds for the growth of a more unified business community. Rather than opposing factions, projecting particular 'interests', a united front emerged which allowed the development of a coherent business strategy. We will now explore the patterns of integration of Manchester's business community and then go on to examine the collective business objectives they attempted to pursue.

There is a connection between Peterloo and the form and pattern of Manchester's business elite. R. J. Morris, for example, has referred to Cobden's belief that the Peterloo outrage would not have happened if Manchester had been incorporated. For Cobden, the massacre was a consequence of country magistrates, 'tory squires or persons coming into town and letting loose a troop of fox hunters disguised as yeomanry cavalry'.[25] Morris is sympathetic to Cobden's argument and asserts, 'The court leet on which Manchester depended for much of its local government excluded the many wealthy merchants and manufacturers who lived in the out-township'.[26] An examination of Manchester's court leet in the 1820s does not bear out this assertion. Table 8.1 lists the members of the jury of Manchester's court leet in 1824, with a description of their main business activity and where possible estimates of their property assets.

Manchester's court leet is clearly dominated by cotton

Table 8.1: Members of the jury of Manchester's court leet, 1824[27]

Name of member	Main business activity[a]	RV of property[b] asset, 1825
John Barton	Merchant (firm of John and Richard Barton)	Warehouse RV £140.00 (6 Mulberry St)
Edward Lloyd	Banker	N/a
Thos. Houldsworth	Fine cotton spinner	Factory RV £1,101.00
John Bradshaw	Manager Bridgewater estates	Bridgewater warehouses RV £800.00
Charles Rider	Gentleman	House, Collyhurst Hall
Peter Ewart	Cotton spinner	Factory RV £337.00
Charles Brandt	Merchant, cotton manufacturer and dealer	Warehouse RV £70.00 (20 Back George St)
Thomas Worthington	Cotton manufacturer and dealer, calico printer, fustian, silk and cotton, muslin and smallware manufacturer, factory cotton spinner	Warehouse RV £200.00 (50–51 High St) Factory RV £255.00 Empty part £74.00
John Powell	Calico printer and merchant in the Peel & Co calico printing empire	N/a
Jonathan Dawson	Gentleman	N/a
Francis Marris	Merchant, cotton manufacturer and dealer, importer of Irish linen, etc.	Warehouse RV £175.00 Warehouse RV £36.00 (36 and 37 Cannon St)
John Kennedy	Fine cotton spinner	Factory RV £943.00
Thomas Heywood	Banker	N/a (house St Anne St)
James Potter[c]	N/a	N/a
Thomas Cardwell	Cotton manufacturer and dealer	Warehouse RV £220.00 (New Market)
Samuel Grimshaw	Gentleman	(house 62 Mosley St)

Sources and Notes: a. *Pigot's Directory*, 1825.
b. Manchester Rate Book 1825.
c. There are numerous Potters listed in the directory — it was not possible to isolate a James Potter with a reasonable degree of accuracy.

businessmen with a roughly equal proportion of warehouse and factory members. There is a need for caution; Morris may not only have underestimated the role of businessmen on the Manchester court leet but he has probably exaggerated its significance as a political organ. Redford, for example, has claimed that during the last half century of its existence, 'the Manchester court leet was an absurd anachronism',[28] and that at the beginning of the nineteenth century 'the administrative function of the court leet was being taken over by the newly reorganised Police Commissioners'.[29] Yet it does not follow that membership of the court leet was akin to political impotence, for as Redford himself conceded 'it was common knowledge that the magistrates, the principal officers of the parish, and the leaders of the Police Commissioners, were all, or almost all, members of a close-knit oligarchy'.[30] The chief officer of the town was the boroughreeve, who was elected by the court leet on an unpaid basis to serve for one year. Between October 1814 and December 1825, of the twelve boroughreeves of Manchester seven were active in the cotton trade either as manufacturers, dealers, factory masters, or calico printers, and an eighth was a cotton machine maker.[31] Of these seven, five were to become directors of the Manchester Chamber of Commerce and Manufacturers after 1820. In 1825, of the 18 non-paid constables of Manchester assisting the boroughreeve, 13 were directly involved in business, either as merchants, manufacturers, factory spinners or calico printers.[32] Not surprisingly these were large-scale businessmen, such as Thomas Cardwell,[33] a cotton manufacturer and dealer, operating a warehouse rated at £220.00, Thomas Worthington (boroughreeve 1822/3) with a warehouse rated at £200.00 and a factory at £255.00, and Gilbert Winter (boroughreeve 1823/4), a cotton twist and weft dealer with a warehouse in St Anne's Street rated at £100.00. The interconnection between local government and the business elite may be further gauged from a decision taken by the directors of the Manchester Chamber of Commerce and Manufacturers, in March 1822, when they agreed that the boroughreeve of Manchester should 'be a member of the Board of Directors, *ex officio*'.[34]

There is little doubt that the business community was closely connected to the circuit of local political power. There were other interconnected circuits, too, which reveal the varied activities of a business elite operating within the political economy of Manchester. These circuits consisted of:

(a) extra business activity (in particular, membership of railway and insurance companies);
(b) municipal utilities and amenities (Manchester gas works, the improvement commission for Market Street[35]);
(c) class-related institutions (Sunday schools, mechanics Institute, the Manchester and Salford Bank of Saving).

What is significant about these institutions is the overlapping membership of both factory and warehouse businessmen who frequently too turn out to be directors of the Chamber of Commerce and Manufacturers. Thus Thomas Cardwell, in addition to his direct business activity and directorship of the Manchester Chamber, was also a committee member of the proposed Manchester and Leeds and Manchester and Oldham railways, a deputy director of the Manchester Assurance Co, a member of the Manchester committee of the North British Fire and Life Assurance Company, a director of the Manchester Gas Works, a commissioner of the Market Street Improvement Bill, a jury member of the court leet, and a Manchester constable.[36] On these committees Cardwell would mix with both warehouse and factory men who made up the majority of the membership. For example, Peter Ewart, a factory spinner, was, like Cardwell, a Chamber director, a director of the Manchester Gas Works and a jury member of the court leet. Table 8.2 shows the pattern of involvement of chamber directors in different Manchester businesses and municipal and socio-political organisations in 1825.

The level of activity in railway and insurance companies reflects, of course, the direction of investment in those activities during the mid-1820s boom.[37] Clearly, too, it was not just factory entrepreneurs who were putting their capital into new joint stock ventures. On the committee of subscribers of the proposed Manchester and Leeds railway, apart from factory men such as Houldsworth, Worthington and Norris, there was a liberal representation of warehouse firms. Of the 28 committee members, 13 operated warehouses in the cotton manufacturing, dealing and calico printing sector.[38] There is a similar combination of factory and warehouse businessmen acting on the committees of the insurance companies. It is interesting to note in this connection that Samuel Stocks Jr, a partner in the firm of S. and B. Stocks and Son (operating two warehouses in 1825 rated at £120.00 and £100.00) was a Manchester committee member of

Table 8.2: Directors of the Manchester Chamber of Commerce and Manufacturers and their various activities, 1825

Organisation	Type of participation	Number of directors involved
Manchester and Leeds Railway[a]	committee of subscribers	10
Manchester and Oldham Railway[b]	committee members	2
Manchester Central Junction Railway[c]	management committee	3
Manchester Assurance Company[d]	directors	3
	auditor	1
Guardian Fire and Life Assurance Company[e]	Manchester committee	3
Norwich Union Fire Insurance Society[f]	Manchester committee	4
Committee of the Friends of Manchester Sunday Schools[g]	committee members	3
Manchester and Salford Bank of Saving[h]	elected trustees	5
Manchester Gas Works[i]	directors	8
Market Street Improvements[j]	commissioners	12
Manchester Court Leet[k]	jury members	5

Sources: a. *Manchester Courier*, 8 January 1825; b. *Manchester Courier*, 29 January 1825; c. *Wheeler's Manchester Chronicle*, 22 January 1825; d. *Manchester Courier*, 26 March 1825; e. *Manchester Courier*, 8 January 1825; f. *Wheeler's Manchester Chronicle*, 19 March 1825; g. *Wheeler's Manchester Chronicle*, 12 February 1825; h. *Manchester Guardian*, 14 August 1825; i. *Manchester Guadian*, 3 July 1824; j. A Prentice, *Historical Sketches and Personal Recollections of Manchester* (Charles Gilpin, London, 1851), p. 209; k. *Court Leet Records of the Manor of Manchester*, vol. X.

the Guardian Fire and Life Assurance Company.[39] As we saw in Chapter 5, his father had been a bitter opponent of the factory system and a supporter of Nathanial Gould. The activities of Samuel Stocks Sr in 1825 supports the idea of a growing convergence of factory and warehouse. In 1816 Stocks Sr had given evidence before the Select Committee examining the condition of children working in factories and had testified that he would not be welcomed by the factory masters to enter their establishments. Visits to the factory were not on the agenda of practical activity for critics such as Samuel Stocks. By 1825 the situation had changed and Stocks was sharing committees with factory masters and joining them in signing petitions on general business policy. Stocks had long been active in the Sunday School movement and in 1825 he was Vice-President of the Subscribers and Friends to the Sunday Schools for Children of all Denominations in Manchester and Salford. The governing committee of this organisation included not only prominent warehousemen such as Thomas and William Townend and Francis Marris, but also large-scale factory masters such as James McConnel, G. A. Lee, George Murray, James Kennedy, Edmund Norris, James Wood and Edward Westhead.[40] The latter two factory men were active from 1819 in the Grosvenor Street Chapel, also regularly attended by Samuel Stocks.[41] Samuel Stocks Jr had chaired the annual general meeting of the Manchester Chamber of Commerce and Manufacturers in February 1823[42] and in June of the same year at a meeting of the Chamber, Stocks Sr signed a petition supporting the recognition of the South American republics.[43] This petition was signed by the principal cotton manufacturers and factory men of their day, including factory masters such as Houldsworth, Hugh Beaver, Jonathan Pollard, T. Ashton, Peter Ewart, Edmund Norris, Harbottle and Richard Clogg. The schism in the cotton trade, reflecting the existence of the separate 'interests' of factory and warehouse, was by 1825 practically closed. The movement towards one common 'interest' group may be gauged from an incident involving the Manchester Chamber of Commerce and Manufacturers. In 1825 the county member of parliament for Lancashire, G. R. Phillips, requested that the Board of Directors of the Manchester Chamber might consider meeting a delegation of three operative spinners[44] wishing to discuss with the Board 'the proposed bill for regulating the hours in factories'.[45] The Board, consisting of six warehouse men[46] and five factory men (Greg, Ewart, Houldsworth, Kennedy and Sterling) agreed to meet the delegation.[47] The initial response was negative, and they stated that 'this Board does not consider it to be within its province to attempt to decide on what are the proper number of hours per day that ought to be employed in work, in any specific trade'.[48] The Board also rejected 'on general principles . . . the regulation of such matters by law', but acknowledged that the introduction of machinery may have given some employers a strong incentive 'to work their people to excess'. They also conceded that 'the factory system renders the labourer less able to regulate his hours of work according to his inclination and his physical powers, than he formerly was'.[49] In the light of these conditions the Board admitted that legislative interference with industrial working hours might be regarded as reasonable, but they added an important caveat. If circumstances justified interference, such interference would necessarily have to be general and not partial. The Board concluded:

> To select one trade for the experiment, whilst others are left free, is injurious to the character, and harsh and offensive to the feelings of those engaged in it, whilst no reason is known to exist, why such an invidious selection should be made.[50]

In 1815, for Nathanial Gould and his followers, the factory represented a special case which called for specific measures of intervention by government. By 1825 some form of intervention might be conceded, but only as a general application. The factory was no longer identified as a separate interest; it was now part of a unified trade. The interlocking activities of both warehouse and factory men made it possible to devise and promote a common set of policies relevant to the Manchester business community as a whole. Let us examine some of these policies.

It might be useful to distinguish between two sets of policies. One set is concerned more with the day-to-day management of business; in particular, they provide the conditions for improving the level of business efficiency. The second set deals more with the long-term development of the trade; with policies and strategies intended to create a business environment conducive to growth. Both sets of policies involve interaction with the state and are thus part of that flow of communication that links national with local political economy. Falling into the first category of policy sets was the interest taken by Manchester businessmen in improved postal services. Redford maintains that for a 'progressive business community like Manchester, efficient postal services were almost as important as the efficient carriage of goods' but he also warns that 'the provincial merchants had to work continuously for the reform of the Post Office'.[51] The efficiency of the postal services was a recurring item on the agenda of the Manchester Chamber of Commerce and Manufacturers.[52] In December 1823 a special meeting of the Chamber was called, which included the boroughreeve and the two senior constables of Manchester, to discuss the postal services. Plans relating to the improvement of Manchester's Post Office were debated and the meeting resolved that 'the merchants of this town are entitled to every possible accommodation and security in the delivery of their letters without being required to incur any increased expense'.[53] The Chamber acted as a forum, both receiving complaints and generating responses in the form of petitions to the Post Master General,[54] holding special meetings and generally increasing the scope for inquiry and debate. Apart from the concern with a more efficient postal service, and therefore improved market information, the business community also focused attention on the management of market transactions. Here, policy discussion centred on such issues as the proper relation between debtors and creditors,[55] the right of bankrupts, and the problem of stamp duties on inland bills of exchange. The Manchester Chamber took a keen interest in the rights of bankrupts, which is not altogether surprising, given the high failure rate of cotton firms. The Manchester Chamber argued that the law should be amended so that each bankrupt would have the right to be brought before a jury, the latter would then determine what form the bankruptcy should take. The Chamber proposed that bankrupts should be placed into three different categories. The first category was defined as 'unfortunate but honest' and these might be allowed to recommence business after a relatively short period; the second category was designated 'Improvident' and these should be 'prohibited for a definite time — to vary according to the amount of dividend and other circumstances — from recommencing business'; and the third category was listed as 'Fraudulent debtors' who should 'be penaly punished and prohibited from trading again for ever, or for a very long period'.[56] As we saw in the previous chapter, it was fashionable in certain circles to welcome commercial crises as purges of the speculative and inefficient. The Manchester Chamber was no enemy to the competitive system but it sought to blur the black and white distinction between success and failure, drawn by political economists and politicians. Business failure was part of the everyday occurrences of the Manchester business system, but not all failures were identical; not all failed businessmen were fools or frauds. In an age lacking the safety net of limited liability, the management and treatment of business failure was a matter of concern to the business community as well as to the legislature.

The operation of a transaction system is also mediated by the instruments used in the settlement of debt, and in Manchester there was 'protracted struggle extending throughout the second quarter of the nineteenth century . . . waged . . . against excessive stamp duties',[57] particularly on inland bills of exchange. Redford argues that this 'apparently minor grievance was attacked with a persistence which suggests that its real importance must have been considerable'.[58] Bills of exchange had carried stamp duty since 1782 and in 1815 the duty had been raised. The charges were felt by Manchester businessmen to be prohibitive, and the directors of the Chamber wrote to Lord Liverpool, in March 1822, complaining that the successive increases of stamp duty on bills had:

> put an almost entire stop to their use in this district for sums of small amount, to the serious inconvenience of business. Payments of from £10 to £50 were formerly made in drafts in London at two months payable to order, for which now Bank of England notes are almost universally substituted, though attended with an increase of risk and trouble.[59]

Yet, in the postwar years, the average duty on a bill of exchange of less than £50.00 was only one-half per cent.[60] The anger generated by the stamp duty may well have been related to the structural pattern of Manchester's warehouse system in the post-Napoleonic period. As was shown in Chapter 7, there was a clear trend towards a smaller size of firm in the warehouse sector after 1815. Small bills of two months credit would have been a significantly more useful financial instrument to small firms than Bank of England notes, but that advantage was neutralised by the duty. The persistence shown by the Chamber, in pursuing this matter, suggests that they were sensitive to the practical needs of the business community in general, and not simply content with serving the needs of a small elite. The Chamber was by no means universally successful in achieving the objectives it set itself. The postal services were improved, particularly as local pressure could be more effectively applied,[61] but the attempt to redefine bankrupts remained on the drawing board, and the petitions to government demanding the reduction of stamp duties 'fell on deaf ears'.[62] There is nothing surprising in this outcome; as the Manchester cotton trade expanded rapidly, a whole series of trade-related issues and policies emerged, and the important task of the business community was to create the means by which dialogue with the state on business issues could be placed on a more formal basis.[63] This process was aided, not only by the formation of the Manchester Chamber of Commerce in 1820, but by the growth of the local press. In addition to the *Manchester Mercury*, *Wheeler's Manchester Chronicle* and *Cowdry's Gazette*, 'Cottonopolis' could boast the *Manchester Observer*, founded in 1818, the *Manchester Guardian* founded in 1821, the *Manchester Iris* founded in 1822, and the *Manchester Courier* founded in 1825.[64] These newspapers by no means followed the same editorial policy; the *Mercury* and the *Courier* were Tory, the *Gazette* (taken over by the Manchester businessman, Archibald Prentice in the early 1820s) Radical, and the *Guardian*, Whig.[65] However, we should not exaggerate these political divisions; in the early 1820s the notion of fixed party positions across a wide range of issues is not really tenable.[66] What was important was that these newspapers provided a forum for debate, which went beyond the purely local, and sought to explore the implications of national policies for the business community. The *Manchester Guardian* in its first issue in May 1821 asserted that,

> no former period in the history of our country, has been marked by the agitation of questions of a more important character than those which are now claiming the attention of the public. To any one who regards for a moment, the conflicting views and wishes of the commercial and agricultural interests — the consideration which may arise out of the existing laws for the regulation of our currency, the present and the anticipated pressure of the national debt and taxation — this statement will be sufficiently apparent.[67]

The *Manchester Guardian* also aimed 'to assist in the diffusion of just principles of political economy'.[68] How were such principles interpreted by the business community and how were they seen to contribute to the health and vigour of the business environment? We are now concerned with the second set of policies.

The competitive conditions and falling price trend, facing the common industry in the 1820s, meant that long-term policies of cotton action, pursued by the business community, were more likely to concentrate on the demand side. From the outset the Manchester Chamber of Commerce and Manufacturers declared that 'the duty of the Association should be to attend the proceedings in parliament affecting the commercial interests of Manchester . . . and to promote . . . by proper means, the removal of existing regulations injurious to the freedom of trade'.[69] This aim links the national to the local, via a political economy which called for the deregulation of constraints on market forces. Deregulation is seen as a prerequisite for expanding market size which is being held back by artificial barriers to trade. This is the clarion call for freer trade, a policy taken up by the Manchester Chamber and important organs of the local press from the early 1820s.[70] Care should be taken not to reduce this campaign to a direct demand for the repeal of the Corn Laws, or to assume that Manchester's business community was demanding trade reforms, immediately after Waterloo. At the public meeting in Manchester, in 1815, to discuss the proposed new Corn Law of that year, the major objections were not directed at agricultural protection itself, but against the increase of duty levied on imported corn.[71] Archibald Prentice, who had set up in the cotton business in Manchester following his arrival from Glasgow in 1815, and who later was to become the proprietor of the radical *Manchester Gazette*,[72] was disappointed at the business community's reaction to the 1815 Act. Prentice reported, 'I did not find many persons of my own class in Manchester, whose opinions in free trade in corn were in accordance with my own . . . I found opposition to the bill had been very faint.'[73] In 1815 the 'interests' of the cotton trade were divided between factory and warehouse and the business community lacked the solid basis to promote a unified and coherent business strategy which was common to the cotton trade. The development of a more vocal, unified and sustained policy on free trade, was necessarily linked, indeed ran parallel to, the convergence of the factory and the warehouse, which as we have seen, rapidly gathered momentum in the early 1820s. There would be little to gain from a detailed description of the various deregulation measures advocated by the Manchester cotton trade in the 1820s,[74] rather let us explore the broad principles which informed and shaped the trade reformers' objectives, and gauge the extent to which they were consistent with Ricardian political economy and the Liverpool government's policy on the regulation of trade. Outlined below are five basic principles which formed the bedrock of business thinking in Manchester on this issue.

(1) The deregulation of trade promotes the growth of manufacturing industry.

(2) The continuation of duties on raw materials, especially raw cotton, places unnecessary costs on competitive industry and threatened employment, prosperity and social order.

(3) When protective measures are removed from manufacturing industry there should be compensatory reductions in agricultural protection.

(4) The private enterprise system has the necessary dynamic to capitalise on the opportunities opened up by trade deregulation.

(5) The protective system is positively harmful, holding back the 'natural' expansion of manufacturers and commerce and distorting the structural balance of the economy.

The first proposition has particular interest in the context of the economic relations between Britain and Ireland. In June 1820 the question of the continuation of the Irish linen duties was raised in the Commons and Vansittart, the Chancellor, defended their continuation on infant industry grounds; the gist of his argument being that Irish manufacturers 'required a few more years before they were ready to face open competition'.[75] This argument was rejected by Ricardo,[76] but the Chancellor of the Irish Exchequer, William Vesey-Fitzgerald, declared that Ireland was a special case. According to Fitzgerald, 'The situation in Ireland was . . . very peculiar . . . as far as related to the provision of the Union, for the protection and encouragement of the manufacturers of that country'.[77] This argument made little impression on the members of the Manchester Chamber of Commerce and Manufacturers. The Manchester merchants, in a memorial to Parliament in 1821, complained bitterly, 'that to levy duties on merchandise passing between parts of the same Empire is injurious to their common prosperity and contrary to the first principles of political economy'.[78] The members also rejected the infant industry argument and asserted that freer intercourse would actually assist the development of Irish manufacturing industry, in particular by encouraging the flow of British capital into Ireland. The Manchester Chamber invited the co-operation of all the principal towns of England to support the deregulation of Anglo-Irish trade, arguing that 'British capital would be used for the object so much desired by parliament — the industrious occupation and comfortable support of the peasantry in

Ireland'.[79] The Chamber was convinced that the removal of restrictions would stimulate manufacturing industry — a claim backed up by their belief that the private enterprise system was ideally suited to capture the advantages of freer trade (proposition 4). Thus the Manchester merchants and manufacturers, referring to the East India trade, claimed in 1822 that, 'since the trade of the East has been opened to the enterprise of private merchants the commerce of this town with India has greatly increased'.[80] Conversely, the continuation of duties on raw materials (proposition 2) and general restrictions on trade (proposition 5) placed unnecessary fetters on the growth of manufacturing. The government's refusal to abolish the duty on raw cotton was a constant irritant to the Manchester cotton trade. The manufacturers complained bitterly in 1820:

> the imposition of heavy duties on those raw materials which form the basis of our manufactures, is in the highest degree impolitic, evidently tending to diminish the labour and reduce the wages of our industrial population, in the full employment and adequate remuneration of which the prosperity of the state essentially depends.[81]

The inference here is clear enough, the manufacturing interest, in terms of its employment generation, is vital to the prosperity, and consequently the stability of the state. The Manchester men in this context are directing their claim at national political economy; a political economy referred to by Cain and Hopkins as 'the management of the national economy and . . . the strategies devised to secure state revenue, domestic employment and public order'.[82] The cotton trade contributed to all three, and it therefore followed that if a policy of deregulation was to be systematically carried out it should be even-handed in its treatment of the manufacturing and agricultural interests (proposition 3). Consequently, when Huskinson brought in his scheme, for the reduction of protective import duties on foreign raw materials and manufactured goods in 1824,[83] the manufacturers demanded 'a quid pro quo' in terms of the treatment of agricultural protection.[84] Such a call for equality of treatment brought the Corn Laws to the centre of debate. They were symbolised as a system of controls which benefited a specific interest group at the cost of the rest of the community (proposition 5). In 1815, as we have seen, Manchester businessmen were muted in their criticisms of the Corn Laws; by the mid-1820s, there were no such reservations. At a special general meeting of the Chamber in 1826 it was unanimously resolved that:

> While the Corn Laws have been highly injurious to the cultivators of the soil, by causing great fluctuations in the value of agricultural produce, they have at the same time been silently and gradually undermining the commerce and manufacturers of the country both by increased British labour costs and by depriving some other countries of their only means of purchasing British manufactured goods, thereby forcing them to manufacture their own sooner than they otherwise would have done.[85]

To the Manchester men the Corn Laws were not only holding back the growth of British manufacturing but they were, in addition, distorting the structural balance of Britain's economic relations with the Continent. It follows that the 'fetters' on trade should be removed, for the prosperity of the country 'depends upon the extension of its commerce'[86] and consequently a structural shift in favour of manufacturing industry. Such a view, it will be argued, is consistent with Ricardian political economy but not with the overview of economic structure held by the Liverpool government. As was stated earlier, in terms of economic performance the government and the Manchester business community accepted the Ricardian notion of spontaneous market recovery, but in terms of economic structure there was not such a harmony of view. Manchester businessmen and the Ricardians advocated the expansion of manufacturing while the Liverpool government, although allowing a progressive revision of the protective system,[87] did not desire major structural change at the level of the aggregate economy. As Berg has claimed, 'the so-called liberal tory governments of 1815–30 . . . were not particularly concerned for the expansion of industry and commerce'.[88] The ministerial aim was to achieve stable employment and although they 'came to recognise — especially after Peterloo — the error of their initial assumption that the best opportunities for growth were to be found in the agricultural sector' they also sought to 'keep growth within legitimate bounds'.[89] But what were these legitimate bounds? According to Boyd Hilton, liberal tories such as Liverpool, Huskinson and Canning accepted the notion of a romantic naturalism which set a 'natural level of economic activity'.[90] This 'worldview' necessarily placed constraints on the movement towards an open economy. As Lord Liverpool stated in 1820:

> We have risen under a very different system than that of free and unrestricted trade. It is utterly impossible, with our debt and taxation, even if they were but half their existing amount, that we can suddenly adopt the system of free trade. To do so would be to unhinge the whole property of the country.[91]

For Ricardo, the liberal tory notion of 'legitimate bounds' was a mystification. Ricardo states clearly in his *Principles* that 'there can be no limits to the capital that may be employed in' producing goods and services 'except that which bounds our power to maintain the workers who are to produce them'.[92] He maintains that there is,

> no limit to demand — no limit to the employment of capital while it yields any profit, and that, however abundant capital may become, there is no other adequate reason for a fall in profit but a rise in wages, and further . . . the only adequate and permanent cause for a rise in wages is the increasing difficulty in providing food and necessaries for the increasing number of workmen.[93]

We are back again here, of course, to the Corn Laws and Free Trade. As Berg has argued, Ricardo's Corn Model 'was a counterfactual, set up precisely in order to emphasise the significance of the factors from which Ricardo abstracted — free trade and technological improvements'.[94] The restraints imposed on the rate of capital accumulation by limited land and therefore rising wages could be avoided by technological change and the abandonment of the Corn Laws. The underlying assumption of the liberal-tory notion of naturalness is a static system, or at least a system based on extensive growth,[95] which will inevitably reach the limits imposed by Ricardo's Corn Model. For Ricardo not only was the 'rising dominance of the manufacturing sector — inevitable for the British economy . . . it was desirable'.[96] The adoption of free trade and the diffusion of machinery breaks the constraints of the stationary state and allows a process of intensive growth. The factory, of course, is the business component which generates intensive growth, and its rapid development in

Manchester in the post-Napoleonic period locates 'Cottonopolis' as the centre for the diffusion of machine technology and the focal point of the attack on the Corn Laws. The convergence of factory and warehouse reinforces this process and by 1825 Manchester has a clearly visible business strategy[97] and a level of business interconnection which contrasts markedly with the schisms of the pre-Peterloo generation.

NOTES AND REFERENCES

1. For a discussion of the major economic issues of this period see A. Boyd Hilton, *Corn, Cash, Commerce: The Economic Policies of the Tory Governments 1815–30* (Oxford University Press, Oxford, 1977); B. Gordon, *Political Economy in Parliament, 1819–1823* (Macmillan, London, 1976); A. Brady, *William Huskinson and Liberal Reform*, 2nd edition (Frank Cass, London, 1967); D. C. M. Platt, *Finance, Trade and Politics in British Foreign Policy 1815–1914* (Oxford University Press, Oxford, 1968), especially Part 2, ch. 1.
2. For a lucid statement of these policy issues see the first edition of the *Manchester Guardian*, 5 May 1821.
3. D. Ricardo, *The Principles of Political Economy and Taxation* (J. M. Dent, London, 1823 edn.), p. 176.
4. Quoted in Gordon, *Political Economy*, p. 77.
5. Hilton, *Corn*, p. 84.
6. Quoted in A. Redford, *Manchester Merchants and Foreign Trade, 1794–1857* (Manchester University Press, Manchester, 1934), p. 158.
7. Quoted in Redford, *Manchester Merchants*, p. 158.
8. G. W. Wood in 1828 operated a warehouse in New High Street rated at £60.00. He was also prominent in local Whig politics in Manchester. See A. Redford *et al.*, *The History of Local Government In Manchester*, vol. 1, *Manor and Township* (Longmans, Green, London, 1939), p. 305.
9. Redford, *Manchester Merchants*, p. 158.
10. Ibid., p. 159.
11. For a list of the principal firms see A. Prentice, *Historical Sketches and Personal Recollections of Manchester* (Charles Gilpin, London, 1851), p. 221.
12. Thomas Sharp later became the partner of Richard Roberts, the inventor of the self-acting mule, in the firm of Sharp, Roberts and Co. At the time of the public meeting in 1821, Thomas Sharp operated a premise in Oxford Street rated at £108.00.
13. Prentice, *Historical Sketches*, p. 223.
14. For a discourse of the political and religious divisions in Manchester during the post-Napoleonic period see Redford, *Local Government*, pp. 194–6.
15. For these petitions see *Journal of the House of Commons*, vol. 75, November 1819 to November 1820, pp. 38–57.

16. The petition was sent by the 'Nobility, Gentry, Clergy, Freeholders and Inhabitants of Westmorland', *Journal of the House of Commons*, vol. 75, November 1819 to November 1820, p. 38.

17. Alexander Baring, of Baring Brothers, was described by Disraeli 'as the greatest merchant England ever had'. See Ralph W. Hidy, *The House of Baring in American Trade and Finance: English Merchant Bankers at Work, 1763–1861* (Harvard University Press, Cambridge, Mass., 1949), p. 48.

18. Gordon, *Political Economy*, p. 2.

19. Ibid., p. 62.

20. Ibid., p. 72.

21. Ibid., pp. 62–3.

22. Ibid., p. 63. Further, Baring agreed to help those in desperate need, 'he would not hesitate to give his vote for the application of one or two millions from the public funds'.

23. Another MP, Edward Ellice, supported Baring arguing that because of uncertainties created by social unrest caused by poverty and unemployment there was a danger of a continuing flight of capital. See Gordon, *Political Economy*, p. 63.

24. Redford, *Manchester Merchants*, p. 68.

25. Quoted in R. J. Morris, 'The Middle Class and British Towns and Cities of the Industrial Revolution 1780–1870'. in D. Frazer and A. Sutcliffe (eds), *The Pursuit of Urban History* (Edward Arnold, London, 1983), p. 299.

26. R. J. Morris, 'British Towns and Cities', p. 299.

27. The list of members is taken from the *Manchester Guardian*, 23 October 1824. See also *Court Leet Records of the Manor of Manchester*, vol. X (Henry Blacklock, Manchester, 1889). The duty of the Michaelmas Court Leet was to elect the officers of the town for the year. 'Of the unpaid officers the first to be elected was the boroughreeve, who was the chief officer of the town'. Redford, *Local Government*, p. 47. The boroughreeve in 1824 was Gilbert Winter, a cotton twist dealer.

28. Redford, *Local Government*, p. 46.

29. Ibid., p. 45.

30. Ibid., p. 258.

31. *Court Leet Records of the Manor of Manchester*, vol. X; also *Pigot's Directory*, 1815, 1820, 1825. The machine maker was Thomas Sharp.

32. For the full list of Constables see *Wheeler's Manchester Chronicle*, 16 April 1825.

33. Thomas Cardwell was a director of the Manchester Chamber of Commerce and Manufacturers.

34. Proceedings of the Manchester Chamber of Commerce and Manufacturers (hereafter P.M.C.C.M.), 20 March 1822 (M.C.L. M8/2/1).

35. The improvement cost £200,000.00 and consisted of a body of 50 commissioners. These were the leading businessmen of their day and are listed in Prentice, *Historical Sketches*, p. 209.

36. For the references to these activities see the sources at the bottom

of Table 8.2.

37. See A. D. Gayer, W. W. Rostow and A. J. Schwartz, *The Growth and Fluctuations of the British Economy*, 2nd edn. (2 vols., Harvester Press, Hassocks, nr. Brighton, 1975), vol. 1, pp. 185–9.

38. These were Fielding, W. Garnett, L. Fort, M. Schunck, G. W. Wood, John Bradshaw, Thomas Cardwell, G. R. Chapell, James Bremner, Wm. Townend, George Frazer, Francis Marris and T. Worthington (a factory and warehouse operator).

39. For the list of committee members of this company see *Manchester Courier*, 8 January 1825.

40. *Wheeler's Manchester Chronicle*, 12 February 1825.

41. J. T. Slugg, *Reminiscences of Manchester 50 years ago* (J. E. Cornish, Manchester, 1881), p. 165. This chapel was also attended by Francis Marris & Son, calico printers, manufacturers and merchants; John Baker, cotton merchants; Thomas Townend, warehouse operator; Luke Gray, manufacturer; and William Burd, calico printer.

42. P.M.C.C.M., 10 February 1823.

43. Ibid., 17 June 1823.

44. The operative spinners were Thomas Foster, Robert Hyde and Daniel McWilliams.

45. P.M.C.C.M., 30 March 1825.

46. The warehousemen were Wood, Bradshaw, Frazer, Jones, Bootham and Bremner.

47. In adition to the factory and warehousemen, also in attendance was the President of the Chamber, H. H. Birley (cotton spinner and also partner in the warehouse firm of Hornby and Birley); Thomas Hoyle (in the printing, dyeing and finishing trade); and two others whose business interests have not been clearly identified, Birch and Matthews.

48. P.M.C.C.M., 30 March 1825.

49. Ibid., also see Redford, *Manchester Merchants*, p. 229.

50. P.M.C.C.M., 30 March 1825.

51. Redford, *Manchester Merchants*, p. 188.

52. The problem of the postal services was discussed in the Chamber on 22 October 1821; 17 April, 22 May, 5 June, 11 December 1822; 26 March, 30 July, 15 December 1823; 12 January, 25 February 1824; 13 July 1825.

53. P.M.C.C.M., 15 December 1823.

54. P.M.C.C.M., 22 May 1822.

55. See P.M.C.C.M., 28 November 1821 and 9 January 1822.

56. P.M.C.C.M., 16 January 1822.

57. Redford, *Manchester Merchants*, p. 209.

58. Ibid., p. 209.

59. P.M.C.C.M., 28 March 1822.

60. This would represent a payment of 5s (25 new pence) on a bill of £50.00. The Chamber recommended 1s 6d (7½ np) on bills of £50.00; 1s (5 np) on bills of £30.00; and 6d (2.5 np) on bills of £20.00.

61. See Redford, *Manchester Merchants*, p. 189.

62. Redford, *Manchester Merchants*, p. 209. However, Redford may have been too dismissive; Gordon has pointed out that at the end of

1824 the government 'had sanctioned reductions in stamp duties'; B. Gordon, *Economic Doctrine and Tory Liberalism 1824–1830* (Macmillan, London, 1979), p. 15.

63. For example, the Manchester and Liverpool chambers were in contact with each other concerning the location of the Assizes, based at that time in Lancaster. Both chambers agreed that the Assizes were '. . . held at so great a distance from the towns of Manchester and Liverpool from which places the principle part of the civil and criminal business arises'. P.M.C.C.M., 23 January 1822.

64. See E. A. Axon, *The Annals of Manchester: A Chronological Record from the Earliest Times to the End of 1815* (John Haywood, Manchester, 1886), pp. 153, 162, 165, 169. Other Manchester papers of the period were the *British Volunteer* and the *Exchange and Herald*.

65. For a discussion of some of these newspapers see Prentice, *Historical Sketches*, p. 262.

66. For the party politics of this period we are indebted to our colleague, Dr B. T. Bradfield.

67. *Manchester Guardian*, 5 May 1821.

68. Ibid.; by 1825 the *Manchester Guardian* was the town's largest circulation newspaper. Prentice estimates the paper's circulation at 2,200, his own *Gazette* at 1,500 and the combined total of the *Mercury*, *Wheeler's Manchester Chronicle*, *British Volunteer* and *Exchange and Herald* at between 3,500 to 3,700. Prentice, *Historical Sketches*, p. 262.

69. Quoted in Redford, *Manchester Merchants*, p. 70.

70. The Manchester newspapers most vocal in their support for trade deregulation were the *Manchester Guardian* and the *Manchester Gazette*.

71. Redford, *Manchester Merchants*, pp. 134–5.

72. For Prentice's involvement in Manchester newspapers, especially the *Guardian* and the *Gazette*, see Prentice, *Historical Sketches*, pp. 202–8.

73. Quoted in Redford, *Manchester Merchants*, p. 135.

74. Measures advocated during this period included the call for the end of the duty on raw cotton, the equalisation of the duty on East and West Indian sugar, free trade with Ireland, the recognition of the South American republics and the appointment of trade consuls, etc. For a survey of these policies see Redford, *Manchester Merchants*, pp. 132–52.

75. Gordon, *Political Economy*, p. 79.

76. Ricardo's complaint was against a duty which had been in existence for 20 years, 'which surely was a period quite long enough to give the Irish manufacturers an opportunity of preparing for their repeal, if any such opportunity were necessary'; quoted in Gordon *Political Economy*, p. 79.

77. Gordon, *Political Economy*, p. 79. For a discussion of the Irish duties see also Boyd Hilton, *Corn*, pp. 186–90.

78. Quoted in Redford, *Manchester Merchants*, pp. 141–2.

79. Ibid., pp. 141–2.

80. P.M.C.C.M., 15 May 1822.

81. Quoted in Redford, *Manchester Merchants*, p. 139.

82. P. J. Cain and A. G. Hopkins, 'The Political Economy of British Expansion Overseas, 1750–1914', *Economic History Review*, vol. XXXIII, no. 4 (1980), p. 465.

83. For the increased momentum towards freer trade, *c*. 1824, see Gordon, *Economic Doctrine*, ch. 2, pp. 14–25.

84. Quoted in Redford, *Manchester Merchants*, p. 136; see also P.M.C.C.M., 15 March 1824, 14 February and 13 April 1825.

85. Quoted in Redford, *Manchester Merchants*, p. 136.

86. P.M.C.C.M., 20 April 1825.

87. See Gordon, *Economic Doctrine*, ch. 2.

88. M. Berg, *The Machinery Question and the Making of Political Economy 1815–41* (Cambridge University Press, Cambridge, 1980), p. 64. For a contrary view, Gordon argues that in 1824 'The Ministry was to heed the advice of the political economists'. He also quotes Robinson, the Chancellor of the Exchequer, who claimed the government would 'cut the cords which tie down commerce to the earth, that she may spring aloft, unconfined and unrestricted'. Gordon, *Economic Doctrine*, p. 14. However, Gordon also acknowledges that in 1825 the Ricardians '. . . began to be more critical of Huskinson and his colleagues. The government was not proceeding far enough, fast enough, nor was it legislating in the rational fashion recommended by the Classical Theory of Economic Policy'. Gordon, *Economic Doctrine*, p. 22.

89. Boyd Hilton, *Corn*, pp. 305, 307.

90. Ibid., p. 307.

91. Quoted in Gordon, *Political Economy*, p. 77.

92. Ricardo, *Principles*, p. 195.

93. Ibid., p. 197.

94. Berg, *Machinery*, p. 47.

95. It is not, therefore, unrelated to the views of Nathanial Gould and his romantic view of the putting-out warehouse system.

96. Berg, *Machinery*, p. 63. This point is also reinforced by Ricardo's disciple, McCulloch, when he states, 'Our great cities, and their increasing and busy thousands, are all produced in proof that commercial and manufacturing industry are inseparably connected with civilisation; and that it is the duty of the state to promote, by all means, their further and unlimited development'. J. R. McCulloch, 'Distress of the Manufacturing Districts: Causes and Remedies', *Edinburgh Review*, vol. clv (1843), pp. 193–4. See also R. Chenevix, 'History and Prospects of English Industry', *Quarterly Review*, vol. XXXIV (1826), p. 99.

97. There was not complete agreement on all areas of policy. This was particularly so over the issue of the export of textile machinery — an issue which will be explored in Chapter 9.

9

The Modern Sector: The Metal, Chemical and Finishing Trades in Manchester

A major theme of this work has been to examine the economic linkages between the factory and warehouse in Manchester's business system, but apart from this central link there are important connections between the factory and other sectors of the Manchester economy. The obvious sectors that spring to mind are the metal engineering trades, the chemical industry and the finishing processes of bleaching, dyeing and printing. For want of a better term, we will call them the modern sector,[1] with the clear implication that these trades provide an ideal base for exploring the economic spin-off of the cotton factory. The technological determinants of growth, in the factory spinning sector, had important repercussions on the modern sector, and as Rostow points out, 'The effects of a sector [cotton] touched by new technology transcend the sector itself'.[2] Of course, there is nothing novel in suggesting a close relationship between cotton and the modern sector, but this does not mean that the form of relationship has been identified or the structural pattern of these trades clearly explored. The interconnections with the factory and the pattern of change in the modern sector will be examined in detail during the crucial years 1815 to 1825. Furthermore, the emergence of a specialist machine making sector opened up a new area of political debate within the cotton trade concerning the exportation of machinery and the emigration of artisans.

Charles Hulbert, a native of Manchester, had no doubt about the expansion of the metal, chemical and finishing sector by 1825, or the intimate connection with the cotton sector:

> The spinning trade is becoming every year more and more

> extensive . . . The weaving is also carried on to a great extent . . . But the erection and keeping up of the various and complicated machinery which is constantly at work is itself a source of very great business in and around Manchester. This gives rise to great iron foundries, and other works of a similar kind, and to the invention even of new machines to facilitate its operations. Besides the weaving and spinning, the printing, dyeing and bleaching businesses are caried on to a very great extent in and around Manchester . . . as are several well-managed sulphuric acid, or oil of vitriol works.[3]

Certainly, the modern literature[4] emphasises the technological interconnections between the cotton trade and the machine sector. The machine industry, situated within the capital goods sector of the economy, was actively stimulated by cotton spinning and as Farnie points out, spinning was 'essentially process-centred rather than product-centred'[5] and 'became a pioneer of machine technology, a seed-bed of indigenous invention, and a school of machine making'.[6] Similarly, Rosenberg alludes to the uniquely important historial role of the capital goods industries in facilitating the diffusion process, in addition to its central role in invention.[7] The Industrial Revolution 'had at its centre a rapidly expanding armamentarium of new technologies involving new power sources, new techniques of metallurgy and machine making', and this new technology was interrelated and mutually reinforcing.[8] For example, Berg observes that the rise of the factory system, 'though based on the breakdown of skills and the division of labour, would not have been possible without an existing foundation of engineering, metalworking and metal-extracting skills'. Thus the rise of the factory was a 'double-edged process'; 'skilled labour was displaced through factory organisation and mechanisation', and in turn 'created an increased demand for both labour and skills in order to create the new capital goods needed by the factory system'.[9]

The role of skilled labour was crucial to the development of the metal trades[10] and in 1815 they employed a wide range of artisans; 'metal workers, iron founders, brass founders, blacksmiths, white smiths, millwrights', who 'produced a wide range of products varying from nails to steam engines'.[11] The continued importance of skilled labour, to the metal trades, is emphasised by Samuel, who argues that even by mid-century the production processes in metalworking and engineering 'was discontinuous and depended on craftsmanly skills'.[12] There is therefore some controversy surrounding the actual level of development of these trades, particularly in the strategically important machine tool industry. For example, William Fairbairn, the prominent Manchester engineer, when he first came to Manchester just before the end of the Napoleonic Wars, claimed that

> the whole of the machinery was executed by hand. There was neither planing, slotting nor shaping machines; and with the exception of very imperfect lathes, and a few drills, the preparatory operations of construction was effected entirely by the hands of workmen.[13]

Nevertheless, Musson and Robinson take a more optimistic view about the development of mechanised engineering, and they claim that from an examination of the evidence 'it seems evident that specialised machine making must have been evolving quite rapidly for at least a quarter century before 1800'.[14] Whatever the level of technological development, there is broad agreement that the 'tremendous growth of Lancashire from about 1770 . . . gave rise to an equally rapid development of mechanical engineering'. Lancashire manufacturers, and more specifically Manchester men, fabricated not only cotton, but also cotton machinery, steam engines, boilers, machine tools, mill gearing, etc.[15]

Similar to the metal industries, the stimulus of cotton's rapid expansion was also felt in the chemical sector and the various finishing trades, which have obvious technological interconnections. As Musson points out, the growth of the cotton trade 'was not based simply on a mechanical revolution in spinning and weaving' but 'The rapidly increasing output of yarn and cloth had to be bleached, dyed and printed, and the processes were more chemical than mechanical'.[16] From the 1790s, the finishing trades demanded increasing quantities of chemicals, especially alkalis for bleaching.[17] Furthermore, the increased 'tempo in textile production, put considerable pressure on cloth finishers' to accelerate the bleaching process via the utilisation of sulphuric acid. In turn, the 'very intimate connections between sulphuric acid and bleaching made progressive bleachers realise that they could with advantage make their own chemicals'.[18] The innovation of chlorine, as a bleaching re-agent, further stimulated the production of sulphuric acid, which was required for the production of chlorine, and as the Clow's point out, 'so sulphuric acid production kept in step with the expanding textile sector'.[19]As early as 1783, the Manchester College of Arts and Sciences was founded and gave special priority to chemistry because of its application 'to so many of the arts, of which our manufacturers depend'.[20]

The link between chemicals and cotton finishing can be demonstrated by the example of Thomas Hoyle, the large Manchester dyer, who in 1789 claimed that 'for some time past' he had 'been bleaching cotton goods by a new, safe and expeditious method and dyed them fancy colours'. Due to the success of this new process, he was intending 'to carry on that branch in a most extensive manner'.[21] Hoyle was 'a prominent pioneer of chlorine bleaching',[22] and his initial optimism was justified, for by 1815 he operated the largest dye works in Manchester, rated at £340.00.[23]

Calico printing was also intimately linked to the spinning and dyeing trades, and a recent study by Chapman and Chassagne[24] points to the 'intimate connection' between the rise of the early leaders of the cotton industry and the printing sector of the rapidly rising textile trade. Eminent pioneering firms such as Livsey, Hargreaves and Company, Arkwright, Strutt, Oldknow, and the Peels[25] 'each . . . combined factory spinning with weaving and printing activities'.[26] Lancashire's rise to industrial prominence 'came when two lines of evolution (spinning and printing) were united under the direction of some of the great textile entrepreneurs of the eighteenth century'.[27] Furthermore, firms integrated dyeing activities with printing. For example, Thomas Hoyle set up a large integrated dyeing and printing works at Mayfield, Ardwick, near Manchester, in the 1790s,[28] and in 1815 the firm operated a print warehouse in Manchester rated at £120.00.

Innovation in printing took two forms, chemical and mechanical. Chemical innovation involved the discovery of new dyes and chemicals for fixing the design in the fabric.[29] Chapman claims that colour-making techniques developed rapidly in the first half of the nineteenth century with the development of new dyes and colours.[30] Thus product innovation, involving the use of new dyes and colours, was obviously important to an industry whose demand was dictated by the vagaries of fashion.[31] On the mechanical side, cylinder machines, patented by Thomas Bell in 1783 to 1784, took some part of calico printing into the factory between the 1780s and 1810, and several Lancashire printing firms installed steam engines in the 1790s. This led to the emergence of specialist calico printing machine makers in Manchester from the 1790s onwards.[32] Thus calico printing was intimately linked to the developments in dyeing and bleaching and the rise of mechanical engineering which characterised the development of the textile industry in the early nineteenth century.

The development of the metal, chemical and finishing trades was characterised by the emergence of large Manchester firms in these activities by the first quarter of the nineteenth century. Certainly, our knowledge of the large engineering firm, in Lancashire, has been advanced by the work of Musson and Robinson, [33] and their study of Peel and Williams offers an interesting insight into the development of a large Manchester machine making firm in the early nineteenth centry.[34] Indeed, by 1825 Manchester could boast

> a string of great iron foundries and general engineering works from Shudehill to Great Bridgewater Street, mostly along the line of the Ashton and Rochdale canals, including the works of Peel and Williams, Ebeneezer Smith, Fairbairn, Hewes and Wren, Ormrods, Radford and Waddington, Galloway and Company.[35]

To this list we could also add the machine making firms of Parkinson and Arrie, W. and J. Creighton, Roberts, Hill and Company and the spindle works of Issac Ripon.[36] Manchester was the centre not only of the world's cotton but also the world's engineering industry, and this development 'made the city . . . a centre of technical innovation, especially in spinning technology'.[37] Similarly, in the chemical and finishing sector, great works such as Thomas Hoyle and Sons, William Newton, William Oliver, Jonathon Whitelegg, Alexandra Lindsey and Company, and Rothwell and Harrison, were amongst the largest of their type in the world.[38]

These firms were obviously leaders in their field, but it may be presumptuous to assume that the business history of these industries can be written in terms of the activities of large-scale firms. We would do well to heed Hannah's observation that the pattern of development in such industries as cotton, iron and chemicals 'favoured the multiplication of small firms rather than the dominance of large ones'.[39] In other words, in order to examine the structure and pattern of change in the modern sector, what is required is a reconstruction of their respective firm populations. How dominant was the large-scale firm; was there any discernible tendency towards increased concentration, and did firm population structure change in response to broad developments in the primary cotton sector?

The problem, of course, is again the lack of any detailed business records on individual firms. In the absence of such empirical data we return to our synchronic perspective which allows us to reconstruct the industrial structure of a given population of firms. From this we can infer a number of propositions concerning firm behaviour and response. For example, a size distribution pattern can be constructed which will provide observations relating to concentration ratios, barriers to entry, economies of scale and market profile. Over the period 1815 to 1825 it was possible to identify 760 firms in the modern sector, each with their RV and a description of their activity. This was done by cross-referencing a firm listed in the Manchester rate-books with the corresponding entry in the Manchester directories. Looking first at the 1815 structure we were able to break down the firm populations into two major categories, and the number of firms, the total and average RV is given in Table 9.1.

Given the data in Table 9.1, it may be surprising that firms in the chemical and finishing sector had a significantly higher average RV than metal sector firms, but it needs to be borne in mind that average figures disguise the wide ranges in size patterns. A simple size distribution pattern provides a more useful guide and this is shown in Table 9.2.

Table 9.1: Industrial profile of the modern sector, Manchester, 1815

Industrial sector	No of firms	Total RV (£)	Average size per firm RV (£)
Metal machinery	77	3,298	42.83
Chemicals/finishing[a]	240	16,710	69.62

Note: a. This figure is higher than that given in Table 9.3 because firms operating warehouses are included.

Source: Manchester Central Library (MCL), Township of Manchester Poor Rate Assessment Book, 1815 (MCL, M9/40/2/78); and *Pigot's Trade and Commercial Directory*, 1815.

Table 9.2: Size, distribution of firms in the modern sector, Manchester, 1815

Size category RV (£)	Metal/machinery No of firms	% of total	Chemical/finishing No of firms	% of total
1–25	37	48.0	60	25.0
26–50	21	27.3	74	30.8
51–75	2	2.6	18	7.5
76–100	8	10.4	36	15.0
101–150	7	9.1	34	14.2
151–200	2	2.6	8	3.3
201–300	—	—	8	3.3
301 +	—	—	2	0.9
Total	77	100.0	240	100.0

Source: Compiled from data in Table 9.1.

Table 9.2 shows clearly the large cluster of metal firms in the small-scale category, with 75 per cent of all firms in this sector being rated at £50.00 or under. The chemical and finishing sector offers a somewhat different profile with 21.7 per cent of firms being rated at £101.00 or above. Nevertheless, the predominance of small firms in both sectors is obvious with 60 per cent of all firms rated at £50.00 or less. Thus the emphasis in the literature on the large firm needs to be modified in the light of this thick undergrowth of small-scale units.[40] But how should we interpret this data to provide insights into firm behaviour patterns at a crucial stage of the Industrial Revolution?

Let us first consider the following observation by M. A. Utton:

> the number and size distribution of firms in individual industries are evidently closely bound up with their behaviour and performance. In particular, where a high proportion of total industry output or sales is made by a small number of firms then the industries' performance is likely to diverge considerably from that predicted for a perfectly competitive industry.[41]

Utton is here concerned with market concentration;[42] can such estimates of market concentration be provided for the two industries under study? Even present-day economists, with their bank of statistical data, find considerable difficulty in measuring market concentration.[43] Firstly, what variable or economic quantity are we going to measure; secondly, what constitutes the basic population which the measurement refers to; finally, what is the appropriate mechanism of measurement?

The contemporary work on concentration ratios have used as many as four different economic variables as their basis of measurement: sales, value added, employment and assets.[44] Obviously, none of these criteria are available to us, but as historians we have to be satisfied with what is left to us and abstract as many nutrients and trace elements as we can. We have already shown that RVs produce a significantly high correlation to employment and property asset valuation. Thus RVs will be used as a proxy for asset valuation[45] with the caveat that the tentative nature of their status as a measurement factor will be kept to the forefront in the process of interpretation.

In terms of the basic population that we are going to measure, then obviously we need a working definition of industry. The concept or notion industry ideally 'seeks to establish spheres of economic activity which are unique and distinguishable from other spheres by a composite of similar characteristics which they have in common. Principle among these characteristics are similarity of process, products, and material used.'[46] The sphere of activity covered by the metal machine sector includes foundry production and metal fabrication; machine making, machine tool production, pipes, boilers, mill gearing, etc. The production of machine components is itself carried out by a variety of producers, ranging from blacksmiths, tinplate workers, braziers, turners, etc.[47] The chemical and finishing sector includes dyers, bleachers, vitriol acid, drysalters, and general chemical producers, calendrers and sizers, and calico printers. In practice, however, the demarcation between different spheres is not easily distinguishable, and there may be an overlapping of business activity as firms diversity their production horizons.[48] Nevertheless, we can offer a breakdown of our two broad industrial categories in 1815, and this is shown in Table 9.3.

Table 9.3 shows that the broad industrial categories disguise the presence of large firms in the various branches of the metal and chemical sectors. Clearly, foundry firms[49] were usually larger business units, reflecting the high capital requirements of this sector. Of the 15 firms operating foundries, seven were rated at £100.00 and above. In the chemical and finishing sector,

Table 9.3: Metal machinery, chemical and finishing trades, disaggregated categories, Manchester, 1815

Industrial sector	Sub-sector	No of firms	Total RV (£)	Average RV (£)
Metal machinery:	Iron founders	15	1,342	89.47
	Brass founders, braziers, copperplate and tinplate workers	19	657	34.58
	Blacksmiths	23	218	19.48
	Pin makers and wire drawers	5	281	56.20
	Machine makers, millwrights, spindle makers	9	472	52.44
	Ironmongers	6	328	54.66
Chemicals and finishing:[a]	Chemical producers[b]	29	1,834	63.24
	Bleachers	10	293	29.30
	Dyers	40	3,298	82.45
	Calendrers, dressers, makers up, sizers	34	1,485	43.68
	Calico printers only	86	5,823	67.71
	Calico printers combined	41	3,977	97.00

Notes: a. A number of these firms, especially bleachers and drysalters, operated warehouse. All firms in the printing trade operated calico printing warehouses.

b. Includes firms engaged in chemical manufacturing (chemists), vitriolic acid manufacturers and manganese manufacturers, and drysalters.

Source: Compiled from data in Table 9.1.

dyeing firms and calico printers had larger average RVs than other firms. Of the 125 firms engaged in calico printing in Manchester,[50] in 1815, 41 firms combined calico printing with other activities,[51] and as one would expect, these firms display a significantly higher average RV than firms engaged in calico printing only.

Turning to the appropriate instrument of measurement for concentration analysis, this has generated some controversy.[52] In the UK the usual practice is to take the three largest firms and estimate the proportion they contribute to total output, employment, value added or assets. On the other hand, the usual convention in the US is to take the top four firms as the measurement of concentration.[53] Adopting our RV proxy, Table 9.4 shows the three and four firm concentration ratios[54] for our two industrial categories in 1815.

Table 9.4: Concentration ratios, three and four largest firms, Manchester, 1815

Industrial category	% of 3 largest firms to total RV	% of 4 largest firms to total RV
Metals machinery	15.7	19.6
Chemicals and finishing	6.5	8.0

Source: Compiled from data in Appendix 7.

What interpretation can we place on these tentative estimates? As a starting hypothesis we may postulate that the lower the concentration ratio the more likely will the industry approximate the conditions of competitive behaviour, as opposed to oligopolistic or monopolistic behaviour. Unfortunately, there is no unambiguous theoretical position which in practice will define a particular pattern of competitive or oligopolistic behaviour. As a consequence, most empirical studies of industrial concentration, which seek to identify those industries most likely to be competitive and those most likely to be oligopolistic, have had to use their own judgement as to the level of concentration that forms the dividing point.[55] The usual practice is to make a threefold distinction between concentrated, medium concentrated and unconcentrated industries, but with different scales of division employed. Table 9.5 shows the estimates offered by the most detailed British and American studies.

Table 9.5: A guideline to industrial concentration ratios

Industry type	Estimates of Everley and Little (3 largest firms)[a] %	Estimates of Kayser and Turner (4 largest firms)[b] %
Concentrated	67	50 +
Moderately concentrated	33–66	25–49
Unconcentrated	– 33	– 25

Notes: a. Everly and Little utilise the contribution of the three largest firms to total output and employment.

b. Kayser and Turner utilise the contribution of the four largest firms to total output.

Source: R. Everly and I. M. D. Little, *Concentration in British Industry* (Cambridge University Press, Cambridge, 1960), p. 51; C. Kayser and D. F. Turner, *Antitrust Policy: An Economic and Legal Interpretation* (Harvard University Press, Harvard, 1959), pp. 295–7.

Clearly, under both schemes of measurement, the industrial sectors would fall into the unconcentrated category (see Table 9.4). From these findings we could interpret the structure of these industries as polypoletic. The major structural characteristics of polypoletic systems are large numbers of sellers, ease of entry, and of 'most importance, the absence of control over a significant share of the market by any individual seller or small group of sellers'.[56] The economic behaviour of business units operating within polypoletic structures has been described by Fritz Machlup as follows:

> Polypoly is defined as the market position (or state of mind) of sellers who know that they have competition, but in making up their own minds about changing their selling or production policies, do not ponder over what their competitor's reactions might be.[57]

If we wish to take the analysis further, then there are three immediate objections that require our attention. Firstly, the status of the RV proxy is a fragile foundation to construct propositions concerning concentration ratios[58] and we therefore need to support our tentative claims with as much empirical evidence as can be collected. But this leads us to the second problem; the amount of evidence relating to individual firm behaviour is extremely limited.[59] Thirdly, the broad industrial categories may disguise the concentration of firms in various branches of these sectors. Referring back to Table 9.3, then this shows clearly the higher RVs of firms in the foundry, machine making, dyeing and printing trades. Was there a higher degree of concentration amongst firms in these particular activities? Table 9.6 shows the concentration ratios for the three and four

Table 9.6: Concentration ratios of the three and four largest firms in the foundry, dyeing and printing trades, Manchester, 1815

Sub-category	% of 3 largest firms to total RV	% of 4 largest firms to total RV
Foundry machinery[a]	27.4	34.0
Dyeing	27.9	33.3
Calico printing[b]	7.5	9.8

Notes: a. These firms include iron and brass founders, machine makers and millwrights.
b. These firms include calico printers only and combined firms.

largest firms in these sub-categories in 1815. Firms engaged in the foundry machine trades, and dyeing, are on the borderline of unconcentrated and moderately concentrated, under both schemes of measurement (see Table 9.5). The calico printing sector is clearly unconcentrated, reflecting the large number of firms of roughly similar size in this activity.

Given the limited amount of evidence available, if we are to offer some observations concerning the behaviour of the population of firms, we are obliged to make such interpretations from observations concerning the structural patterns of the population itself. We can, for example, pose questions related to those forces which allegedly enhanced concentration, namely the role of economies of scale, barriers to entry, shifts in concentration ratios, and the influence of the market. Thus the existence of important economies of scale might be inferred from rising concentration ratios which may also raise barriers to entry and the optimum size of plant.

A possible influence on the pattern of concentration may be associated with economies arising from large-scale plant. A number of factors may act as sources for plant economies, but one of the commonest known, 'and most hallowed in economic analysis is the division of labour, which, as it proceeds, allows the quantity of work done by a given labour force to rise'.[60] This point may be reinforced by employing Sargent Florence's principle of 'multiple' which holds that 'the smaller the scale of operation and the fewer the total number of persons dividing and diffusing their labour, the less chance there is for all of them being fully made use of as specialists'.[61] This principle is clearly applicable to the metal trades and in particular the machine making sector.[62] Certainly Peter Ewart, giving evidence before the 1824 Select Committee on Artisans and Machinery, was well aware of the division of labour in the manufacturing of textile machinery. Ewart attributed the superiority of English cotton machinery over its continental rivals to 'the high state of the sub-division of labour to which it is carried, and that is owing to the extent to which it is carried on'.[63] That such a process was cumulative, Ewart was in no doubt:

> I must refer again to experience; we never had any sub-division of labour till it was carried on to a great extent [in machine making], and it is impossible to have a great sub-division of labour, but in proportion to the extent of the business.[64]

The upswing of cotton production in the 1820s, culminating in the 1824–5 boom, stretched the resources of Manchester machine makers to the extent that newly built factories were left empty due to the shortage of machines.[65] John Lee Bradbury, 'a prominent Manchester calico printer',[66] giving evidence before the 1824 Select Committee, claimed that a considerable number of cotton mills had been built in the past two or three years 'and are now building and . . . I am assured by the first machine maker in Manchester[67] that it will require three years to supply those mills with machinery'. In Manchester and its neighbourhood 'there are supposed to be upwards of 70 mills unsupplied with machinery now', and Bradbury did not know of any other area of the country that could supply them with machinery.[68] A number of witnesses to the 1824 Select Committee maintained that no application was made by Manchester factory operators to the London engineering firms, 'as the latter are quite out of the practice of making cotton machinery', a fact which Ewart attributed to the lack of the sub-division of labour in the London industry.[69] T. C. Hewes, one of the largest engineering and mill constructing firms,[70] confirmed Ewart's observation. He claimed that over the period 1810 to 1824 'there have been great improvements, greatly increased sub-division of labour in making articles and better establishments created'.[71]

Over the period 1815 to 1825, the number of firms in the metal machine sector increased by 85.7 per cent, and the total RV by 121.3 per cent. Was this associated with any significant increase in the degree of concentration? Table 9.7 shows the three and four firm concentration ratios for 1815 and 1825. Despite a significant increase in the total RV, there was no discernible movement in concentration. The average firm size increased from £42.83 to £51.03, the number of firms rose sharply and there is evidence to suggest increasing specialisation from the early

Table 9.7: Concentration in Manchester's metal machinery sector, 1815–1825

Year	No of firms	Total RV (£)	% of 3 largest firms to total RV	% of 4 largest firms to total RV
1815	77	3,298	15.6	19.7
1825	143	7,298	17.1	21.3

Source: Compiled from Table 9.1 and M.C.L., Township of Manchester Poor Rate Assessment Book, 1825 (M.C.L., M9/40/2/92.93).

1820s, as the demand for cotton machinery and millwork increased rapidly. It is clear, too that some of the larger firms increased their plant size and operated more than one plant.[72] Furthermore, over the period a number of large firms had entered the industry. Among the most prominent were Fairbairn and Lilley, with a foundry rated at £130.00 and workshops at £60.00 in 1825; Roberts Hill and Company, machine makers, rated at £415.00; and George Calvert and Company, general metal fabricators and ironmongers, rated at £340.00. Nevertheless, increasing plant size, increased division of labour, and a rapidly growing market between 1820 and 1825, did not lead directly to a process of rapid concentration; a polypoletic structure remained the dominant characteristic. Certainly what evidence is available denies any form of collusion amongst the large firms. T. C. Hewes stated to the 1824 Select Committee that,

> The combination among masters do not exist with others; I do not think they can in our trade . . . so little do we know of each other, that I do not know more than two in my line, as townsmen, I do not know them personally; and I have never, in the whole course of my business, met but once on our business and that was because the men were going to turn out, and we met as the millwright branch about 17 years back; the result of it turned out to be nothing, and we never saw each other again on the subject, and there has never been a meeting since.[73]

Musson and Robinson describe Hewes as 'one of the most outstanding' engineers and millwrights of his generation and there is no reason to doubt his evidence before the Select Committee.[74] While the expansion of the market allowed a more extensive division of labour, in terms of industrial structure, this worked itself out in the form of the growth of specialist component firms rather than the dominance of large-scale plants. Thus Peter Ewart, referring to the Manchester spindle makers, claimed that

> there are two or three classes of spindle makers, separate and distinct trades, masters and men. Before the demand was so great as it is, one master spindle maker would make several kinds of spindles; now . . . he confines his work to one kind of spindle only.[75]

The Hyde cotton spinner and power loom manufacturer, J. Bremner, stated that the manufacture of rollers had become 'a business by itself',[76] and T. C. Hewes, despite his extensive activities,[77] relied upon outside component firms for his supply of rollers and spindles.[78] For example, William Fairbairn, when he first set up business in Manchester in 1815, succeeded in getting an order for driving shafts from A. and G. Murray, the large Manchester spinners,[79] 'who pleased with the product, recommended him to his friends; he got many orders and ten years later his was one of the largest engineering firms in the country'.[80] This pattern of development is consistent with the high level of entry in the metal machine sector. Over the period 1815 to 1825, 103 new firms entered the industry, representing 72 per cent of the 1825 population. Clearly, the opportunities for capitalists to enter the industry were plentiful and barriers to entry in terms of capital were low. For example, the famous Manchester engineer, Joseph Naysmith, writing about his arrival in Manchester in 1834, claimed that,

> I could settle down with my limited capital and tools, and in course of time contrive to get on, helped by energy, self-reliance and determination . . . the making of machine tools might be carried on with little expenditure of capital, as the risks were small and the returns were quick, I resolved to cultivate that moderate and safe class of mechanical business.[81]

Often a position as a partner could be obtained by providing technological expertise to the firm.[82] Crouzet has argued that there was 'an abnormal proportion of industrialists who started their career as manual workers', and entered the industry on the basis of their technological knowledge.[83]

The pattern of development in the metal sector is consistent with George Stigler's model of industrial organisation.[84] Stigler begins his analysis by invoking Adam Smith's famous dictum that the division of labour is limited by the extent of the market,[85] a fact clearly appreciated by Peter Ewart in his statement quoted earlier. But Smith's theorem, for all its potential richness, also created a dilemma. If the opportunities for a further extension of the division of labour exist, and offer lower costs for larger outputs, entrepreneurs would gain by combining or expanding, and driving out rivals. As Stigler put it, 'here was the dilemma; either the division of labour is limited by the extent of the market, and, characteristically, industries are monopolised; or industries are characteristically competitive, and the theorem is false or of little significance.'[86] Stigler's solution to the dilemma is directly related to his notion of the firm, which he argues is engaged in a series of distinct operations: purchase, storage, fabrication, marketing, selling and distribution. That is, the firm is defined in terms of 'the functions or processes which constitutes the scope of its activities'.[87] The cost pattern of these individual functions will be related to technology, and if we assume that the cost of each function depends only on the rate of output of that function, a unique cost curve for it can be drawn. Furthermore, Stigler claims that

> if there is a constant proportion between the rate of output of the final product, we may draw the cost curve of all these functions on one graph, and the (vertical) sum of these costs of various functions will be the conventional average cost curve of the firm.[88]

It follows therefore that we would expect to find different patterns of average costs of functions, some rising continually (C2), some falling continually (C1), and some displaying the conventional U shape (C3). Figure 9.1 reproduces Stigler's simple geometric illustration.

If we now return to consider Smith's observation, and given that certain processes are subject to increasing returns (C1), the obvious question arises: why doesn't the firm exploit these processes to a greater extent and take up a monopolistic position? However, Stigler argues that things are not as simple as this, for there are other functions subject to diminishing returns, and they may, on balance be so costly as to ensure that average costs do not necessarily continually fall in line with increased output. This, in turn, raises the question of why the firm does not abandon the functions subject to increasing returns, thus allowing another firm, or industry, to specialise in them and to keep the advantages of increasing returns. Stigler offers three principal reasons for this. First, in the initial stage of development these functions are too small to support a group of specialist firms; secondly, the sales of the product are too small; thirdly, the output of a by-product may be too small to support a specialist fabricator. However, as the industry expands the

Figure 9.1: Stigler's model of functional average costs

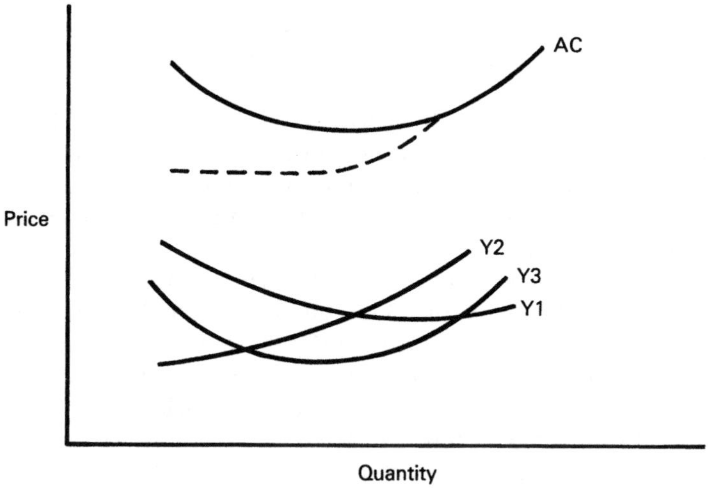

Source: Compiled from G. Stigler, *The Organisation of Industry* (Richard D. Irwin, Homewood, Illinois, 1968), p. 132.

magnitude of the functions subject to increasing returns may become sufficient to permit a firm to specialise in performing it. The firm will then abandon the process (C1), and a new firm will take over. With the continual expansion of the industry the number of firms supplying process C1 will increase, so that the new industry becomes competitive and may, in turn, abandon parts of the process C1 to a new set of specialists.[89]

If we take C1 to be cotton machine making, then we can trace a trajectory which both clearly follows Stigler's pattern and integrates it initially with cotton spinning. The major Manchester cotton spinners, McConnel and Kennedy, A. and G. Murray, and Peter Ewart, all combined machine making with cotton spinning.[90] Lee points out that in the boom period of cotton spinning in the late eighteenth and early nineteenth centuries,

> The major capital outlay would be in machinery, and this probably accounts for the predominance of apprenticeship in machine making as the route of entry into the cotton trade[91] . . . It seems likely that machine making became separated

> from spinning only when production reached such proportions that it was cheaper to purchase machines and more profitable to devote all available space to spinning. Before then McConnel and Kennedy, and probably many other firms, continued to make their own machinery.[92]

Thus, McConnel and Kennedy ceased to fabricate machines for sale at the beginning of the nineteenth century,[93] and with the rapid expansion of spinning activities the spinning only firm and the specialist machine firm emerged. In the post-Napoleonic period the second stage of specialist component firms, concentrating on a narrow range of sub-parts, rapidly developed following the Stigler path. Once this process had been set in motion, it could be extremely difficult to reverse, as entrepreneurs found to their cost. J. Bremner, the Hyde cotton spinner and manufacturer, informed the 1824 Select Committee that his brother had recently decided to produce his own castings but the iron founders had combined and would 'not work for persons who make their own castings'. Bremner's brother was forced to abandon his plans and put the work out to a specialist firm. Bremner observed that the object of the combination was that cotton manufacturers 'should employ the master founders to do the work'.[94]

There is no doubting the enormous impact of the spinning factory on the emerging metal machine sector. As T. C. Hewes put it, 'our employment keeps pace with the prosperity of the cotton trade'.[95] Between 1815 and 1825 the total RV of the factory sector increased by 141 per cent,[96] and structural change expanded the market for machinery.[97] Lloyd-Jones and Le Roux have shown that the period 1815 to 1841 witnessed the emergence of the medium-sized spinning firm as the optimum business unit in the Manchester cotton industry.[98] Indeed, this pattern was already evident by 1825, with the decline of the shared part factory firm and the growing predominance of middle-sized units. The growth of medium-sized firms will be explored in more detail in Chapter 10, and as will be shown a major factor stimulating growth was an improvement in mule technology, which increased the number of spindles per machine.[99] This, in turn, increased the demand for components supplied by the machine sector.

Furthermore, the prosperity of the mid-1820s, and the easy availability of long-term credit,[100] had, in the words of George

Smith, a partner in the spinning and manufacturing firm of James Massey and Company, 'brought a great deal of capital into it [the cotton trade], and the demand never has overtaken the supply'.[101] However, the reversal of prosperity and falling profit margins after 1825 led master spinners to introduce new cost-cutting processes.[102] Henry Houldsworth informed the 1833 Select Committee on Manufacturers and Commerce that,

> There has been an increased demand for machinery; for instance cotton mills were so exceedingly reduced in their profits, that they were obliged to lay out additional capital, in order to accomplish the object of bringing the manufacture into the market cheaper, this they could only do with improved machinery.[103]

Houldsworth also claimed that the increased productivity in cotton spinning, since 1815, required '15 per cent more machinery in order to effect that improvement in quality which enables us to do the extra quantity'.[104] But clearly, in the mid-1820s, there were severe bottlenecks in the supply of machinery, and particularly components to the spinning sector. This supply restraint hindered the cost-cutting efforts of the spinners, and Thomas Ashton informed the 1824 Select Committee that the shortage of machinery has led to 'a considerable rise in the price of some articles, especially rollers and spindles'.[105] According to T. C. Hewes, the price of machine parts had increased by 20 per cent between 1823 and 1824, 'because of the greatly increased demand for machinery'.[106] At the same time as spinning factories were attempting to cut costs, the basic machine components were increasing in price. Clearly, in this respect, we can agree with Rosenberg, who claims that 'at the most advanced stage of capitalist development, inter-industry relationships come to play a most important role, because the rate of profit in one industry now becomes the function of the labour productivity in other industries'.[107]

Two reasons can be put forward to explain the machine shortage of the mid-1820s. Firstly, the shortage of skilled labour in the machine sector and the problem of recruitment. On the one hand the increased sub-division of labour increased output and reduced costs. On the other hand, however, it called into increasing demand specialist skills in machine making.[108] Peter Ewart informed the 1824 Select Committee that the great difficulty in meeting the increased demand for machinery was 'the deficiency of hands brought up to the separate parts of the machinery, which is a work of time'.[109] Similarly William Fairbairn claimed that 'I do not think in two, three, or four years, hands can be trained to supply a greater quantity of machinery than what is now in demand', as 'It requires a considerable length of time, before a man can become an expert workman at that business'.[110] The problems of recruitment and training were further compounded by the sectional division of labour into craft combines. T. C. Hewes, for example, complained bitterly that he could not meet the increased demand for machinery because,

> We cannot get a supply of men. The men now engaged in that sort of work will not allow other workmen to come into the trade; machine makers, more particularly, in our manufactories, are not allowed by those people to come in, unless they have worked five years at cotton mills, flax mills, or woollen mills. Myself and most of the machine makers in the neighbourhood have completely given up on this point.[111]

Mechanics were usually employed in the factory to repair and maintain machinery, and this provided a potential pool of skilled labour for firms engaged in machine making.[112] Hewes had no objection to the recruitment of mechanics from the factory, 'for we want to increase the numbers'. However, his workforce opposed the recruitment of inexperienced or apprenticed factory labour, and 'this has existed for ten or a dozen years'. Hewes was forced to recruit from other skilled trades and 'the men who are now leaders in that [machine making], I have taken from cabinet makers and clock makers and things of that kind'.[113]

This example again brings to light the organisational problems facing entrepreneurs in the early Industrial Revolution. According to Hewes the day wages of mechanics had increased from 28s to 30s between 1821 and 1824, resulting in an increased price for machine components. The solution to this was to introduce a new system of work organisation, and 'the increased demand for machinery obliged us to change from day to piece rates'. In 1821, two-thirds of Hewes' workforce were engaged in day work, however by 1824 this had been reversed, and now 'a man working by day work earns 30s, a man working by piece earns 36s to 40s'. However, the introduction of this system brought forth new problems of supervisory control, and Hewes admitted that if they reverted to a complete piece system, 'we should prepare more, but it would not be done so well; some of the men are apt to slight their work'.[114]

Secondly, there is evidence to suggest that the Manchester machine makers were slow to introduce new machine tools and techniques into the construction of machines.[115] Jeremy points out that the Lancashire manufacturers had 'an unshakable belief in their superiority', and quotes Peter Ewart on the greatly increased sub-division of labour.[116] Nevertheless, this was in marked contrast to the ingenuity of the London engineers, who 'dispensed with the handicrafts of turning and filing and their intensive sub-division. Instead, they relied on a new range of machine tools, handled by skilled operatives, to accomplish the same job.'[117] There were some exceptions to this in Manchester, notably Sharp, Roberts and Company, who were operating new machine tools in the 1820s. However, the 'Northern manufacturers seem to have been unaware of this, assuming that the locus of technology still resided in terms of specialist craftsmen. In fact, it had shifted from men to machines'.[118] This may be so, but it fails to consider the fact that London was not a specialist producer of cotton machinery, a fact which Peter Ewart was aware of when he claimed that the London mechanists 'are quite out of the practice of making cotton machinery'.[119] Furthermore, as Jeremy himself points out, the important area of spindle making 'remained beyond the capacity of the new machine tools', and remained a manual operation well into the 1830s.[120]

The interconnections between the factory and the development of the machine sector reinforces our argument that the factory impacted a dynamic on other sectors of the economy. Similarly we would expect a substantial increase in the chemical and finishing trades, in the wake of the post-1815 factory expansion. Table 9.8 shows the growth of this sector between 1815 and 1825. The number of firms in this sector increased by 25.0 per cent, but the total RV by only 16.1 per cent, suggesting a movement towards smaller scale units. Indeed, the average RV of firms in the sector fell from £69.62 in 1815 to £64.68 in 1825. Clearly, the small firm remained the optimum business unit. For example, in the dyeing trade the typical new entrant by 1825 remained a small-scale firm with an RV of £50.00 or less. Of the 61 new firms entering dyeing between 1815 and 1825, 46 firms

Table 9.8: Growth of the chemical and finishing sector, Manchester, 1815–1825

No. of firms		Total RV (£)		% increase	
1815	1825	1815	1825	No	RV
240	300	16,710	19,404	25.0	16.1

Source: Compiled from data in Table 9.1, and Manchester Rate Book, 1825.

fell into this category. The high entry rate in dyeing[121] suggests that the pattern of development was highly volatile, and indeed, between 1815 and 1825 there was a 55 per cent failure rate.[122]

Given the lack of empirical evidence for individual firms in dyeing, it is difficult to go beyond this broad outline. However, there is more information on the related trade of calico printing, and for this we are indebted to the excellent work of Chapman. This allows us to make some observations concerning the development of calico printing in Manchester between 1815 and 1825. Chapman argues that because spinning and weaving took an early technological lead, it 'does not necessarily mean that another . . . set of firms at the next stage of production [i.e., calico printing] felt the need to shift to steam power'.[123] Indeed, the new technique of roller printing by power was slow to replace the older process of hand-block printing. Roller printing was only justified by long runs which did not interest producers at the fashion end of the market.[124] For example, Chapman shows that the leading Blackburn calico printers, Thompson, Chippendale and Company (who operated a print warehouse in Manchester *c.* 1815–25),[125] had, by 1820, only seven roller printing machines with 110 hand block printing tables.[126] Thus new technology went hand in hand with the proliferation of old techniques; the number of block printing tables employed by Thompson and Chippendale was only 37 in 1812.[127]

The close of the Napoleonic Wars saw the first major reversal in the fortunes of calico printers, with the change in fashion from 'colourful patterned fabrics to white dresses made in cambrics and muslins'.[128] The change in the demand schedule, conditioned by the vagaries of fashion,[129] put increasing pressures on Manchester calico printers faced by a declining market for high-cost printed goods. As Chapman points out,

> the Lancashire calico printing industry was reaching a point where the various firms had to make far reaching decisions

> about their future commercial policies . . . Experience evidently persuaded most to remain at the cheap end of the market and hope that thinner profit margins would be compensated for by growing turnover.[130]

The adverse conditions faced by calico printers is reflected in the high rate of exit in Manchester between 1815 and 1825. This is shown in Table 9.9. Two characteristics of growth can be discerned from Table 9.9. Firstly, the rate of exit amongst combined firms was lower than for calico printing only firms. This

Table 9.9: Number of firms exiting from calico printing, Manchester, 1815–1825

Activity	Exit[a]		Survival		Total
	no of firms	% of total	no of firms	% of total	no of firms
Calico printing only	52	60.5	34	39.5	86
Calico printing combined	21	51.2	20	48.8	41

Note: a. The term exit is meant to represent those firms exciting from calico printing; they may of course move into other business activities.

Source: Compiled from data in Table 9.3 and Manchester Rate Book, 1825.

suggests that combined firms could transfer their resources into other activities when the market dictated.[131] Secondly, and following on from this, one option open to entrepreneurs was to drop calico printing and move into other activities. Of the 73 firms withdrawing from calico printing, 14 survived by branching out into other areas[132] (for a list of these firms see Appendix 7). For example, in 1815 the large firm of Haigh, Marshall and Company, with a print warehouse in Brown Street, Manchester, rated at £220.00, were listed in the commercial directory as calico printers, manufacturers and dealers and merchants. By 1825, however, they had dropped calico printing and were now listed as manufacturers and dealers and merchants.[133]

Thus we can hypothesise that the most logical option for printing firms, faced with adverse market conditions, was not necessarily to innovate but rather to diversify into other activities. We would therefore expect an increase in the number of combined printing firms by 1825. This expected trend is shown in Table 9.10.

Table 9.10: Reconstruction of the Manchester calico printing trade, 1825, and a comparison with 1815

Activity	No of firms	Total RV (£)	% change from 1815 No	RV
Calico printing only	59	3,887	−45.8	−33.2
Calico printing combined	74	6,406	+80.5	+61.1

Source: Manchester Rate Book, 1825, and data in Table 9.3.

Table 9.10 clearly shows that there was a substantial increase in the number of combined firms (80.5 per cent) by 1825. On the other hand, single process firms declined by 45.8 per cent, reflecting the adverse conditions affecting firms engaged in calico printing activities. The typical new entrant to the printing trade was a combined firm, reflecting the desire to spread risks over a wider business area.[134] Between 1815 and 1825, 79 new firms entered the industry, and of these 51 firms, or 64.5 per cent, were combined firms. Unlike the metal sector, calico printing firms did not follow a path of increasing specialisation, along the lines portrayed by Stigler's theory. Instead, calico printing developed through a process of increasing diversification in the face of changing market conditions for printed goods. Thus we can agree with Chapman that the options open to entrepreneurs in calico printing did not necessarily follow a trajectory of innovation, and the adoption of new techniques,[135] but there was a wide scope for the expansion and diversification of business activities.

The growth of these new business sectors, in the post-Napoleonic period, brings us back to the question of business structure and the political economy of Manchester cotton. In Chapter 8 we argued that the schism between the factory (spinning) and the warehouse (manufacturing) had been closed by 1825. However, continued development of new business sectors, especially the strategically important machine industry, opened up the possibilities of further political controversy. According to Peter Mathias, the development of machine making along specialist lines brought into existence a 'business interest group' which could press 'its claims for export markets for capital goods'.[136] The political debate on the export of machinery and the emigration of artisans was an on-going affair between 1824 and 1841.[137] However, it first found its political expression in the 1820s, culminating in the Select Committee on Artisans and

Machinery of 1824.[138] We are not here concerned with the ultimate outcome of the debate,[139] but rather with the respective argument of the factory masters and the machine makers. What was the major arguments put forward and was there a unity of interest in the trade?

Maxine Berg has claimed that,

> The debate hinged on the recognition of machine making as the pivot of the whole system of production. Previously, free trade had always been conceived in terms of manufactured commodities. The actual process of manufacturing had not been looked on as a market product in its own right. Now contemporaries saw that the tools, machines, sources of power, and expertise out of which they fashioned their exportable consumer goods were also attractive in foreign markets.[140]

Certainly, in 1824, the Manchester Chamber of Commerce was in unison concerning its agitation against the repeal of the export prohibition on machinery. In February 1824, they unanimously declared that 'it would be highly inexpedient and injurious to the interests of this country, to allow the export of machinery and tools'.[141] Similarly, the Manchester textile manufacturers and machine makers, giving evidence before the 1824 Select Committee, all registered strong opposition to the free export of machinery.[142] Given this apparent unity, what were the main themes of the debate?

The debate focused on four main themes. Firstly, it was argued that the free export of machinery was detrimental to the manufacturing interest in general. For example, the Manchester Chamber concluded, in March 1824, that 'the matters submitted to the Select Committee . . . are in the nature of the utmost importance to the manufacturing interests of this Kingdom in general, and to those of this district in particular'.[143] This appeal to the national interest, as Berg points out, explains the seeming anomaly between the 'free trade rhetoric' of the Manchester manufacturers and their unanimous support for protectionist policies in the export of machinery. It was not simply 'a question of protecting one industry against international economic development, but of protecting all industries by controlling the markets of one key industry — the capital goods or machine making industry'.[144] It therefore followed that the free export of machinery was detrimental, in the long run, to the national economic interest. In 1824, the 'primary concern was the course of overall industrial prosperity'.[145]

Secondly, it was argued that the free export of machinery would, in the long run, lead to a loss of overseas markets for British manufactured goods. Peter Ewart informed the 1824 Select Committee that the exportation of machinery would aid the expansion of foreign cotton spinning techniques, and the opening up of the market for British cotton machinery would reduce the gains achieved by Britain's superiority in the manufacturing of cotton machinery. At present 'what enables us to compete is the superior cheapness which we produce our cotton goods', claimed Ewart. The competitive gains of superior machinery were counterbalanced by the advantages of continental manufacturers in 'cheaper provisions, lower labour costs in the manufacturing towns, and lighter taxes'.[146]

Thirdly, it was claimed that the export of machinery would lead to the curtailment of business expansion. Thomas Sharp, the Manchester machine maker, presented a motion to the Chamber of Commerce to the effect that,

> at the present period, it is an undoubted fact, that the demand for machinery for our own use cannot by any means be adequately supplied and the first effect of a free exportation would be to admit foreigners as rivals in the market, who would willingly pay higher prices for machines, than could be afforded by the British manufacturers.[147]

Similarly, Peter Ewart informed the 1824 Select Committee that 'Many cotton spinners have great difficulty in getting their orders promptly and punctually executed and the admission of foreign orders into the market would greatly increase that difficulty'.[148] This would ultimately curtail the expansion of cotton factories as 'they would not build mills if they could not get machinery to fill them'.[149] Furthermore, it was argued that the export of machinery would only produce short-term gains to the machine makers. T. C. Hewes claimed that,

> if there was a free trade a quantity of machines would be ordered from the continent, and in consequence . . . the manufacturers on this side of the water would take alarm, and would not be inclined to enlarge their mills or erect others; and I conceive the demand on the other side, would be merely

> for single machines of different descriptions, not more than one of a sort to one manufactory.[150]

Fourthly, the theme of debate moved towards the role of artisan skill in the production of machinery. Not surprisingly, given the shortage of skilled labour discussed earlier, the machine makers were solid in their support against the repeal of the laws on the emigration of artisans. However, 'Over the question of artisan emigration, witnesses [to the 1824 Select Committee] from the textile industry . . . were divided. Those opposed feared the loss of technical secrets, a shortage of skilled workers, or the development of foreign competition'.[151] For the supporters of repeal, the terms of debate were conducted around the theme of 'justice and property rights'.[152] It was argued that the law was 'an unjust infringement on their rights to dispose of their labour to the best advantage'.[153] Thus the laws infringed on the right of labour freely to choose its most profitable outlet, and restricted the free mobility of labour.

To counteract this argument, the opponents of repeal turned the question towards 'the role of artisan skills in technical change' and 'away from the artisan himself to the machine'.[154] It was argued that the new machines could not be successfully introduced abroad 'without the artisan skills needed to erect them, adapt them, and repair them'.[155] Thus William Fairbairn claimed that,

> If France were to receive our machinery free of all restrictions, and they got the machinery over from this country, they would require also workmen to keep it in repair and those workmen . . . would also be competent to make improvements and construct new ones.[156]

Furthermore, it was argued that, at present, there was no grounds for repeal given the higher rate of wages offered to machine artisans in comparison to other types of labour. Thus James McConnel, although supporting the rights of labour to choose freely, concluded that,

> no efficient ground can be shown for a repeal of the existing law, so long as the wages of this description of workmen (mechanics) are above the ordinary rate of wages for every other description of labour, as is the case at present.[157]

Undoubtedly, the major factor conditioning the views of machine makers and manufacturers in 1824 was the prosperous nature of the cotton trade. Both spinners and machine makers fervently agreed that the production of machinery was inadequate to meet home demand, let alone supply export markets. However, this unity was short lived, and with the downturn of the cotton trade during 1825 to 1826 the depression led Manchester machine makers to break their alliance with the manufacturers who used their machinery.[158] By 1826, the Manchester machine makers were vigorously petitioning Parliament, complaining that,

> unexampled distress now prevails in . . . Manchester, amongst machine makers and mechanics, for want of employment in the home trade; that the petitioners could at present have extensive orders for the purpose of exportation, but are prohibited from taking the benefits of an export trade; that whilst every other class of manufactures are allowed to export the produce of their labour, the petitioners are bound with fetters . . . and are not placed on an equal footing with the great body of His Majesty's Subjects.[159]

The downturn of trade after 1825 opened up a new schism in the cotton trade between the factory men, who supported the maintenance of Britain's superiority in the production of machinery, and machine makers who were clamouring for the advantages of export markets in the face of a falling home demand for textile machinery. As Arthur Redford put it 'manufacturers and merchants were in alliance for the maintenance of prohibition, their common enemies being the new class of machinery makers'.[160] The debate now hinged on the particular interests of competing sectors of Manchester's business community, and witnessed the opening up of a new political schism. Employment for machine makers, via export, was interpreted by cotton manufacturers as unemployment for the factory. However, as Jeremy argues, by the mid-1820s the factory 'held the whip hand' politically, and the alienation of a powerful group of wealthy textile entrepreneurs (reinforced by the convergence of factory and warehouse) was not a step which government was willing to take. In consequence, and in the face of economic depression, the government postponed repeal until the 1840s.[161]

NOTES AND REFERENCES

1. These sectors are normally associated with the diffusion of innovation and economic growth which underpins the technological change interpretation of the Industrial Revolution.

2. W. W. Rostow, 'Leading Sectors and the Take-Off', in W. W. Rostow (ed.), *The Economics of Take-Off Into Self-Sustained Growth* (Cambridge University Press, Cambridge, 1961), p. 3. The importance of technological linkage effects, in explaining economic growth, is further emphasised by Rosenberg, who claims that 'technological progress in one sector of the economy has become increasingly dependent upon technological change in other sectors'. N. Rosenberg, *Inside the Black Box: Technology and Economics* (Cambridge University Press, Cambridge, 1982), p. 73.

3. Quoted in W. H. Thompson, *History of Manchester to 1852* (John Sherratt and Son, Altrincham, 1967), p. 316.

4. See, for example, M. Berg, *The Age of Manufactures, 1700–1820* (Basil Blackwell, Oxford, 1985), p. 188; D. Landes, *The Unbound Prometheus: Technological Change in Western Europe from 1700 to the Present* (Cambridge University Press, Cambridge, 1969), ch. 2; Rosenberg, *Black Box*, pp. 46, 73–4.

5. In particular, Rosenberg stresses the need to consider both process innovation (new methods or technologies of production) and product innovation (new goods and services). In practice, both types of innovation are intermingled; process innovations typically involve new machinery or equipment in which they are embodied and this machinery constitutes a product innovation to the suppliers of new machinery (i.e. machine makers) but a process innovation to the users of new capital equipment (i.e. cotton spinners). See Rosenberg, *Black Box*, pp. 4, 14, 237.

6. D. A. Farnie, *The English Cotton Industry and the World Market 1815–1896* (Clarendon Press, Oxford, 1979), pp. 35–6.

7. Rosenberg, *Black Box*, p. 21.

8. Ibid., p. 246.

9. M. Berg, 'Introduction', in M. Berg (edited documents), *Technology and Toil in Nineteenth Century Britain* (Humanities Press, New Jersey, 1979), pp. 7–8.

10. The importance of skill in the division of labour amongst Manchester machine makers will be discussed later in this chapter.

11. A. E. Musson and E. Robinson, *Science and Technology in the Industrial Revolution* (Manchester University Press, Manchester, 1969), p. 428.

12. R. Samuel, 'The Workshop of the World; Steam Power and Hand Technology in Mid-Victorian Britain', *History Workshop*, Issue 3 (1977), p. 19.

13. Quoted in Musson and Robinson, *Science*, p. 427.

14. Ibid., p. 427.

15. Ibid., pp. 427–8.

16. A. E. Musson, *The Growth of British Industry* (B. T. Batsford, London, 1978), p. 84. This is not to suggest, however, that there was no

mechanisation in these processes. For example, both bleachworks and dyeworks used waterwheels and later steam engines to power wash and dash wheels. See S. D. Chapman, *The Cotton Industry in the Industrial Revolution* (Macmillan, London, 1972), p. 25.

17. Farnie, *English Cotton Industry*, p. 33. For a discussion of the development of chemical technology see Musson and Robinson, *Science*, pp. 231–371; Landes, *Unbound Prometheus*, pp. 108–14; A. Clow and N. L. Clow, 'Vitriol in the Industrial Revolution', *Economic History Review*, vol. XV (1945), pp. 44–55.

18. Clow and Clow, 'Vitriol', p. 49.

19. Ibid., p. 49.

20. Quoted in Musson and Robinson, *Science*, p. 242.

21. *Manchester Mercury*, 23 June 1789, cited in Musson and Robinson, *Science*, p. 316.

22. David J. Jeremy, *Transatlantic Industrial Revolution: The Diffusion of Textile Technologies Between Britain and America, 1790–1830s* (Basil Blackwell, Oxford, 1981), p. 109.

23. See Appendix 7.

24. S. D. Chapman and S. Chassagne, *European Textile Printers in the Eighteenth Century: A Study of Peel and Oberkamf* (Heinemann Educational: Pasold Fund, London, 1981).

25. Clearly the Peel family were the predominant pioneers in this field and 'eventually the various branches of the Peel family owned about 14 cotton mills, and their concerns were vertically integrated, extending from spinning to printing'. In 1795 the Peels operated 23 cotton mills and eight print works. F. Crouzet, *The First Industrialists: The Problem of Origins* (Cambridge University Press, Cambridge, 1985), pp. 16, 159 n. 83. Two branches of the company, Thomas Peel and Brothers and Peel, Yates and Company, operated print warehouses in Peel Street, Manchester, in 1815, both rated at £250.00 each.

26. Chapman and Chassagne, *European Textile Printers*, p. 3.

27. Ibid., p. 20.

28. Jeremy, *Transatlantic Industrial Revolution*, pp. 109–10.

29. Chapman and Chassagne, *European Textile Printers*, p. 11. See also H. Clark, 'The Design and Designing of Lancashire Printed Calicoes During the First Half of the 19th Century', *Textile History*, vol. 15, no. 1 (1984), pp. 102–5.

30. S. D. Chapman, 'Quantity Versus Quality in the British Industrial Revolution: The Case of Printed Textiles', *Northern History*, vol. XXI (1985), pp. 180–1.

31. For a discussion of the impact of fashion on calico printing see Chapman and Chassagne, *European Textile Printers*, pp. 3–4; Berg, *Age of Manufactures*, pp. 205, 216–17; Clark, 'Design and Designing', pp. 101–2.

32. Jeremy, *Transatlantic Industrial Revolution*, p. 52. Calico printing by cylinder was 'extraordinarily labour saving' compared with the old techniques of block printing. See Jeremy, p. 104. There is evidence to suggest, however, that the application of steam power to printing machinery was a slow affair. In 1837, the bleaching, dyeing and printing trades in Manchester used only 756 horse power compared

with 5,272 horse power in the spinning and weaving sectors. A. E. Musson, 'Industrial Motive Power in the United Kingdom, 1800–70', *Economic History Review*, vol. XXIX, no. 3 (1976), p. 430. See also Clark, 'Design and Designing', pp. 105–9.

33. See Musson and Robinson, *Science*, ch. 13.

34. See Ibid., ch. 14. See also A. E. Musson, 'An Early Engineering Firm: Peel Williams and Co, Manchester', *Business History*, vol. 3 (1960); and A. E. Musson, 'Peel Williams and Co., ironfounders and engineers Manchester', *Transactions of the Lancashire and Cheshire Antiquarian Society*, vol. 69 (1959).

35. Musson and Robinson, *Science*, p. 454.

36. For the RV and the activities of these firms see Appendix 7.

37. Farnie, *English Cotton Trade*, p. 63.

38. For the RV and the activities of these firms see Appendix 7.

39. L. Hannah, *The Rise of the Corporate Economy* (Methuen, London, 1976), p. 10.

40. As Samuel points out, 'increased investment was by no means synonymous with the growth of large capitalist firms or the installation of elaborate plant. In some trades . . . it was accompanied by a proliferation of small producers'. Samuel, 'Workshop of the World', p. 13.

41. M. A. Utton, *Industrial Concentration* (Penguin, Harmondsworth, 1970), p. 14.

42. Ibid., p. 15.

43. Ibid., p. 35.

44. Ibid., p. 36.

45. Musson and Robinson, in their study of Peel and Williams, use RV data to formulate an approximate capital valuation of the firm in 1820. Factories and workshops were assessed at about 5½ to 6 per cent of such valuation, and this gives an approximate valuation of £4,000.00 for Peel and Williams Soho foundry (RV, £230.00), and £3,650.00 for their Phoenix foundry (RV, £210.00), a total of £7,650.00. Musson and Robinson, *Science*, p. 466. A similar technique is employed by Katrina Honeyman to measure the capital value of Bolton cotton factories. See K. Honeyman, *Origins of Enterprise: Business Leadership in the Industrial Revolution* (Manchester University Press, Manchester, 1982), pp. 100–3.

46. J. Blair, *Economic Concentration* (Harcourt, Brace, Jovanovich, New York, 1972), p. 8. A similar definition is provided by Nightingale who defines an industry as 'any grouping of firms which operate similar processes and could produce technically identical products within a given planning horizon'. J. Nightingale, 'On The Definition of Industry and Market', *Journal of Industrial Economics*, vol. XXVII, 1978, p. 35.

47. Musson and Robinson, *Science*, pp. 433–4.

48. For example, Peter Ewart, a large Manchester entrepreneur, was at one time or another an engineer, millwright, bleacher and calico printer, and cotton spinner. In 1780 he was Boulton and Watts' agent in Manchester, and in 1792 went into partnership with Samuel Oldknow in a bleaching and calico printing business, which was dissolved after a year. Ewart returned to engineering and in 1798, in partnership with Samuel Gregg, entered the cotton spinning business. See Musson and

Robinson, *Science*, p. 443. In 1815, Ewart is designated as a cotton spinner, because this is where his main business assets were directed. Also see W. C. Henry, 'A Biographical Note on the late Peter Ewart Esq.', *Memoirs of the Literary and Philosophical Society of Manchester*, 2nd series, vol. VII (1846).

49. These firms are described in the 1815 directory as iron founders, but it is probable they produced a wide range of machinery and millwright work. For example, Peel Williams and Company were by 1806 producing water wheel castings, mill gearing and engine work, weighing machines, spinning rollers and general millwork. Musson and Robinson, *Science*, p. 462.

50. These firms operated from print warehouses and one suspects that the printing of calico took place in these warehouse establishments. However, there is no evidence to suggest that the print warehouses used mechanised power. A number of prominent outside printers operated warehouses in Manchester such as the Peels, Thompson, Chippendale and Co, Brookes and Oughton, Haigh, Marshall and Co, J. and J. Bury, to name a few, and one suspects that these warehouses were utilised for display and marketing purposes. For a history of these firms see M. M. Edwards, *The Growth of the British Cotton Trade 1780–1815* (Manchester University Press, Manchester, 1967); S. D. Chapman, 'Quantity Versus Quality'; Chapman and Chassagne, *European Textile Printers*.

51. Of these 41 firms, 17 combined calico printing with manufacturing and dealing suggesting that they were actively involved in the putting-out system.

52. See Utton, *Industrial Concentration*, pp. 42–50.

53. Ibid., pp. 42–3.

54. For an interpretation of concentration ratios see Utton, *Industrial Concentration*, pp. 43–6.

55. Ibid., p. 70.

56. Blair, *Economic Concentration*, p. 3.

57. Quoted in Blair, *Economic Concentration*, p. 3.

58. An obvious objection is that RVs may provide a poor proxy for output and thus it may well underestimate the contribution of the larger plants. Further, it does not allow for non-fixed components which may well be proportionally greater in larger firms compared with small.

59. Musson and Robinson conclude, from their study of the leading Manchester engineering firms, that their sample constitutes 'only a few of the growing number of such firms . . . almost all their names have been forgotten and little historical evidence of their activities have survived, but they played a most important role in manufacturing the early textile machines of the Industrial Revolution in Lancashire'. Musson and Robinson, *Science*, p. 443. We hope that our reconstruction will secure some of their names for posterity.

60. Utton, *Industrial Concentration*, p. 19. Writing in 1835, Charles Babbage concluded that 'perhaps the most important principle on which the economy of a manufacture depends, is the division of labour amongst the persons who perform the work'. For Babbage, the division of labour meant cheapening the individual parts of the production

process. C. Babbage, *On the Economy of Machinery and Manufactures* (1835), reprinted in Berg, *Technology and Toil*, pp. 41, 45.

61. P. Sargent Florence, *The Logic of Industrial Organisation* (Routledge and Kegan Paul, London, 1933), pp. 19–20.

62. For a discussion of the importance of the division of labour, and the role of skill, in the metal trades, see Berg, *Age of Manufactures*, pp. 264–86.

63. PP, 1824 (51), V, *Select Committee on Artisans and Machinery*, p. 252.

64. Ibid., p. 258.

65. See, for example, ibid., evidence of Peter Ewart, p. 255, and evidence of Thomas Ashton and J. Bremner, the Hyde cotton spinners, p. 299. A particular shortage was to be found in the supply of rollers and spindles; for example, T. C. Hewes, a Manchester machine maker and millwright, was declining orders for these components, 'for those are parts that we cannot procure ourselves'. Ibid., pp. 347–8.

66. Jeremy, *Transatlantic Industrial Revolution*, p. 67.

67. Most probably Peel, Williams and Company, the largest foundry and engineering firm in Manchester in 1825, with two plants rated at £190.00 and £300.00.

68. PP, 1824 (51), V, p. 547. William Fairbairn confirmed the general observation and concluded that 'The demand for machinery at home is so very considerable, that in the cotton districts the machine makers are not capable of supplying the home demand' for the last twelve months, 'when the trade in Manchester has been very brisk'. Ibid., p. 568.

69. Ibid., p. 253.

70. In 1815 Hewes' plant was the fourth largest in Manchester rated at £130.00. See Appendix 7.

71. PP, 1824 (51), V, p. 341.

72. For a list of firms operating more than one plant in Manchester, in the metal sector, see Appendix 7.

73. PP, 1824 (51), V, p. 346. This view is supported by Farnie, who claims that competition amongst the machine makers 'encouraged a long-term reduction in the price of machinery since engineers were too jealous of their competers ever to consider united action, least of all in the maintenance of prices'. Farnie, *English Cotton Industry*, p. 55.

74. Musson and Robinson, *Science*, p. 445.

75. PP, 1824 (51), V, p. 253.

76. Ibid., p. 301.

77. Hewes described his activities as chiefly making cotton machinery, but was 'extensively engaged in erecting mills and filling them with machinery'. He employed 140 to 150 men 'about 40 may be employed on heavy mill work and 110 on machinery, the heavy gearing and the fire proof mills'. Ibid., p. 340.

78. Ibid., p. 343. See also evidence of John Lee Bradbury, p. 545.

79. Similarly, in cotton spinning, Chapman has claimed that the small firm was dependent on larger firms for 'its conception and survival'. Economies of scale in factory spinning enabled entrepreneurs of little capital to enter, functioning as commission agents. These firms were dependent on large firms for supplies and markets and were shed

when trade fell off. S. D. Chapman, 'Financial Restraints on the Growth of Firms in the Cotton Industry, 1790–1850', *Economic History Review*, vol. XXXII, no. 1 (1979), p. 66.

80. Quoted in Crouzet, *The First Industrialists*, p. 91. In 1825, the firm of Fairbairn and Lilly operated two foundries, rated at £65.00 and £130.00. For a biography of William Fairbairn see P. A. Pole, *The Life of Sir William Fairbairn* (David and Charles, Newton Abbot, 1970).

81. Quoted in Crouzet, *The First Industrialists*, p. 90.

82. For a discussion of the importance of technological expertise to the firm see Chapters 6 and 10.

83. Such examples include William Fairbairn, T. C. Hewes, Peter Ewart, and William Galloway. See Musson and Robinson, *Science*, pp. 98–9; and Crouzet, *The First Industrialists*, p. 195.

84. G. Stiegler, *The Organisation of Industry* (Richard D. Irwin, Homewood, Illinois, 1968), ch. 12.

85. Ibid., p. 129.

86. Ibid., p. 129.

87. Ibid., p, 131. This fits in with our contention that the two industrial sectors are separable and distinguishable.

88. Ibid., p. 132.

89. Ibid., pp. 132–3.

90. C. H. Lee, *A Cotton Enterprise 1795–1840: A History of McConnel and Kennedy, Fine Cotton Spinners* (Manchester University Press, Manchester, 1972), p. 13.

91. For example, William Fairbairn and his brother, Peter, were initially apprenticed as engineers and millwrights in London. See Crouzet, *The First Industrialists*, p. 91.

92. Lee, *McConnel and Kennedy*, p. 15.

93. Ibid., p. 21.

94. PP, 1824 (51), V, p. 307.

95. Ibid., p. 345.

96. For a discussion on the growth of the factory sector between these dates see Chapter 7.

97. Especially the demand for machine components such as rollers and spindles.

98. R. Lloyd-Jones and A. A. Le Roux, 'The Size of Firms in the Cotton Industry: Manchester 1815–41', *Economic History Review*, vol. XXXIII, no. 1 (1980), pp. 74–5. The medium-sized firm is defined as one employing between 151 and 500 workers. The rise of the medium-sized factory firm is explored in Chapter 10.

99. As Catling has observed, 'Inevitably the application of power to drive the spindles during the draw was exploited by making mules with more and more spindles'. The number increased from 100, when manually driven, to 350 when powered, and by 1830 mules of 600 spindles were the optimum size, with a few being built to a capacity of 1,200. H. Cattling, 'The Development of the Spinning Mule', *Textile History*, vol. 9 (1978), pp. 41–2. See also Chapter 10 for a discussion of the introduction of the long mule.

100. For a discussion of credit availability in the 1820s see, Chapman, 'Financial Restraints'.

101. PP, 1833 (690), VII, *Select Committee on Manufactures, Commerce and Shipping in the United Kingdom*, p. 554.

102. According to Cattling, 'Despite the developments which had taken place, the final stage of spinning remained by far the most expensive single operation and it was here that efforts of cost reduction were concentrated'. H. Cattling, *The Spinning Mule* (David and Charles, Newton Abbot, 1970), p. 48.

103. PP, 1833 (690), VII, p. 310. This view was supported by Holland Hoole, a Manchester cotton spinner, who informed the factory inspectors in 1833 that 'Few if any cotton mills have been erected in Manchester since 1825, but every man has been trying to make his fixed capital more productive by filling up his spare rooms, speeding or destroying old and substituting new and improved machinery'. PP, 1833 (450), XX, *Report of the Royal Commission on the Employment of Children in Factories*, p. 98.

104. PP, 1833 (690), VII, p. 313.

105. PP, 1824 (51), V, p. 299. See also evidence of Peter Ewart, p. 253.

106. Ibid., p. 341.

107. Rosenberg, *Black Box*, p. 46.

108. Thus Peter Mathias points out that 'Industrialisation bred the need for new skills faster than it destroyed old ones. The pace of diffusion of new techniques was limited by the scarcity of skill as much as by the scarcity of capital'. P. Mathias, *The First Industrial Revolution* (Methuen, London, 1969), p. 144.

109. PP, 1824 (51), V, p. 258.

110. Ibid., pp. 568, 569. This was further supported by Robert Bremner, the Hyde cotton spinner, who claimed that 'We cannot make machine makers so quickly as any other description of persons; they require a long time to learn'. Ibid., pp. 301.

111. Ibid., p. 341.

112. This further supports the notion of linkages between the factory and the machine sector. Baines reproducing Stanway's returns of 151 cotton factories for the Factory Commissioners shows that out of a total of 48,645 operatives, 989 were employed as engineers, firemen and mechanics. E. Baines, *History of the Cotton Manufacturer in Great Britain* (Frank Cass, London, 1966, 2nd edition), p. 372.

113. PP, 1824 (51), V, p. 341.

114. Ibid., p. 345.

115. This fits in with Marx's notion of technological progress, where 'The realisation of the full productive possibilities of modern industry required that machine techniques be employed in the construction of machines themselves'. Rosenberg, *Black Box*, p. 44.

116. Jeremy, *Transatlantic Industrial Revolution*, p. 66.

117. D. J. Jeremy, 'Damming the Flood: British Government Efforts to Check the Outflow of Technicians and Machinery, 1780–1843', *Business History Review*, vol. 5, no. 1 (1977), p. 21. According to Jeremy, this position only changed gradually in the 1830s. See Jeremy, *Transatlantic Industrial Revolution*, p. 67.

118. Jeremy, 'Damming the Flood', pp. 21–2. The slow adoption of

new machine tools finds some support from our empirical reconstruction. In 1825 we were able to identify only two small specialist tool and lathe manufacturers: Edward Green, with a works rated at £25.00, and Francis Lewis, with a works rated at £18.00. However, it is probable that the large machine makers produced their own machine tools, but it is clear from the available evidence that in the case of tool manufacture the industry did not follow the Stiegler path of increasing specialisation.

119. PP, 1824 (51), V, p. 253.

120. Jeremy, *Transatlantic Industrial Revolution*, pp. 67–8.

121. The 61 new entrants accounted for 79 per cent of the population of 77 dyeing firms in 1825.

122. This, of course, reflects the fluctuating nature of trade in the post-Napoleonic period.

123. Chapman, 'Quantity Versus Quality', p. 176.

124. Ibid., p. 179. Furthermore, the print unions were solid in their agitation against the introduction of mechanisation. See Ibid., pp. 179–80; and Tina Bruland, 'Industrial Conflict as a Source of Technical Innovation: Three Cases', *Economy and Society*, vol. 11, no. 2 (1982), pp. 104–11.

125. The RV of this warehouse was £140.00 in 1815 and £125.00 in 1825.

126. Chapman, 'Quantity Versus Quality', p. 185.

127. Ibid., p. 185.

128. Ibid., p. 184.

129. Changes in fashion were important factors in shaping entrepreneurial judgements, as shown in Chapter 7. See for example the activities of John Heywood and Son. Also Clark 'Design and Designing', pp. 103–5.

130. Chapman, 'Quantity Versus Quality', p. 182.

131. This business behaviour mirrors the activities of manufacturing firms such as John Heywood and Owens Owens shown in Chapter 7.

132. Eight combined firms (19.5 per cent of the total of combined firms), and six calico printing only firms (7.0 per cent of such firms) had dropped calico printing by 1825. Thus these firms survive to 1825, but are recorded as exit firms from the calico printing industry.

133. *Pigot's Directory* for 1815 and 1825.

134. This trend is also clearly shown in the cotton spinning sector with the combination of spinning and weaving. See Chapters 7 and also 10.

135. Chapman, 'Quantity Versus Quality', p. 176.

136. P. Mathias, *The Transformation of England: An Economic and Social History* (Methuen, London, 1979), p. 13.

137. M. Berg, *The Machinery Question and The Making of Political Economy* (Cambridge University Press, Cambridge, 1980), p. 204.

138. PP, 1824 (51), V. Jeremy points out that until the 1820s the emigration of artisans seems to have been more important in the international diffusion of technology than the export of machinery; but 'Even so there was a sizeable traffic of undetermined volume in the export of tools, machinery, parts and plans, a fact acknowledged by the 1824 Select Committee'. Jeremy, 'Damming the Flood', p. 12.

139. The outcome of the Select Committee of 1824 was the repeal of the restrictions on the movement of skilled artisans, but the prohibition on machinery remained, under a discretionary licence from the Board of Trade. See Berg, *Machinery*, pp. 203–4; Jeremy, 'Damming the Flood', p. 18.

140. Berg, *Machinery*, p. 205.

141. Proceedings of the Manchester Chamber of Commerce and Manufacturers (hereafter P.M.C.C.M.), 25 Feb. 1824.

142. See Jeremy, 'Damming the Flood', p. 19. In fact, the Manchester Chamber of Commerce subscribed £100.00, out of Chamber funds, to pay the expenses of witnesses to the *Committee*. P.M.C.C.M., 10 March 1824.

143. P.M.C.C.M., 10 March 1824.

144. Berg, *Machinery*, p. 209.

145. Ibid., p. 209.

146. PP, 1824 (51), V, pp. 251–2. This echoes the arguments put over by warehouse manufacturers against the export of yarn, discussed in Chapter 5. In fact, 'Peter Ewart was hard put to explain the difference between the two debates. He feebly argued that in exporting cotton yarns one did not export the means of making them, forgetting that yarn was also the means of making piece goods'. Berg, *Machinery*, p. 219.

147. P.M.C.C.M., 24 March 1824. The motion was seconded by James McConnel of McConnel and Kennedy.

148. PP, 1824 (51), V, p. 253.

149. Ibid., p. 255. For example, Thomas Ashton, the Hyde cotton spinner, informed the Committee that he was presently engaged in constructing a mill but 'would not have thought it prudent if he knew beforehand that the exportation would be allowed'. Ibid., p. 300.

150. Ibid., p. 342.

151. Jeremy, 'Damming the Flood', p. 19.

152. Berg, *Machinery*, p. 210.

153. P.M.C.C.M., 24 March 1824. The motion was put forward by J. E. Taylor and was in fact seconded by Thomas Sharp, the Manchester machine maker. This suggests that the machine makers themselves were not entirely united over the question of artisan emigration.

154. Berg, *Machinery*, p. 212.

155. Ibid., p. 212.

156. PP, 1824 (51), V, p. 569.

157. P.M.C.C.M., 24 March 1824. Motion by James McConnel, supported by Thomas Hoyle.

158. Jeremy, 'Damming the Flood', p. 20.

159. *Journal of the House of Commons*, vol. 82, July 1825 to Jan. 1826, p. 99.

160. A. Redford, *Manchester Merchants and Foreign Trade, 1794–1857* (Manchester University Press, Manchester, 1934), p. 131.

161. Jeremy, 'Damming the Flood', p. 20.

10

Business Strategy and the Firm in the Industrial Revolution

The general approach of this book has been to explore the interconnections between business components and their roles as part of a holistic business system. The exercise has been concerned with establishing both the economic structure and the political economy of the overall business system in which firms operate. It seems to us little point in merely reiterating the findings explored in the previous chapters; rather we intend to relate those findings to the business behaviour of the basic unit of business activity, the firm. Returning again to the metaphor, of Peter Mathias, we employed in the Introduction, having reconstructed the business system in which firms operated (the 'wood') let us speculate on the pattern of behaviour of the individual trees (firms) and their role in the Industrial Revolution.

THE FIRM AND THE INDUSTRIAL REVOLUTION

It has been fashionable for same time to conceptualise the Industrial Revolution as a long-run process, having its antecedents over an extended historical period.[1] The idea of the Industrial Revolution as a sharp discontinuity has faded, in part as a consequence of the critical attack directed against the ill-fated Rostowian notion of the 'take-off'.[2] While production expanded it has been stressed that traditional methods of work persisted in many industries and reflected the labour-intensive bias of the Industrial Revolution.[3] Yet our contention is that this view has been taken too far. As was argued in Chapter 6, the expansion of those labour-intensive systems were themselves a function of the dynamic of the factory and in a timely corrective Maxine Berg has placed the machine back at the centre of the Industrial Revolution. She claims:

> it must be admitted that the shocks of a rapid process of mechanisation were there, albeit confined to particular sectors and regions, and these pointed the way of future developments. It was also evident that the economic and technical transformation of the 1820s and 1830s happened at a much faster pace than any previous change.[4]

If the machine can be re-established as the catalyst of the Industrial Revolution, the predominant form it took was the factory, the sector that it most radically transformed was cotton and the vehicle that both captured and expressed its dynamic was the business firm. The importance of the firm as a key agent of industrial change should not be underestimated. Decisions relating to the amount and direction of investment, the type of commodity produced, the operation of plant and the hiring of labour (see Chapter 9) took place at the level of the firm and were, in most cases, the prerogative of the capitalist entrepreneur. The entrepreneur was either an owner or occupier of the property asset utilised as a production unit and the forms of occupation were both complex (see Chapter 3) and could undergo rapid change (see Chapter 7). In certain operations where the scale of capital was large the single owner-occupier might be inappropriate and control and operation of the enterprise might be vested in a more complicated structure. Even in industries where relatively small amounts of capital ensured ease of entry, the firm, in terms of control, might and did take the form of a partnership.[5] Nevertheless the single proprietor tended to be the most characteristic form of control. Of the 90 cotton factory firms operating in Manchester in 1815, 27 operated as partnerships and the remainder were single proprietors. Certainly the foremost manufacturing industry of the Industrial Revolution was characterised by a large number of small and medium-sized firms and this structure was by no means untypical of industry generally.[6] The success of the process we term the Industrial Revolution was in large part the result of individual initiative, and as the scale of business activity grew this involved a dynamic proliferation of those who became involved in the entrepreneurial function. The reconstruction of Manchester's business system has demonstrated the breadth of business activity at the very centre of the process. The typical business unit tended to be largely independent of external sources of capital and consequently of the social groups that controlled such funds.[7] Growth was generated by the process of reinvested profits and it was the need of working capital rather than fixed capital which more than probably taxed the acumen of the entrepreneur.[8] Survival could well depend on the successful insertion of the firm in the circuit of short-term credit[9] and accounts for the concern displayed by the Manchester business community over such issues as local bank notes, the stamp duty on small inland bills of exchange and the rules of bankruptcy (see Chapter 8). Industrial structure was composed of large numbers of small and medium-sized firms and it follows that one of the main structural features of the Industrial Revolution was that of a highly decentralised economic system.[10] At the same time the firms making up that system were not separate atomised units, each making their decisions in splendid isolation; rather they were part of a business system, which as we have seen in the various chapters, mediated the relationships between business units and imposed broad structural patterns on the mode of business change. We saw, for example, in Chapter 5 the attempt by the manufacturing interest to impose barriers to the growth of factory firms, and thus if we are to explore the behaviour of the specific units to which decisions are delegated we need always to keep in mind the particular business structure in which they operate. This caveat is important for it may help shape our choice of the appropriate theoretical perspective; that is, in order to proceed with our study of the business unit we require some kind of theory of the firm.[11] But what theory should the business historian select? There is an embarrassment of choice. Certainly there is more than one theory of the firm, in fact, there are a multitude of theories.[12] These range from standard neo-classical profit maximisation models, to managerial and behavioural theories, through to radical and neo-Marxian models.[13] Whilst there is a proliferation of theories, clearly the dominant framework informing the general work in economic and business history in recent years has been the neo-classical system.[14] Let us turn first to the neo-classical approach in the search for an appropriate analytical framework.

Richard Jones[15] has argued that the concept of the firm

employed in neo-classical or received theory tends to abstract from most of the characteristics of the real world firm. The role of the firm 'is to convert inputs into outputs and the firm is envisaged as an accounting point at which transactions occur'.[16] Four basic assumptions define the concept of firm in received theory: (a) the sole objective of the firms' activities is to maximise profits; (b) progress towards this goal is made by the manipulation of perfectly known and given cost and revenue functions; (c) the external environment is taken as given; (d) there is perfect knowledge.[17] These assumptions stretch the credulity of the business historian. We have argued throughout this book for the necessity of specifying the business system in which the firm operates, that is the external environment needs to be reconstructed rather than given. The assumption of perfect knowledge also poses major problems for the historian. A basic condition of human societies, never mind capitalist economies, is the uncertainty of future outcomes. As Joan Robinson puts it,

> In reality today is a break in time. Yesterday lies in the past, and has ceased to be relevant to what happens today, except insofar as experience of it colours expectations about what happens next. Tomorrow lies in the future and cannot be known.[18]

The perfect knowledge assumption freezes time and locates analysis in a static set of conditions. It is important to note that this view abstracts from a synchronic approach, for the firm in received theory remains an atomised unit and the interrelationships between firms are not specified, whereas a synchronic perspective seeks to identify the causal interconnections between systems components.[19] Radical writers have attacked the static assumptions of received theory suggesting that the neo-classical system underpinning it has tended to elevate the capitalist system to a natural universal system. Hunt and Schwartz have argued that 'radicals, perceiving at a glance that something is missing — namely private property, capitalists, workers — have tended to regard the whole of neo-classical theory as an apologetic'.[20] The neo-classical firm is a disembodied creature which ghost-like fabricates inputs into outputs. It has no correspondence to the real firm of the historically concrete. But in an important sense the radical critique misses the point. The received theory of the firm does not attempt to disguise its basic assumptions, on the contrary, they are clearly and unambiguously stated. As Machlup puts it, the theory is not 'designed to explain and predict the behaviour of real firms, instead it is designed to explain and predict changes observed in prices . . . as effects of particular changes in conditions'.[21] If theorists, be they economists or historians, are concerned with the set of objectives outlined by Machlup, received theory is a perfectly acceptable framework of analysis. On the other hand for the business historian, concerned with the structure of firm interrelationships at a given moment of time, and the growth and development of the firm over time, received theory, as an analytical framework, is inappropriate.

THE THEORY OF BUSINESS STRATEGY

As an alternative line of approach the theory of business strategy, developed by Scott Moss,[22] will be explored and utilised. The value of Moss's framework, to the business historian, is that he specifically makes the case for firm theory to be located within an historical context.[23] The antecedents of his theory are to be found in the works of Penrose, Chandler and Andrews. These works are linked, according to Moss, because of

> their common concern with the growth and development of actual firms and markets — their concern in other words with history and the historical process by which business as an activity and as a collection of institutions grows, develops and perhaps decays.[24]

This perspective allows the exploration of business, 'in all its ramifications'; that is it takes up Roy Church's approach to business history, outlined in Chapter 1. Moss identifies, as the key role of the economic theory of business strategy, the need to demonstrate 'the broad forces which constrain firms and which create business opportunities'.[25] The firm is defined as a collection of productive resources, physical and human, and these resources in turn will determine the range of activities undertaken by the firm. For example, such physical resources as the firm's plant and equipment 'determine the technology it employs, the commodities it produces and the inputs required to produce them'.[26] This is consistent with the notion of property asset, for, as was shown in Chapter 2, the form of property asset adopted will shape the pattern of business activity, and its utilisation, for example, allows for the distinction between factory firm and warehouse firm. For the property asset to be effectively utilised the firm requires the usage of human resources, that is the firm must include workers with skills[27] and temperament which are appropriate to the working of its plant and equipment. Again this mirrors our earlier contention that labour controls and technology are synchronic properties of the factory firm.[28]

The combination of the firm's physical and human resources requires, for the purpose of co-ordination, a central unifying principle which for Moss takes the form of the organisational structure. As Moss states:

> As a matter of practice, the various resources comprising the firm cannot be coordinated without an organisational structure delineating responsibilities for particular kinds of decisions and the nature and direction of various information flows. Thus, for both practical and logical reasons, we require to specify the organisational structure as a distinct part of the definition of the firm, for the organisational structure is not itself a resource but rather derives from the services which are rendered by the human and physical resources of the firm.[29]

Applying Moss's framework, it might be considered that the organisational structure of the typical cotton firm was relatively simplistic, in many cases as we have shown, identical to that of the single proprietor. Yet on reflection there was nothing simple about the organisational demands placed on the firm. The cotton factory firm, after all, was the basic business unit of the world's first mechanised industry and was required, if it was to survive and prosper, to train and control a mass labour force appropriate to the needs of machine technology. Such a task called for considerable organisational innovation which, in the spinning factory, often took the form of sub-contracting where the adult operative spinner was frequently the task and paymaster.[30] As Landes has recently pointed out the adult spinner was also a boss taking his 'share of surplus product'.[31] Such organisational modes were adopted by factory firm masters because, 'it was obviously worth it to them to shift the responsibility for much of the hiring and firing, as well as the bulk of the supervision to others'.[32] What the sub-contracting system reflected was 'the inability of centralised management to extract "full" labour for wages',[33] and is a reminder of the mystification of factory work, which, as we saw in Chapter 5, warehouse capitalists such as Nathanial Gould laboured under. In addition to the complexities of its human resource management, the cotton firm was obliged to import its major input, raw cotton, from across the Atlantic and therefore was inserted into a sophisticated supply system. Its final product was frequently marketed on an international scale (note the agitation concerning the exportation of yarn in Chapter 5 and the call for freer trade, Chapter 8) and consequently required specialist support and market information.[34] Such organisational complexities help to explain, on the one hand the proliferation of different types of specialist firms,[35] and on the other the problem of the political economy of firm development, witnessed by the struggle between the factory and the warehouse over the control of the industry's resources. The mediation of that struggle, resulting in the convergence of the warehouse and the factory, increased the degree of organisational complexity of the cotton firm.

Moving from this preliminary outline of Moss's theory to a more direct exploration of the process of business strategy we will now examine its impact on firm behaviour in the 1820s and 1830s, that is, during Berg's decades of 'rapid economic and technical transformation'. Competitive conditions in the 1820s and 1830s imposed severe constraints on profit-seeking entrepreneurs. While the number of firms in the cotton industry grew rapidly there was a high turnover of business units.[36] Margins were driven down and a substantial number of firms failed the test of the competitive struggle and left the industry. As Chapman has pointed out, 'after 1825 there can be little doubt, in the industrial north, spinners', manufacturers', merchants' and shippers' profit margins were equally under pressure'.[37] Margins in the cotton trade were highly sensitive to movements in raw cotton prices as well as influenced by changes in the level of productive capacity. The former factor could, and did, cause severe short-term fluctuations[38] while the latter was more a long-term process of supply outstripping effective demand as markets failed to absorb rapidly rising output.[39] It is difficult to gauge the magnitude of the fall in margins as the available empirical data tends to be fragmentary or too general for specific use. One approach which may offer us some idea of the direction of movement in the margin is to take a firm operating the best practice technique and assume that while upward movements in its margins would probably run ahead of the general trend, downward movements would be unlikely to exaggerate and indeed probably understate the general fall. The firm chosen is one referred to earlier in the text, J. Massey and Sons of Manchester.[40] Already established as cotton agents and handloom manufacturers before the early 1820s, this enterprise entered the cotton spinning business in 1825 erecting a new mill at a cost of £20,000.00 and filled its factory 'with the best constructed machinery'.[41] One of the firm's partners, George Smith, testifying before the 1833 Select Committee on Manufactures estimated that between 1825 and 1833 the margin on 30 water twist had fallen by 36 per cent; on four cut warp by 29 per cent and on printed calicoes by 24 per cent.[42] If Massey's firm experienced such a fall in margins then firms with older and less efficient plant must have been operating under considerable competitive pressure. Indeed, of the 82 cotton firms listed in the Manchester Rate Books for 1825, 36 had left the industry by 1831, a fall of 44 per cent.[43] Yet in terms of output the industry did not contract. On the contrary, Matthews has claimed that while the aggregate value of the cotton industry's output, between 1825 and 1834, 'showed a mild upward trend of rather less than one per cent per annum', in terms of volume 'output by 1827 had far surpassed that of the boom year of 1825'.[44] New firms were not deterred from entering the industry and added to the increased competitive pressures which combined rapidly rising output with falling prices.[45] As Farnie has observed,

> The ranks of employers were swelled during each successive phase of expansion by a new influx of recruits with limited means and were then decimated during the subsequent depression, so creating a market in second-hand machinery, facilitating entry by new aspirants and exposing the trade to repeated bouts of over-production and underselling.[46]

Not surprisingly firm population structure in the 1820s was highly volatile with high exit and entry rates, yet there was also an underlying trend which, as Lloyd-Jones and Le Roux have shown, shifted the profile of industrial structure away from the small and large firm towards the medium-sized unit, i.e. a firm employing between 151 and 500 operatives.[47] These shifts in firm size are closely connected to the competitive process, and we might well explore these developments by conceptualising two broad areas of response which Moss would recognise as providing a basic understanding of the behaviour of firms under competitive conditions.

According to Moss, growing competitive pressures will lead first of all to changes in the constraints under which firms operate in the short run. That is conceptually it leads to 'problems, which arise in the day-to-day operation of the firm and which cannot be handled within the routine procedures adopted for those operations'.[48] Constraint changes may be associated with changes in input supply, increasing pressure on existing plant and equipment, or on the existing administrative structure of the firm. Secondly, increasing competition is associated with uncertainty. Uncertainty may be conceptualised as partly subjective — what Penrose has called temperament and Keynes, 'animal spirits' — and partly objective, in the sense we are objectively ignorant of the future. 'Lack of information about the present increases one's feeling of ignorance about the future and one's temperament, or "animal spirits", or nervous energy will determine the extent to which such ignorance predisposes one to inaction'.[49] Summarising Moss's two response mechanisms, it would appear that on the one hand competitive pressures increase the constraints on day-to-day operations, which stimulate the need for decisive action if the firm is to survive, and on the other hand growing uncertainty may engender a mood of excessive caution and entrenched conservatism in relation to change. What was the outcome in the cotton industry? The competitive pressures of the 1820s and 1830s triggered a set of changes by cotton firms which were vigorous, far-reaching and suggestive of a dynamic business strategy. Three sets of broad changes may be identified: market expansion, resource development and structural change.

Commenting on the post-1815 cotton trade, Chapman refers to 'A large and constantly changing body of entrepreneurs trying to sell increasing quantities to more distant and dispersed markets'.[50] By 1829 Latin America had overtaken Europe as a market for British piece goods and by 1840 had reached its peak of relative importance as an absorber of British manufactured cottons.[51] Unfortunately Lancashire's 'production of textile goods outpaced the capacity of domestic and overseas markets to absorb them, especially in the second quarter of the nineteenth century'.[52] As the *Manchester Gazette* informed the business community in 1829, 'you can sell neither cloth nor twist at any price that will cover your expenses . . . you cannot make profits; you cannot save yourself from loss. Your eyes are wandering over the map of the world for new markets.'[53] Such a state of affairs underpinned the growing demand for trade deregulation: a policy area which was explored in Chapter 8 and one taken up with increasing vigour in Manchester from the mid-1820s. As the German historian of the Lancashire cotton industry, Schulze-Gaevernitz, put it, the cotton manufacturers of Lancashire fought the Corn Laws in the first instance in the interest of exports.[54] The objective was to stimulate foreign incomes via the export of grain to Britain with the expectation that a portion of that enhanced income would be spent on British cotton textile products.[55] Alongside this long-term strategy Lancashire entrepreneurs also sought to penetrate foreign markets by increasing cost efficiency and thus lowering export prices. Paradoxically this had the effect of rapidly increasing output and thus intensifying the competitive pressures. This policy is related to the second main area of response, resource development.

Firm resource development in the 1820s and 1830s may be sub-divided into three categories. Firstly, the development of the firm's physical resources was associated with rapid rises in productivity. Schulze-Gaevernitz estimates that on no 40 yarn (the commonest number spun) the number of hanks spun per spindle per day rose from 2 in 1820 to 2.75/3.00 in 1830 and further increased to 3.73/4.12 in 1834.[56] The main factor underlying this doubling of productivity inside 15 years was not a major innovational breakthrough[57] but a set of sub-innovatory techniques in preparatory and spinning activity. Probably the most significant sub-innovation was the increase in the number of spindles per mule, or long mule (or sometimes long wheel) as it was known. The increasing diffusion of the long mule during the 1820s is referred to by the Webbs,[58] Schulze-Gaevernitz,[59] S. J. Chapman,[60] Musson and Kirby[61] and Blaug.[62] While at the beginning of the 1820s, 300 spindles per mule was the upper limit, by 1832 some of the more progressive Manchester firms were operating mules of 600 spindles[63] and Blaug claims that in the early 1830s the average number of spindles per mule was approximately 350 to 400.[64] Not all firms however adopted this sub-innovation and thus in terms of Moss's typology of competitive response some firms chose a policy of inaction rather than a dynamic business strategy. Kirkby and Musson point to technically progressive firms introducing long mules after 1826, but they also refer to small-wheel manufacturers resisting change and persisting with their existing vintage mules.[65] In the late 1820s and early 1830s there is good evidence to suggest collusion between small-wheel manufacturers and operative spinners in order to inhibit the rapid diffusion of the long mule. John Doherty, the spinners' leader in Manchester, argued in 1830 that,

> it was to the advantage of employers with old fashioned machinery . . . to oppose all discounts, or all increased discounts, on the newest machines, or otherwise their markets would be secured by new men, or by masters renewing old machinery who would natually buy the latest wheels.[66]

According to S. J. Chapman, these 'views were undoubtedly accepted by numerous employers'.[67] Small-wheel masters gave support to strikers facing piece rate reductions introduced by progressive masters in 1826[68] and in 1830, 'some spinners at Hyde had combined with the men against an individual employer on the machinery question'.[69] In 1830 Nassau Senior, in his report to the Commission inquiring into the need for a new Combination Law, asserted that 'combinations enabled rival manufacturers to oppose their competitors by fomenting resistance to lower piece work rates which the best machinery rendered equitable, and that in consequence the motive to increase speed and methods was extinguished'.[70] This is of course an exaggeration; the operative spinner's fight, against piece rate reductions brought by the long mule, had crumbled by the early 1830s, as had the resistance of the small-wheel men to the rapid diffusion of the long mule.[71] This victory of the more progressive elements associated with a dynamic business strategy increased the pressure on the second resource category, the firm's human resources. The main change here was a concerted attempt to drive down piece rates and thus reduce labour costs. Large-wheel masters quickly attempted to implement lower piece rates on their improved machines and not surprisingly long mules were at the centre of most labour disputes in the second half of the 1820s and early 1830s.[72] Overall piece rates were driven down, but not content with this success masters sought to further lower labour costs by substituting female and adolescent labour for that of adult males. In the first issue of the *United Trades Cooperative Journal* on 6 March 1830 an adult male spinner complained that he had lost his job earning 25s to 30s per week to a female spinner, who would be paid only half that amount. John Doherty commented 'that this practice was harmful both to the females, who must perform fatiguing labour . . . and also to the workmen who were thereby supplanted'.[73] At a general meeting of Manchester fine spinners in April 1830 the chief complaint was that, 'several members of the employers association had adopted the practice of employing boy and women spinners in the place of men . . . at a reduction of from five to ten hanks in the lb'.[74] That such developments alarmed the operative mule spinners and led leaders such as Doherty to complain that the 'natural roles of males and females were being reversed to suit the avarice of greedy employers',[75] there is little doubt. Yet this trend, too, can be easily exaggerated. It has already been commented upon that the sub-contracting system in the spinning factory placed a constraint on managerial control and therefore limited the extent to which employers could force through labour substitution policies. As Lazonick has argued, 'For the mule spinner . . . the sub-contracting system had the advantage of permitting him to maintain within the context of factory production, a significant degree of control over division of labour on his mule'.[76] Female mule spinners never became widespread.[77] In 1833 a survey of 151 Lancashire cotton factories was compiled by a Manchester accountant, S. Stanway, for the Factory Commissioners and his returns showed that of the total number of spinners employed only 22.8 per cent were female.[78] Although during the 1830s and 1840s, 'a higher proportion of women were employed as minders (on the self-acting mule) than had been . . . employed on common mules . . . the vast majority of self-acting minders . . . were males entering adulthood'.[79] There were therefore constraints on the employers' ability to shift the composition of the labour force in the direction of lower labour costs. Consequently employers sought alternative policies.

A third category associated with firm resource development concerned a more intensive use of both physical and human resources. This involved more effective use of raw materials, increased spinning efficiency, the use of waste as a by-product and the increased utilisation of existing plant and labour via long hours of work, night work, etc. Most of these changes were summarised by Schelze-Gaevernitz, nearly a century ago, when he claimed that the pressure of competition had

> taught the spinner to use raw materials to a greater extent than before, to spin equally good yarn from poorer cotton by improved preparatory machinery, to lessen the loss during spinning and to utilise the waste itself for lower qualities of yarn.[80]

Quite naturally this greater intensity of plant use had important implications for the human resources of the firm. In February 1830 approximately 140 master spinners and power-loom weavers met in Manchester to discuss the state of the cotton trade.[81] The main item on the agenda was the squeeze on profit margins and the main proposal advocated to counteract this was a call for a cut in wages. C. Hindley, a Dukinfield cotton master, put the majority view when he stated, 'All capital was invested for the sake of profit, and if it did not yield that, the spinners must either stop their mills, or lower the rate of wage'.[82] Not all employers accepted this policy and underlying their objection was their disquiet with the increased intensity of labour utilisation. Rejecting the option of wage cuts masters such as George Chapell and Aron Lees argued for short-time working. Thomas Harbottle, the Manchester spinner and manufacturer, also favoured output restriction but he took the argument further. He claimed that there was a great disproportion of time worked in different mills and declared himself to be, 'almost ashamed to be connected with the cotton masters, on account of the long hours they worked their hands'.[83] Such was the problem of the over intense use of plant and labour for Harbottle that he called for parliamentary intervention to restrict the hours of labour to 12 hours per day (6 am to 6 pm). He admitted his proposals were long term and in the immediate situation he suggested a signed agreement whereby manufacturers would pledge themselves to restrict work to daylight only. This attack on the system of night work received scant support, and the *Manchester Mercury* reported that the proposed 'agreement gained little support from the floor and at the close only 20 manufacturers had signed'.[84] Undeterred by this set-back, Harbottle, with the support of Chapell and Lees, lobbied the Manchester Chamber of Commerce arguing that long hours of work and the persistence of night working were the underlying causes of overproduction and overstocked markets.[85] George Chapell, at a Chamber meeting, called for the restriction of night work but he received little support. These attempts to restrict the more intensive use of the firm's human resources echo the arguments of Nathanial Gould 15 years earlier,[86] except they were no longer dressed up in a moral rhetoric. The paradox of more intensive use of plant and labour and the problems of overproduction were clearly recognised by entrepreneurs such as Harbottle but they were unable to persuade the bulk of the employers that it was in the long-term interest of the trade to forego strategies of increased labour intensity. In any case proposals to handle the problems of competitive pressure and overproduction by limiting the hours of work ran against the major structural change which had been set in train during the 1820s. This is the final response category and it involves a new type of cotton firm created by the process of vertical linkages.[87] This was the integrated spinning and weaving firm often referred to as the combined firm.

It was argued in Chapters 7 and 8 that the process of convergence involved both hand and power-loom production being increasingly integrated with factory spinning. Matthews, for example, claims that the installation of power weaving equipment by cotton firms, 'was probably the most important form of investment undertaken by the industry between 1825 and 1834'.[88] This trend towards vertical integration is closely associated with the rise of the medium-sized firm noted earlier and is also an important factor in the process of increased plant utilisation. A significantly higher proportion of vertically integrated firms were medium sized compared with single-process spinners (fine or coarse spinners) and power-loom weaving only firms. In 1841, 72.2 per cent of all combined-process firms employed between 151 and 500 operatives while 43.3 per cent of single-process coarse spinners employed less than 150 operatives[89] (small size). If the typical firm was a medium-sized unit, employing between 151 and 500 operatives, the typical medium-sized firm was a combined spinning and weaving concern. What is the link between the vertically integrated unit, medium size and capacity utilisation? Moss has outlined a basic framework which appears to fit the cotton industry of the 1820s and 1830s. He states as follows:

> In those industries in which technical change had led to highly mechanised production, the capital and running costs of the plant and equipment embodying those techniques have resulted in very high operating leverages which to be profitable require that plant and equipment must be operated at, or very close to, full capacity. If the firm which is investing in high fixed cost plant and equipment is doing so in order to grow, then its management team would do well to consider incorporating vertical integration in its growth strategy in order to reduce the uncertainties attaching to that strategy and thereby to render less vulnerable the survival of the firm.[90]

Quite clearly from the middle of the 1820s vertical integration and greater plant utilisation[91] was a growth path followed by cotton firms. Nevertheless there were restraints operating on this strategy which tended to limit firms to the medium-size category. That is industrial structure did not become dominated by a few giant integrated firms. Essentially we can point to two factors which shaped business strategy in limiting firms to medium size: the market and management. Market pressures led to a greatly intensified use of plant, long hours of work, and night working but this in turn acted to increase output and further exacerbate market pressures. The result was falling prices and a squeeze on margins; in this situation, coupled with the absence of convincing technical economies of scale,[92] there was little premium in embarking on an expansion programme which pushed the firms beyond medium size. Between 1815 and 1841 the share of large cotton firms in Manchester's total factory labour force fell from 44.24 per cent to 31.68 per cent while the corresponding share of medium firms rose from 27.3 per cent to 55.8 per cent.[93] Further, while market pressures did encourage a more intensive use of the firms' physical resources at the same time there were a group of organisational parameters which acted to constrain growth. These parameters have been referred to as the 'Penrose effect'[94] and therefore takes us to the antecedents of Moss's theory of business strategy. The 'Penrose effect' is associated with the idea that growth requires preparation and consolidation and therefore is subject to some upper limit over a long period of time. That is there is some mechanism which 'causes a fast growing firm in one period to slow down in the next'.[95] Growth requires 'surplus resources or new resources, management awareness and the willingness of management to accept risks'.[96] T. Y. Shen has maintained that these requirements are least likely to be fulfilled after a plant has just expanded considerably; or as he puts it more technically 'in profit calculation terms, there exist a collection of friction costs related to various rates of growth and this functional relationship shifts upwards for plants that have temporarily strained their growth resources'.[97] In the context of the cotton industry it may well have been the case that combined spinning and weaving firms, which as we have seen, expanded rapidly in numbers from the 1820s,[98] had by the beginning of the third decade of the nineteenth century began to experience friction costs associated with rapid growth. Combined units as was shown above tended to be larger firms than single-process units, and while the decision to combine both processes may have aided profitability, it increased organisational complexity and demanded greater management skills and awareness. It may well have been the case that available management resources acted to restrain growth beyond a given size. Pollard, for example, refers to the absence of a strongly professional group among cotton spinners and points out that it was not until 1835 that the first guide book on cotton factory management, including technical and managerial advice, was published. He further adds that 'even in the 1820s and 1830s the youthfulness of many of the managers of the largest [cotton] mills was striking'.[99] A hiatus in firm growth would be an appropriate response for at this point the firm was exposed to a central weakness as the limited supply of managerial talent dovetailed with the restraint placed on the supervisory controls exercised by central management. As we have seen, a sub-contracting system, organised by the adult operative spinner, remained at the core of factory activity. This placed a structural constraint on the degree to which management could fully implement its policy of plant integration[100] and consequently tended to limit combined firms to the medium-sized range. Thus in terms of firm size and strategy a focal point is the struggle for the control and effective management of human resources. Cotton 'Lords' were not feudal barons any more than spinners were serfs. Moss's approach, emphasising the firm as a collectivity of both physical and human resources, allows the development of a political economy which moves beyond a simplistic labour-capital confrontation. The pattern of relationships inside the factory firm was no less complex than the set of relationships outside, i.e. to the overall business system. Those contemporaries who espoused the inhumanity of the factory were just as one-dimensional as those visitors who came to Manchester to gaze at the smoke-stacks and factories of Ancoats and thought they had seen all the secrets of Cottonopolis.

NOTES AND REFERENCES

1. Perhaps the most extreme examples of this form of approach are to be found in the writings of the neo-Marxists such as Robert Bremner and I. Wallerstein. See for example I. Wallerstein *The Capitalist World Economy* (Cambridge University Press, Cambridge, 1979).
2. W. W. Rostow, *The Stages of Economic Growth* (Cambridge University Press, Cambridge, 1960), pp. 31–5, 139–42, 189–99. For a recent overview of the Rostowian system see C. P. Kindleberger and G. di Tella (eds), *Economics in the Long View, Essays in Honour of W. W. Rostow*, vol. 1., *Models and Methodology* (Macmillan, London, 1982).
3. See particularly R. Samuel, 'The Workshop of the World: Steam Power and Hand Technology in mid-Victorian Britain', *History Workshop*, issue 3, Spring (1977).
4. Maxine Berg, *The Machinery Question and the Making of Political Economy 1815–1848* (Cambridge University Press, Cambridge, 1980), p. 21.
5. Often the requirement of a particular type of expertise necessitated an entrepreneur taking on a partner. See Chapters 6 and 9.
6. Berg, *Machinery*, p. 27.
7. See Peter Mathias, *The Transformation of England, Essays in the Economic and Social History of England in the Eighteenth Century* (Methuen, London, 1979), p. 92.
8. See M. M. Edwards, *The growth of the British Cotton Trade 1780–1815* (Manchester University Press, Manchester, 1967), p. 215.
9. P. L. Cottrell, *Industrial Finance 1830–1914: The Finance and Organisation of English Manufacturing Industry* (Methuen, London, 1980), p. 33.
10. As Farnie has observed, 'The representative unit of enterprise in the cotton industry was the small rather than the large firm and the representative employer was a yeoman of industry rather than a captain of industry'. D. A. Farnie, *The English Cotton Industry and the World Market 1815–1896* (Oxford University Press, Oxford, 1979), p. 209.
11. R. Marris 'Why Economics needs a Theory of the Firm', *Economic Journal*, vol. 82 (1972).
12. M. C. Sawyer *Theories of the Firm* (Weidenfeld and Nicolson, London, 1979), p. 3.
13. For an outline of Marxist models of the firm see J. Steindl, *Maturity and Stagnation in American Capital* (Blackwell, Oxford, 1952), and D. P. Levine, *Contributions to the Critique of Economic Theory* (Routledge and Kegan Paul, London, 1977), pp. 130–2,

137–40, 253–4, 256–7, 260–4. For perhaps the clearest outline of the neo-classical approach see George J. Stigler, *The Organisation of Industry* (Richard D. Irwin, Homewood, Illinois, 1968), especially Part II, chs. 6 to 11, and part II, chs. 12 to 19.

14. Neo-classical theory has had a major influence on the so-called New Economic History, indeed it might be better referred to as the New Neo-Classical Economic History. See for example the influence of the neo-classical approach in a recent major text-book. R. Floud and D. N. McCloskey (eds), *The Economic History of Britain Since 1700*, vols. 1 and 2 (Cambridge University Press, Cambridge, 1981).

15. R. Jones, *Supply in a Market Economy* (George Allen and Unwin, London, 1976).

16. Ibid., p. 22.

17. Ibid., p. 23.

18. Joan Robinson, *The Accumulation of Capital* (Macmillan, London, 1956), p. 181.

19. For the distinction between static and synchronic approaches in economics see Chapter 2.

20. E. K. Hunt and Jesse G. Schwartz (eds), *A Critique of Economic Theory* (Penguin Educational, Harmondsworth, 1972), p. 17.

21. Quoted in Sawyer, *Firm*, p. 5.

22. Scott J. Moss, *An Economic Theory of Business Strategy. An Essay in Dynamics Without Equilibrium* (Martin Robinson, Oxford, 1981).

23. Ibid., p. 13.

24. Ibid., p. 13.

25. Ibid., p. 14.

26. Ibid., p. 17.

27. For the importance of workers' skills see Chapter 9.

28. See Chapter 2.

29. Moss, *Business Strategy*, pp. 17–18.

30. See M. M. Edwards and R. Lloyd-Jones, 'N. J. Smelser and the cotton factory family: a reassessment', in N. B. Harte and K. G. Ponting (eds), *Textile History and Economic History, Essays in Honour of Miss Julia de Lacy Mann* (Manchester University Press, Manchester, 1973).

31. D. S. Landes 'What Do Bossess Really Do?', *Journal of Economic History*, vol. XLVI, no. 3 (1986), p. 610.

32. Ibid., p. 610.

33. Ibid., p. 610. See also W. Lazonick, 'Industrial Relations and Technical Change: The Case of the Self Acting Mule', *Cambridge Journal of Economics*, iii (1979), p. 223.

34. See Farnie, *English Cotton Industry*, especially chs. 1 and 3.

35. For example in Chapter 7 we showed 21 different types of combinations of warehouse manufacturing and dealing firms. For an overview of the different types of specialisms see the trade directories of the period, especially Pigot's.

36. R. Lloyd-Jones and A. A. Le Roux, 'Marshall and the Birth and Death of Firms: The Growth and Size Distribution of Firms in the Early Nineteenth-Century Cotton Industry', *Business History*,

vol. XXIV, no. 2 (1982).

37. S. D. Chapman, 'Financial Restraints on the Growth of Firms in the Cotton Industry, 1790–1850', *Economic History Review*, vol. XXXII, no. 1 (1979), pp. 61–2.

38. For example, rapidly rising raw cotton prices, early in 1830, led to a meeting in February of that year of master spinners and power-loom weavers in Manchester to discuss the fall in margins. The outcome of the meeting was a call for wage reductions to offset rising raw cotton prices. See *Manchester Mercury*, 2 February 1830.

39. Chapman claims that all cotton firms *c.* 1815–50 'suffered at one time or another from glutted markets and hence slow returns'. Chapman, 'Financial Restraints', p. 64.

40. This firm is explored in Chapters 7 and 8.

41. Evidence of George Smith, a partner in the firm, before the *Select Committee on the Present State of Manufacturers, Commerce and Shipping in the UK*, P.P. 1833 (690), VI, p. 129.

42. Ibid., p. 129.

43. Figures calculated from Manchester rate books of 1825 and 1831. A list of all factory firms in Manchester between 1807 and 1841 is available on computer data bank at Sheffield City Polytechnic.

44. R. C. O. Matthews, *A Study in Trade Cycle History: Economic Fluctuations in Great Briatain 1833–1842* (Cambridge University Press, Cambridge, 1954), p. 130.

45. For the role of entry firms in this period see Lloyd-Jones and Le Roux, 'Marshall and the Birth and Death of Firms', pp. 148–50, and R. Lloyd-Jones and A. A. Le Roux, 'Factory Utilisation and the Firm: the Manchester Cotton Industry *c.* 1825–40', *Textile History*, vol. 15, no. 1 (1984), pp. 119–20.

46. Farnie, *English Cotton Industry*, p. 210.

47. R. Lloyd-Jones and A. A. Le Roux, 'The Size of Firms in the Cotton Industry: Manchester, 1815–41, *Economic History Review*, vol. XXXIII, no. 1 (1980), pp. 74–80.

48. Moss, *Business Strategy*, p. 38.

49. Ibid., p. 32.

50. Chapman, 'Financial Restraints', p. 50.

51. Farnie, *English Cotton Industry*, p. 93.

52. Chapman, 'Financial Restraints', p. 55.

53. Quoted in Chapman, 'Financial Restraints', p. 56.

54. G. von Schulze-Gaevernitz, *The Cotton Trade in England and on the Continent* (Simpkin, Marshall, Hamilton, Kent and Co, London, 1895), p. 58.

55. For an outline of this strategy see P. J. Cain and A. Hopkins, 'The Political Economy of British Overseas Expansion', *Economic History Review*, vol. XXXIII, no. 4 (1980).

56. Schulze-Gaevernitz, *Cotton Trade*, p. 42.

57. These shifts in productivity pre-date the diffusion of the self-acting mule.

58. Webb MSS., vol. XXXIV (London School of Economic).

59. Schulze-Gaevernitz, *Cotton Trade*, p. 42.

60. S. J. Chapman, *The Lancashire Cotton Industry* (Manchester

University Press, Manchester, 1904), pp. 78–80.

61. R. G. Kirby and A. E. Musson, *The Voice of the People, John Doherty, 1798–1854* (Manchester University Press, Manchester, 1975), pp. 28, 29, 43, 100, 109.

62. M. Blaug, 'The Productivity of Capital in the Lancashire Cotton Industry During the 19th Century', *Economic History Review*, vol. XIII, no. 3 (1960–1), p. 366.

63. *Tables on the Revenue, Population, Commerce of the United Kingdon*, 1820–1833. P.P., no. 300, (46), p. 406.

64. Blaug, 'Productivity of Capital', p. 366.

65. Kirby and Musson, *Voice of the People*, p. 43.

66. Quoted in Chapman, *Lancashire Cotton*, p. 80.

67. Ibid., p. 80.

68. Kirby and Musson, *Voice of the People*, p. 43.

69. Chapman, *Lancashire Cotton*, p. 30. Chapman also refers to a 'joint committee of employers and men being formed in 1831', which was in fact a conspiracy on the part of the small wheel masters and the men against the possessors of large wheels, p. 80.

70. Quoted in Chapman, *Lancashire Cotton*, p. 80.

71. See Kirby and Musson, *Voice of the People*, pp. 100–9.

72. Ibid., pp. 28–9.

73. Quoted in ibid., p. 109.

74. Ibid., p. 109.

75. Ibid., p. 109.

76. Lazonick, 'Industrial Relations', p. 233.

77. There was a greater proportion of women spinning on throstles in the 1830s compared with the hand mule. The throstle, used for spinning low counts (i.e. coarse yarn), was an improved version of the water frame. The throstle was driven by steam but the yarn produced was still called water twist. For a survey of the technology of throstle spinning see E. Leigh, *The Science of Modern Cotton Spinning*, vol. 11 (Palmer and Howe, Manchester, 1873), p. 207.

78. *Supplementary Reports of Factory Commissioners*, P.P. (XIX), pp. D[1] 124–125.

79. Lazonick, 'Industrial Relations', p. 238.

80. Schulze-Gaevernitz, *Cotton Trade*, p. 41.

81. *Manchester Mercury*, 2 February 1830.

82. Ibid.

83. Ibid.

84. Ibid.

85. Proceedings of the Manchester Chamber of Commerce and Manufacturers, 24 February 1830 (Manchester Central Library).

86. See Chapter 5.

87. For an examination of the process of vertical linkage which suggests a more widespread linkage than the Manchester data shows, see J. Lyons, 'Vertical Integration in the British Cotton Industry, 1825–1850', *Journal of Economic History*, vol. 45, no. 2 (1985). Our own data for Manchester, however, clearly shows a trend towards vertical linkage from the early 1820s rather than before. See Chapters 3 and 7.

88. Matthews, *Trade Cycle History*, p. 131.

89. Lloyd-Jones and Le Roux, 'The Size of Firms', p. 80. Power-loom weaving-only firms were smaller than single-process spinners. 85 per cent of this category employed less than 151 workers.

90. Moss, *Business Strategy*, p. 149.

91. Matthews, for example, argues that 'In the representative cotton mill of the period (1820s–1840s) overhead costs were so high in relation to prime costs that, however low the price of the product, it was in general bad policy to reduce output below the level of full capacity'. Matthews, *Trade Cycle History*, p. 130.

92. V. A. C. Gatrell, 'Labour, Power and the Size of Firms in Lancashire Cotton in the Second Quarter of the Nineteenth Century', *Economic History Review*, vol. XXX, no. 1 (1977), p. 97.

93. Lloyd-Jones and Le Roux, 'The Size of Firms', p. 76.

94. For a discussion of the 'Penrose effect' see T. Y. Shen, 'Economies of Scale, Penrose Effect, Growth of Plant and their Size Distribution', *Journal of Political Economy*, vol. 78 (1970), pp. 702–16. See also E. Penrose, *The Theory of the Growth of the Firm* (Basil Blackwell, Oxford, 1959), chs. 3, 9.

95. Shen, 'Penrose effect', p. 702.

96. Ibid., p. 709.

97. Ibid., p. 709.

98. There were only a handful of combined power firms in 1820. By the early 1830s they were beginning to outnumber single-process spinners. Ure, for example, outlines a list of 151 Lancashire firms for 1833, and 68 (the largest category) are combined units,. 62 single-process coarse spinners, 17 fine spinners and 4 power-loom weaving-only. A. Ure, The Cotton Manufacturers of Great Britatin (H. G. Bohn, London, 1861), vol. 1, pp. 390–9.

99. S. Pollard, *The Genesis of Modern Management* (Penguin, Harmondsworth, 1968), pp. 149–50.

100. For the wide variation in the pattern of integration of combined firms see Gatrell, 'Labour, Power', pp. 118–20.

Appendices

APPENDIX 1

Fifty-five Sub-categories of the General Industrial Classification

Code	Category
1:	Production/General[a]
1:1	Cotton Spinning Factories
1:2	Metal/Sector/Machines, Foundries and Smithies
1:3	Chemical Works, Dye Works, Calender Houses
1:4	Rope Works
1:5	Unspecified Works and Factories or Empty Factories
2	Building Trade: Construction
2:1	Joiners Shops
2:2	Saw Pits
2:3	Timber Yards
2:4	Brickworks and Yards
3	Food and Drink Processing
3:1	Distillers
3:2	Breweries
3:3	Cooperage
3:4	Bakehouse
3:5	Slaughterhouse
4	Retail/general
4:1	Shops
4:2	Stalls
5	Retail: Drink Trade/Hostelry
5:1	Public Houses and Inns
5:2	Vaults
5:3	Lodging Houses and Hotels
6	Wholesale/Distribution
6:1	Warehouses
6:2	Store Rooms
6:3	Store Cellars
6:4	Stables and Coach Houses Adjoining Warehouses
7	Finance/Commerce/Services
7:1	Offices
7:2	Counting Houses
7:3	Banks
8	Transport Services/Distribution
8:1	Canals, Locks and Appendages
8:2	Wharfs and Docks
8:3	Toll Gate of Market

Code	Category
9	Residential: Housing (Private)
9:1	Houses
9:2	Occupied Cellars
9:3	Stables Adjoining House
9:4	Gardens Adjoining House
9:5	Outhouses
10	Public Utilities/Leisure
10:1	Post Office
10:2	Public Offices and Buildings
10:3	Council Offices
10:4	Hospitals
10:5	Poor House
10:6	Waterworks
10:7	Schools
10:8	Public Gardens
10:9	Portico
10:10	Panorama
10:11	Assembly Rooms and Meeting Rooms
10:12	Libraries
10:13	Theatres
11	Extractive Industry
11:1	Coal Pits
12	Land and Agriculture
12:1	Land
12:2	Farms
12:3	Farmhouse and Barns
12:4	Cow Houses
12:5	Crofts
12:6	Agricultural Land and Fields
12:7	Stables Adjoining Farms

Note: a. The number of sub-categories in the *Textile History* article was originally 13, but since then our cross-referencing with the directory has enabled us to combine the property assets to form 5 distinct industrial activities.

Source: R. Lloyd-Jones and M. J. Lewis, 'The Economic Structure of Cottonopolis: Manchester in 1815', *Textile History*, vol. 17, no. 1 (1986), p. 84.

APPENDIX 2

Distribution of Manchester Warehouses by District, 1815, with a Description of their Business Activities

Rate district	No. warehouse units	Total RV (£)
1	—	—
2	7	154
3	82	2,278
4	15	1,311
5	151	7,336
6	663	29,750
7	5	190
8	73	2,673
9	421	20,402
10	7	618
11	17	942
12	90	3,374
13	24	1,453
14	22	3,146
Total	1,577	73,627

Districts

(1) Ancoats District, including districts of New Cross, Beswick and Holt Town. The largest factory district in the township, including the extensive cotton spinning factories of McConnel and Kennedy and A. & J. Murray (RV £933.00 and £924.00 respectively). This district also contained the largest concentration of housing and the only coal mine in Manchester, that of the Bradford Colliery Co (RV £280.00).

(2) St Michael's District, includes Shudehill and New Town. A newly developing area at this period.

(3) Collegiate Church District, including Strangeways, Manchester Cathedral and Exchange Areas. The medieval section of the town. The warehouses in this district were largely utilised for the warehousing of food, provisions and miscellaneous goods.

(4) St Clement's District. The second largest factory district in Manchester and the second largest concentration of housing. A number of large foundries were also situated in this district. Few warehouses were located here, but notably the large carriers warehouse of the Rochdale Canal Co (RV £600.00).

(5) St Paul's District. A centrally situated area merging into the central warehouse district. The warehouses in this district were concentrated on Church street and Upper High Street, and were mainly utilised for the warehousing of cotton goods (44 per cent of the identified warehouse units in this district being utilised for that purpose).

(6) Exchange District. The central warehouse district and the most important for the warehousing of cotton goods (68 per cent of the warehouse units in

district 6 being utilised for this purpose, and 55 per cent of all identified cotton warehouses were located in this district). The majority of calico printing warehouses were also situated here (64 per cent of all identified calico printing warehouses). The warehousing was highly concentrated in and around Cannon Street, Peel Street, Lower High Street and Marsden Square. The adjoining courts, notably Blue Boar Court and Abrahams Court, contained numerous outside manufacturers who rented warehouse space and operated in the Manchester market. This district also possessed the largest public houses and was an important retail centre with a number of large shops.

(7) Mynshul District. The fourth largest factory district in Manchester. Unimportant for warehousing in 1815, although there is a general movement of warehouses to this district after 1830.

(8) St James's District. On the perimeter of the central warehousing district, the warehouses being centred in and around George Street, Charlotte Street and Lower Fountain Street.

(9) St Anne's District. The second most important district for the warehousing of cotton goods (64 per cent of the identified warehouse units in district 9 being utilised for this purpose, and 32 per cent of all identified cotton warehouses were located here). This district was especially important for warehouse firms specifically dealing in cotton goods, providing a further indication of the geographical specialisation of activity within the township. Unlike district 6, the concentration of warehouses was more widely dispersed, although here again numerous outside manufacturers rented warehouses, notably in Ormrod's Court. Situated within the district were the residences of the business and professional men of the town (the average RV of houses in the district was £24.00, the highest for any Manchester district); and this was the commercial and administrative centre of the town, with banks, offices and the town hall located here.

(10) Oxford Street District. This district was largely concerned with the carriage of goods by water, with wharfs and dock yards and the large carriers warehouse of Thomas and Matthew Pickford (RV £350.00).

(11) St Peter's District. The third largest factory district and the third largest concentration of housing.

(12) St Mary's District. A wide range of warehousing activity in this district.

(13) Old Quay District. Mainly concerned with the inflow of goods from Salford.

(14) St John's District. This district contained the biggest warehouses in Manchester (those of the Old Quay Co and the Trustees of the Duke of Bridgewater, both rated at £800.00 each), and was particularly concerned with the transportation of goods by the Bridgewater Canal.

Source: See Lloyd-Jones and Lewis, 'Economic Structure', pp. 85–6.

Map: The township of Manchester in 1815, showing the rating districts and the number of warehouse units in each district

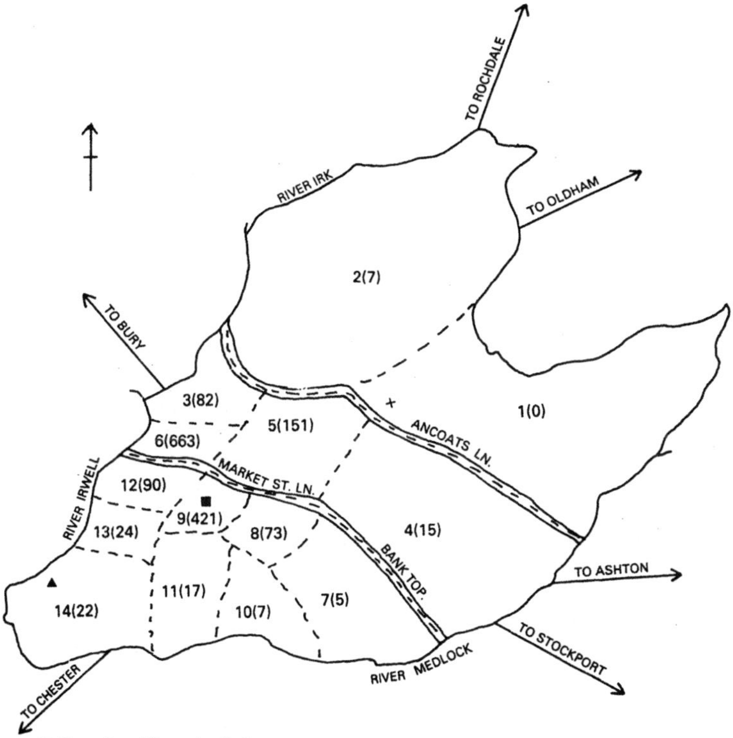

× = McConnell and Kennedys Factory
■ = Manchester Town Hall (Fountain St.)
▲ = Warehouse of the Duke of Bridgewater (Knott Mill and Castlefield)
---- Denotes the rating areas in 1815

APPENDIX 3

Thirty-two Manchester Warehouse Firms Specialising in Cotton Twist and Weft Dealing, 1815

Firm		RV £	Location
1	Thomas Milner & Co	220	2 Back Square
2	I. Withington	160	13 Back Square
3	G. Winter & Co	140	St Ann's Street
4	William Stewart	110	New Market Buildings
5	J. Aspinall & Co	100	18 New Market
6	John Fazy	100	2 Cheapside
7	James Bayley Jnr.	100	1 Red Cross Street
8	Dean & Co	100	3 Marsden Square
9	Thomas Harrop & Co	70	15 New Market
10	Charles Metcalf	55	10 Blue Boar Court
11	John Lees	50	1 New Market Lane
12	Thomas Phillips	50	Wrights Court
13	J. Ashworth	48	2 Red Cross Street
14	L. & G. Cooper	48	18 New Cannon Street
15	Smethurst & Co	45	Cannon Street Buildings
16	Samuel Walker	45	2 Ridings Court
17	John & Thomas Birch	40	5 Red Cross Street
18	Joseph Potter	40	Half Moon Street
19	John Williamson	32	16 Pall Mall
20	J. T. Linney	30	7 Back Square
21	Samuel Sinister	30	4 Wright Court
22	Joseph Beckett	25	6 Pool Street
23	John Edenson	24	Clevelands Buildings
24	Robert Goring	20	11 Half Moon Street
25	Samuel Halliday	20	9 New Market Place
26	F. Phillips	20	Back Parade
27	James Pollett	20	Bancroft Court
28	Abraham Watkin	18	17 Cannon Street
29	John Wood Jnr.	12	3 Bateman Buildings
30	Appleton	7	7 Sickle Street
31	Simon Townsend	6	Blue Boar Court
32	N. Gerrard	4	Ormrods Court

Source: Rate Book, 1815, and *Pigot's Commercial Directory*, 1815.

APPENDIX 4

Cotton Manufacturers, Merchants and Calico Printers Operating Manchester Warehouses and Objecting to a Proposed ad valorem tax on the Export of Cotton Manufactured Goods, Manchester, 9 May 1815

Name	RV warehouse (£)	Description of business activity
John Parkin and Co	45	Merchants
N. and G. Gould and Co	280	Fustian manufacturers
J. T. & N. Touchett	140	Fustian manufacturers and merchants
Burrows and Farrington	70	Merchants
Haigh, Marshall and Co	220	Manufacturers and dealers and calico printers
Wm. Boyd	200	Manufacturers and dealers
J. and R. Millington	160	Manufacturers and dealers
Jonathan Kelsall	90	Irish linen merchant
Wilson and Williams	110	Cotton and silk manufacturers
Hole, Wilkinson and Co	110	Calico printers
Locke, Hindley and Co	140	Manufacturers and dealers and merchants
Robert Parker and Nephew	250	n/a
Blaire, Gatrix and Co	60	Cotton manufacturers
Roe, Gray, and Roe	90	Calico printers
Worthington, Parker and Co	250	Manufacturers and dealers
James Bury and Co	30	n/a
Samuel and S. Stocks and Co	175	Manufacturers and dealers
Terry and Sykes	110	Manufacturers and dealers
Darbyshire, Leigh and Co	100	Manufacturers and dealers
Thomas Slater	130	Manufacturers and dealers
Wm. Townend and Sons	110	Merchants
Thomas Coates and Co	150	Manufacturers and dealers and calico printers
Arrowsmith and Rider	136	Calico printers, Irish linen merchants
Baxter and Croft	120	Manufacturers and dealers, Scotch warehouse
Hoskins and Hand	130	Calico printers
L. Parsons	50	Calico printers
Jonathan Atkinson and Co	150	Cotton twist and weft dealer, cotton dealer
D. Grant	150	Manufacturer and dealer, calico printer
Thomas and Richard Potter	140	Manufacturers and dealers
Gallimore, Johnson and Brooks	110	Cotton dealers, calico printers
Peach and Stanway	90	Fustian manufacturers
Watkins and Harbottle	120	Manufacturers and dealers

Name	RV warehouse (£)	Description of business activity
Broadbent, Marris and Co	190	Calico printers, Irish linen merchant
Otto Hulme and Son	110	Manufacturers and dealers, calico printers
Warren, Leese and Co	122	Manufacturers and dealers
Miles Clayton	75	Calico printers
Thomas Moseley	30	Manufacturer and dealer
Rea and Lomax	120	Calico printer
Clay and Cullingworth	240	Manufacturers and dealers, calico printer
John Mosley	30	Cotton manufacturer
Blair, Everall and Co	120	Calico printer
Jonathan Wood and Bros	60	Cotton manufacturers?
Dickinson and Wild	90	Cotton and silk manufacturers
John Wilson	150	Fustian manufacturers
Nicholls, Marsey, Nicholls	211	Manufacturers and dealers
Carbutts, Thomas and Hayliffe	100	Calico printers
John Grafton and Son	65	Manufacturers and dealers, calico printers
Edward Hall	100	Manufacturers and dealers
Edward Salterthwaite	132	Manufacturers and dealers
D. Speakman	45	Manufacturer and dealer
Jonathan B. Homefield	20	Manufacturer and dealer
Litt, Radcliffe and Co	80	Calico printer
Skickelthorpe and Thomasson	90	Fustian manufacturers
Thomas Andrew and Sons	130	Calico printer
Joseph Thorley and Co	80	Irish linen merchants
Amies and Robinson	65	Manufacturers and dealers
Brooks and Oughton	150	Manufacturers and dealers, calico printers
Hugh Greaves	70	Manufacturers and dealers
Robert Ranson and Co	80	Calico printers
George Neden	110	Manufacturers and dealers
William Padmore	120	Fustian manufacturer
Heaton, Ingham and Co	80	Calico printers
Joseph Docker	100	Fustian manufacturer and merchant
Thomas and John Johnson	60	Manufacturers of check
Richard Blackstock and Co	115	Fustian manufacturers
Cockbain and Ogden	80	Cotton and silk manufacturers
William Bateman	230	Manufacturer and dealer
Thorpe and Boulton	50	Manufacturer and dealer
James Bayley and Co	35	Manufacturers and dealers and calico printer
John and George Holford	28	Fustian manufacturer
Peter Crompton	20	Merchant

Name	RV warehouse (£)	Description of business activity
James Molineaux	10	Manufacturer and dealer (cotton twist and weft)
T. B. Sanderson and Co	40	Fustian manufacturer
P. Trueman	40	Manufacturer and dealer
John Greenwood	100	Manufacturer and dealer
Peter Watson	50	Manufacturer and dealer, calico printer
T. and R. Saunders	180	Irish linen merchants
Lancaster and Burgess	165	Calico printers
Batt and Barker	150	Calico printers
Craven, Kirk and Co	100	Manufacturers and dealers
Appleby and Faulkner	70	Cotton and silk manufacturers
Bridge, Tomlinson and Co	70	Manufacturers and dealers
Hall and Travis	9	Manufacturers and dealers
Webb and Warmsley	50	Manufacturers and dealers
Jas. and Josh. Wright	35	Manufacturer and dealer and calico printer
C. B. and O. Potter	50	Manufacturers and dealers
T. and J. Todd	30	Cotton and silk manufacturers
Thomas and John Dawson and Co	50	Manufacturers
H. C. Frederick Brandt	130	Merchant
Jonathan Ratcliffe	90	Cotton dealer
Daniel and Shelley	25	Calico printer
Thomas Walker	30	Manufacturer and dealer
Jonathan and Ab. Milne	20	n/a
Christopher Openshaw	18	Pillow manufacturer
Haslam, Plummer and Co	24	Muslin manufacturer
Christopher Ainsworth	15	Muslin manufacturer
Jonathan and George Jones	100	Calico printer
J. and T. Ramsbotton	90	Manufacturers and dealers (and factory occupiers)
Weight, Armitage and Co	80	Manufacturers and dealers
Henry and W. Burgess	80	n/a
Joshua Bowman	30	n/a
J. and W. Magnall	100	Fustian manufacturer
George Fletcher	50	Fustian manufacturer
Richard Crumbleholme	12	Drysalterer
Dawson Bros	44	Fustian manufacturer
Jasper Milne	45	Merchant
Jonathan Lees	100	Cotton dealer
Jonathan Rigby and Son	44	Cotton and silk manufacturer
Gardner and Dawson	180	Cotton and silk manufacturer
Jas. Walker	18	Nankeen manufacturer
Total Number of Firms	110	Total RV of Warehouses £10,533.00

Sources: *Manchester Mercury*, 9 May 1815; Manchester Poor Rate Assessment Book, 1815 (M.C.L. M9/40/79); *Pigot's Manchester and Salford Directory*, 1815.

APPENDIX 5

Warehouse Growth By District, Manchester, 1807–1815

Rate district	No warehouse units 1807	Total RV £ 1807	No warehouse units 1815	Total RV £ 1815
1	4	40	–	–
2	5	154	7	154
3	50	1,300	82	2,278
4	33	1,619	15	1,311
5	110	4,692	151	7,336
6	501	18,821	663	29,750
7	8	196	5	190
8	45	1,875	73	2,673
9	319	15,262.75	421	20,402
10	–	–	7	618
11	18	838.50	17	942
12	63	2,216.25	90	3,374
13	14	539.75	24	1,453
14	12	1,778.5	22	3,146
Total	1,182	49,333	1,577	73,627

Source: Lloyd-Jones and Lewis, 'Economic Structure', p. 85.

APPENDIX 6

Firms Operating Both Factories and Warehouses in Manchester, 1825

Name of firm	Factory RV £	Warehouse RV £	Warehouse address
Sandford and Green[a]	330	70	New Market
Gallimore and Johnson[a]	149	120	9 Cannon Street
R. Schofield	227	50	50 Henkinson Court
Chadwick and Clegg	415/339	140/16	Marsden G. and 32 York Street
J. Latham	250	6[b]	McDonald Lane
J. Fairweather[a]	269	60	2 Phoenix Street
Oxley, Sutcliffe and Gough	234	8	Swan Court
Dacca Twist Co	289	100	22 Cannon Street
Houghton and Leeming[a]	128	28	32 Water Street
Hugh Beaver	415	80	27 Cannon Street
Bowerfield and Co	29	60	New High Street
R. Barnes	236	16	McDonald Lane
Clarke and Jones	243	100	2 York Street
J.C. Dyer	106	34	Dale Street
E. and Y. Dodgson	143	50/15	Bridgewater Place and 6 McDonald Lane
Fernley and Swindels	438	120	12 High Street
Gardner and Bindloss	104	80	1 Cheapside
S. Gregg	62	25/50	Chancery Lane
N.L. Gardner	70	130	15 High Street
Greenwood and Co	195/20/91	90	6 Cromford Court
J. Massey	218	100	17 Marsden Square
S. Motterhead	230	20	Kings Arms Entry
R. Rothwell	131/369	40	McDonald Lane
W. Shaw	56	10	Blue Boar Court
Tatlock and Love	129	45	2 Spear Street
T. Worthington	255	200	50 High Street
Thackery and Russell	417	10	Harrison Terrace
J. Varley	8	20[b]	St James Street
C. Ruddock	16	80	10 Church Street
Taylor and Shatwell	399	14/20	Ancoats Bridge and Marrick Court
Thomas Walker	112 ep 36	90	New Blue Boar Court
Welch and Sells	48/21/ep 32	24	12 New Cannon Street
J. Pollard	627	10	13 Cannon Street
T. Marriot	537/96	50/60	Back Water Street
J. Petty	87	40	4 New Market Lane
T. Smith	104	16	4 Lees Street
J. Shaw	16	3	Falstaff Yard
Wm. Reed	234	20	St Mary's Gate

Notes: a. Firms also operated warehouses in 1815.
b. Firms described in the Rate Book as operating rooms.

Source: Township of Manchester Rate Book 1825 (M9/40/2/92,93); Computer data bank Manchester Factories 1807 to 1841, Sheffield City Polytechnic; Computer data file Manchester Warehouses, 1825, Sheffield City Polytechnic; *Pigot's Commercial Directory*, Manchester, 1825.

APPENDIX 7

A Profile of the Modern Sector in Manchester

Table A: Manchester firms in the metal machine sector, 1815 (RV £100+)

Firm		Property asset	RV (£)	Business activity
1	Peel and Williams	Foundry	178	Ironfounders, machine makers and millwright
2	James Howard & Co	Works	150	Ironfounders and pin makers
3	Hulme and Walker	Foundry	120	Ironfounders
4	Radford and Waddington	Works	130	Iron and brass founders
5	T.C. Hewes	Works	130	Millwright and machine makers
6	Ebeneezer Smith	Works	100	Ironfounders
7	R. Ormrod	Foundry	190	Iron and brass founders and copper smiths
8	Isaiah Horton & Co	Foundry	100	Ironfounders
9	Bateman & Branthwaite	Workshops	108	General ironmongers
10	W. and J. Creighton	Works	100	Machine makers
11	Thomas Sharpe and Co	Workshops	120	Iron merchants and general ironmongers
12	Thomas Sefton	Works	116	Iron founders

Source: Manchester Rate Book, 1815; *Pigot's Commercial Directory*, 1815.

Table B: Manchester firms in the chemical finishing sector, 1815 (RV £100+)

Firm		Property asset	RV (£)	Business activity
1	R. Mutrie	Works	100	Chemical manufacturer
2	Thomas Wood	Works	120	Chemical manufacturer
3	J. and R. Christie and Co	Warehouse	190	Drysalterers
4	P. and C. Pole	Warehouse	300	Dysalterers
5	Richard Walker	Works	320	Dyers
6	Horrocks and Hobson	Works	100	Dyers
7	Joseph Trayford	Works	110	Dyers
8	William Olliver	Works	150	Dyers
9	Thomas Hoyle	Works	340	Dyers
10	William Newton	Works	140	Dyers
11	Whitelegg, Bradburn and Co	Works	150	Dyers
12	T.I. Smith	Works	130	Dyers
13	P. Feeling	Works	120	Dyers
14	Rotherwell and Harrison	Works	260	Dyers
15	James Holt	Works	178	Dyers
16	John Radford	Works	120	Dyers
17	Edward Dewhurst	Warehouse	125	Callenderers
18	Goodiers and Fowden	Warehouse	200	Callenderers
19	Whitehead and Wilcoxon	Callender House	110	Callenderers
20	Bailey and Myatt	Warehouse	100	Calico printers and manufacturers and dealers
21	B. Beddome	Warehouse	100	Calico printer, manufacturer and dealer and fustian manufacturer
22	Brierley, Harrison and Co	Warehouse	100	Calico printer and manufacturer and dealer
23	Brookes and Oughton	Warehouse	150	Calico printer, manufacturers and dealers and merchants
24	David Burton	Warehouse	180	Calico printers and manufacturers and dealers
25	Clay and Cullingworth	Warehouse	240	Calico printers and manufacturers and dealers
26	Thomas Coates and Co	Warehouse	150	Calico printers and manufacturers and dealers
27	Haigh, Marshall and Co	Warehouse	220	Calico printers, manufacturers and dealers and merchants

Firm		Property asset	RV (£)	Business activity
28	Hudson and Blencoe	Warehouse	100	Calico printers and manufacturers and dealers
29	Otto Hulme	Warehouse	110	Calico printers and manufacturers and dealers
30	T. S. Jones	Warehouse	100	Calico printers and manufacturers and dealers
31	Oakden and Taylor	Warehouse	105	Calico printers and manufacturers and dealers
32	Thomas Worthington and Co	Warehouse	250	Calico printers, manufacturers and dealers, fustian manufacturers and silk and cotton manufacturers
33	Thomas Peel and Bros	Warehouse	250	Calico printers and manufacturers and dealers
34	Peter Watson	Warehouse	150	Calico printers and manufacturers and dealers
35	Benjymin Binyon	Warehouse	110	Calico printers and fustian manufacturers
36	Arrowsmith and Rider	Warehouse	136	Calico printers and Irish linen merchants
37	Blackwall, Hunter and Co	Warehouse	150	Calico printers and Irish linen merchants
38	Broadhurst and Marris	Warehouse	190	Calico printers, Irish linen merchants, merchants
39	Thomas Carbutt and Son	Warehouse	100	Calico Printers and Irish linen merchants
40	Thomas Hoyle and Son	Warehouse	120	Calico printers and dyers
41	Peel, Yates and Co	Warehouse	250	Calico printers and merchants
42	Thomas Andrews Jnr	Warehouse	130	Calico printers
43	Bates, Winks and Bates	Warehouse	240	Calico printers
44	Batt, Barker and Denby	Warehouse	150	Calico printers
45	J. and J. Bury	Warehouse	200	Calico printers
46	Blair, Gratrix and Co	Warehouse	120	Calico printers
47	R.I. and E. Clayton	Warehouse	100	Calico printers
48	Henry Fielding and Bros	Warehouse	120	Calico printers
49	R. Ford and Sons	Warehouse	150	Calico printers
50	Greenway and Potter	Warehouse	120	Calico printers
51	Hargreaves and Dugdale	Warehouse	110	Calico printers

Firm		Property asset	RV (£)	Business activity
52	Hole, Wilkinson and Co	Warehouse	110	Calico printers
53	Hoskins and Hand	Warehouse	150	Calico printers
54	William Howe	Warehouse	100	Calico printers
55	Lancaster and Burgess	Warehouse	165	Calico printers
56	John Lowe	Warehouse	120	Calico printers
57	S. Matley and Son	Warehouse	140	Calico printers
58	G. Palfreyman	Warehouse	150	Calico printers
59	Rea and Lomas	Warehouse	120	Calico printers
60	John Slingsby	Warehouse	100	Calico printers
61	Thompson and Chippendale	Warehouse	140	Calico printers
62	Robert Turner Jnr	Warehouse	120	Calico printers
63	Warren, Richards and Co	Warehouse	130	Calico printers
64	John Whitehead	Warehouse	100	Calico printers
65	B.E. and J. Wilson	Warehouse	100	Calico printers
66	William and J. Wright	Warehouse	100	Calico printers

Source: Manchester Rate Book, 1815; *Pigot's Commercial Directory*, 1815.

Table C: Increase in size of large Manchester metal machinery firms, 1815–1825[a]

Firm	Plant size 1815		Plant size 1820		Plant size 1825	
	No	RV (£)	No	RV (£)	No	RV (£)
Peel and Williams	(1)	178	(1)	230	(1)	190
			(2)	210	(2)	300
Hulme and Walker	(1)	120	(1)	120	(1)	152
Radford and Waddington	(1)	130	(1)	130	(1)	162
T.C. Hewes[b]	(1)	130	(1)	130	(1)	130
Adam Parkinson[c]	(1)	89	(1)	65	(1)	65
			(2)	75	(2)	95
R. Ormrod	(1)	190	(1)	210	(1)	280
Bowman and Galloway	(1)	80	(1)	170	(1)	207
			(2)	40	(2)	100
W. and J. Creighton	(1)	100	(1)	100	(1)	270
Thomas Sharp and Co	(1)	120	(1)	120	(1)	150

Notes: a. Four firms listed in Table A are not included in this table. The RV of the firm of Ebeneezer Smith and Co fell from £100.00 in 1815 to £45.00 in 1825. In 1820 the firm's foundry (RV £100) was recorded as half empty. The RV of the firm of I. Horton and Co fell from £100.00 to £36.00 *c.* 1815–20. By 1825 the firm had exited from the industry. No rate book entry was found for the firm of Bateman and Branthwaite in 1820 or 1825. The firm is listed, however, in the directories as general ironmongers, Salford. The firm of Thomas Sefton had left the industry by 1820.

b. By 1820 the firm is recorded as T. C. Hughes and Wren.

c. By 1820 the firm is recorded as Parkinson and Arrie.

Source: Manchester Rate Books, 1815, 1820, 1825.

Table D: Fourteen survival firms, 1815–1825, who drop calico printing

Firm		RV 1815 (£)	RV 1825 (£)
1	Benjamin Beddome	100	50
2	Brookes and Oughton	150	130
3	Haigh, Marshall and Co	220	220
4	J. and J. Wright	35	30
5	Williams, Holford and Co	85	106
6	Arrowsmith and Rider	136	90
7	Blackwall, Hunter and Co	150	150
8	William Smith and Co	34	110
9	Bates, Winks and Co	240	200
10	William Birch	32	30
11	George Lockwood	50	40
12	John Lyon	60	22
13	James Robinson	40	25
14	John Slingsby	100	65

Source: Manchester Rate Books, 1815, 1825; *Pigot's Commercial Directory*, 1815, 1825.

Table E: Pattern of activity shift, 1815–25, of fourteen survival firms

Firm	Business activity, 1815	Business activity, 1825
1	Calico printers and fustian manufacturers	Drysalterers
2	Calico printers, manufacturers and dealers and merchants	Manufacturers and dealers and merchants
3	Calico printers, manufacturers and dealers and merchants	Manufacturers and dealers and merchants
4	Calico printers and manufacturers and dealers	Dyers
5	Calico printers and silk and cotton manufacturers	Cotton and silk manufacturers
6	Calico printers and Irish linen merchants	Irish linen merchants
7	Calico printers and Irish linen merchants	Irish linen merchants
8	Calico printers and drysalterers	Drysalterers
9	Calico printers	Merchants
10	Calico printers	Dyers
11	Calico printers	Commission agents
12	Calico printers	Cotton dealers
13	Calico printers	Manufacturers and dealers and fustian manufacturers
14	Calico printers	Bombasine manufacturers

Source: Manchester Rate Books, 1815, 1825; *Pigot's Commercial Directories*, 1815, 1825.

Select Bibliography

This select bibliography is organised in the following manner:

I Primary sources
- A. Rate books, computer data files and trade directories
- B Manuscript collections
- C. Government publications and official papers and reports
- D. Newspapers and miscellaneous reports and transactions

II Secondary sources
- A. Books
- B. Articles

I PRIMARY SOURCES

A. Rate books, computer data files and trade directories

Township of Manchester Poor Rate Assessment books 1807–1825 (M9/40/2 Manchester Central Library)

Data File Manchester Cotton Factories, 1807 to 1841 (data includes name of firm, RV, type of occupancy and type of utilisation, Sheffield City Polytechnic)

Data File Manchester Warehouses, 1825 (data includes name of firm, RV, location and type of business activity, Sheffield City Polytechnic)

Data File Manchester Calico Printers utilising warehouses, 1815 and 1825 (data includes name of firm, RV, location and business activity and exit, entry and survival estimates)

Data File Manchester Metal Sector Firms, 1815 and 1825 (data includes name of firm, RV of premise, location and business activity and exit, entry and survival estimates, Sheffield City Polytechnic)

Pigot's Commercial Directory of Manchester and Salford, 1815, 1818, 1820 and 1825 (Manchester Central Library)

B. Manuscript collections

A Comparative Statement Relating to the Assessment of Factories, Houses and Shops, Warehouses and other property in the Township of Manchester made by Messrs Bellhouse, Wallis and Johnson, July 1812 (M9/40/1/20), Manchester Central Library

Inventories of Fixtures Ashton's warehouse, New Cannon Street. Piece Account Book John Mawson, 1794–1797 (Misc/551) Manchester Central Library

List of the 14 Districts of the Town of Manchester as Divided by the Commissioners Under the Police Act, 18 July 1782 (M9/30/1/1), Manchester Central Library

Master Cotton Spinners Memorial Sent to the Church Wardens and Overseers of the Poor Law in Manchester, 10 July 1810 (M3/3/7), Manchester Central Library

Tables of assessment to the poor rates in Manchester . . . tables of number of houses and inhabitants, 1821–31 (M63/7/12), n.d., Manchester Central Library

Minutes of the Proceedings of the Manchester Chamber of Commerce and Manufacturers, 1822–1827 (M8/2/1), Manchester Central Library

The Bury Papers. Letters, Accounts concerning the activities of the Pendel Hill calico printers, John and James Bury, Manchester Central Library

The John Heywood Papers. Letters concerning the business activities of John and Robert Heywood, fancy quilt and india jean manufacturers, Bolton and Manchester (Z.H.E/1–30), Bolton Reference Library

The Irving Collection. Manuscript relating to the Life of Samuel Crompton, Bolton Museum

The McConnel and Kennedy Papers. Business papers relating to the Manchester fine spinners, John Rylands Library, University of Manchester

C. Government publications and official papers and reports

P.P., 1802–03 (114), 111, part 4, *Minutes of Evidence Taken Before the Committees on Petitions on the Law Relating to Disputes Between Masters and Workmen in the Cotton Manufacture*

P.P., 1816 (397), 111, *Report of the Select Committee on the State of Children Employed in the Manufactories of the United Kingdom*

P.P., 1817 (141), XIV, *Statement of the Quantity of Cotton Yarn Exported from Great Britain*

P.P., 1817 (482), XIV, *Copies of all the Memorials Presented to H.R.H. The Prince Regent during the Present and Last Year, on the Exportation of Cotton Yarns*

P.P., 1820–33, No. 300 (46), *Tables on the Revenue, Population, Commerce of the United Kingdom*

P.P., 1824 (51), V, *Report of the Select Committee on Artisans, Machinery and Combinations*

P.P., 1833 (XIX), Part 1, *Supplementary Report of the Factory Commissioners*

P.P., 1833 (690), VI, *Report of the Select Commitee on the Present State of Manufactures, Commerce, and Shipping in the United Kingdom*

P.P., 1836 (24), XLV, *A Return of the Number of Power Looms Used in Factories . . .*

Court Leet Records of the Manor of Manchester, vol. X (Henry Blacklock, Manchester, 1889)

Journal of the House of Commons, vols. 70, 72, 83, 75, 82

Hansard Parliamentary Debates, vols. 28, 32, 37

D. Newspapers and miscellaneous reports and transactions

Manchester Guardian
Manchester Mercury
Manchester Courier
Wheeler's Manchester Chronicle
Manchester Gazette
United Trades Cooperative Journal
Mercator, A Letter to the Inhabitants of Manchester on the Exportation of Cotton Twist (Manchester, 1800), Manchester Central Library
J. Kennedy, 'Observations on the Rise and Progress of the Cotton Trade in Great Britain, particularly in Lancashire and the adjoining Counties', *Memoirs of the Literary and Philosophical Society of Manchester*, 2nd series, vol. III (read November 1815)

II SECONDARY SOURCES

A. Books

Anderson, G. *Victorian Clerks* (Manchester University Press, Manchester, 1976)
Ashton, J. *The Manchester Guide: A Brief Historical Description of the Town of Manchester and Salford* (Joseph Ashton, Manchester, 1804)
Ashton, T. S. *The Industrial Revolution: 1760–1830* (Oxford University Press, Oxford, 1948)
Axon, E. A. *The Annals of Manchester: A Chronological Record from the earliest times to the end of 1815* (John Haywood, Manchester, 1866)
Bamford, S. *Early Days* (T. Fisher Unwin, London, 1849)
Baines, E. *History of the Cotton Manufacture in Great Britain* (Frank Cass, London, 1966, 2nd edition with a bibliographic introduction by W. H. Chaloner)
Berg, M. *The Machinery Question and the Making of Political Economy, 1815 to 1848* (Cambridge University Press, Cambridge,1980)
—— *The Age of Manufactures, 1700 to 1820* (Basil Blackwell, Oxford, 1985)
—— (ed.) Technology and Toil in 19th Century Britain (Humanities Press, New Jersey, 1979)
Blair, J. M. *Economic Concentration: Structure, Behaviour and Policy* (Harcourt Brace Jovanovich, New York, 1972)
Boyson, R. *The Ashworths Cotton Enterprise. The Rise and Fall of a Family Firm, 1818 to 1880* (Oxford University Press, Oxford, 1970)
Brady, A. *William Huskinson and Liberal Reform* (2nd ed., Frank Cass, London, 1967)
Braverman, H. *Labour and Monopoly Capital. The Degradation of Work in the Twentieth Century* (Monthly Review Press, New York, 1974)

Brown, W. E. *Robert Heywood of Bolton, 1786 to 1856* (S.R. Publishers, Wakefield, 1970)
Burton, J. *Effective Warehousing* (Macdonald and Evans, London, 1973)
Bythell, D. *The Handloom Weavers. A Study in the English Cotton Industry During the Industrial Revolution* (Cambridge University Press, Cambridge, 1969)
Catling, H. *The Spinning Mule* (David and Charles, Newton Abbot, 1970)
Chapman, S. D. *The Cotton Industry in the Industrial Revolution* (Macmillan, London, 1972)
—— (ed.) *The History of Working Class Housing: A Symposium* (David and Charles, London, 1971)
—— and Chassagne, S. *European Textile Printers in the 18th Century: A Study of Peel and Oberkamf* (Heinmann Educational: Pasold Fund, London, 1981)
Chapman, S. J. *The Lancashire Cotton Industry* (Manchester University Press, Manchester, 1904)
Clapp, B. W. *John Owens Manchester Merchant* (Manchester University Press, Manchester, 1965)
Cottrell, P. *Industrial Finance 1830–1914. The Finance and Organisation of English Manufacturing Industry* (Methuen, London, 1980)
Crouzet, F. *The First Industrialists. The Problem of Origins* (Cambridge University Press, Cambridge, 1985)
Daniels, G. W. *The Early English Cotton Industry* (Longman, Green, London, 1920)
van Duijn, J. J. *The Long Wave in Economic Life* (George Allen and Unwin, London, 1983)
Edwards, M. M. *The Growth of the British Cotton Trade, 1780 to 1815* (Manchester University Press, Manchester, 1967)
—— and Lloyd-Jones, R. 'N. J. Smelser and the Cotton Factory Family: a reassessment', in Harte, N. B. and Ponting, K. G., *Textile History and Economic History: Essays in Honour of Miss Julia de Lacy Mann* (Manchester University Press, Manchester, 1973)
Engels, F. *The Condition of the English Working Class* (George Allen and Unwin, London, 1892 ed.)
Eversley, R. and Little, I. M. D. *Concentration in British Industry* (Cambridge University Press, Cambridge, 1960)
Farnie, D. A. *The English Cotton Industry and the World Market 1815 to 1896* (Oxford University Press, Oxford, 1979)
Fielden, J. *The Curse of the Factory System*, with an introduction by Ward, J. T. (Frank Cass, London, 1969 ed.)
Freeman, C. *Structural Determinants of Employment and Unemployment* (O.E.C.D., Paris, 1979)
—— Clarke, J. and Soete, L. *Unemployment and Technological Innovation: A Study of Long Waves and Economic Development* (Frances Pinter, London, 1982)
Gayer, A. D., Rostow, W. W. and Schwartz, A. J. *The Growth and Fluctuation of the British Economy*, 2 vols. (Harvester Press, Hassocks, nr Brighton, 1975)

Gerschenkron, A. *Economic Backwardness in Historical Perspective* (Harvard University Press, Cambridge, Mass., 1966)
Gordon, B. *Political Economy in Parliament, 1819 to 1823* (Macmillan, London, 1976)
—— *Economic Doctrine and Tory Liberalism 1824 to 1830* (Macmillan, London, 1979)
Hannah, L. *The Rise of the Corporate Economy* (Methuen, London, 1976)
Hartwell, R. M. *The Industrial Revolution and Economic Growth* (Methuen, London, 1971)
Helm, E. *Chapters in the History of the Manchester Chamber of Commerce* (Simpkin, Marshall, London, 1897)
Hidy, R. W. *The House of Baring in American Trade and Finance: English Merchant Bankers at Work* (Harvard University Press, Cambridge, Mass., 1949)
Hilton, A. B. *Corn, Cash, Commerce: The Economic Policies of the Tory Governments 1815 to 1830* (Oxford University Press, Oxford, 1977)
Hirschman, A. O. *The Strategy of Economic Development* (Yale University Press, New Haven, 1958)
Hobsbawm, E. J. *Industry and Empire* (Penguin, Harmondsworth, 1969)
Honeyman, K. *Origins of Enterprise. Business Leadership in the Industrial Revolution* Manchester University Press, Manchester, 1982)
Hunt, E. K. and Schwartz, Jesse G. (eds) *A Critique of Economic Theory* (Penguin Educational, Harmondsworth, 1972)
Jeremy, D. *Transatlantic Industrial Revolution. The Diffusion of Textile Techniques between Britain and America, 1790 to 1830* (Basil Blackwell, Oxford, 1981)
Jones, R. *Supply in a Market Economy* (George Allen and Unwin, London, 1976)
Kay, Neil M. *The Innovating Firm* (Macmillan, London, 1979)
—— *The Evolving Firm: Strategy and Structure in Industrial Organisation* (Macmillan, London, 1982)
Kayser, C. and Turner, D. F. *Antitrust Policy: An Economic and Legal Interpretation* (Harvard University Press, Cambridge, Mass., 1959)
Kindleberger, C. P. and di Tella, G. (eds) *Economics in the Long View. Essays in Honour of W. W. Rostow*, vol. 1, *Models and Methodology* (Macmillan, London, 1982)
Kirby, R. G. and Musson, A. E. *The Voice of the People: John Doherty, 1798 to 1854. Trade Unionist, Radical and Factory Reformer* (Manchester University Press, Manchester, 1975)
Kydd, S. *The History of the Factory Movement* (Burt Franklyn, New York, n.d., reprint of London edition of 1857)
Landes, D. S. *The Unbound Prometheus. Technological Change from 1780 to the Present* (Cambridge University Press, Cambridge, 1969)
Lee, C. H. *A Cotton Enterprise 1795 to 1840: A History of McConnel and Kennedy — fine cotton spinners* (Manchester University Press, Manchester, 1972)

Leigh, E. *The Science of Modern Cotton Spinning*, 2 vols (Palmer and Howe, Manchester, 1873)
Levine, D. P. *Contributions to the Critique of Economic Theory* (Routledge and Kegan Paul, London, 1977)
McCloskey, D. N. 'The Industrial Revolution, 1780 to 1860: A Survey', in Floud, R. and McCloskey, D. N. (eds), *The Economic History of Britain Since 1700*, vol. 1 (Cambridge University Press, Cambridge, 1981)
Mantaux, P. *The Industrial Revolution in the Eighteenth Century* (Methuen, London, 1964, ed.)
Matthews, R. C. O. *A Study in Trade Cycle History. Economic Fluctuations in Great Britain, 1833–42* (Cambridge University Press, Cambridge, 1954)
Marx, K. *Capital: A Critical Analysis of Capitalist Production*, vol. 1 (Lawrence and Wishart, London, 1974 ed.)
Mathias, P. *The First Industrial Nation* (Methuen, London, 1969)
——— *The Transformation of England: Essays in the Economic and Social History of England in the Eighteenth Century* (Methuen, London, 1979)
Mensch, G. *The Stalemate in Technology. Innovations Overcome the Depression* (Balinger, New York, 1979)
Millington, A. F. *An Introduction to Property Valuation* (Estate Gazette, London, 1972)
Mitchell, B. R. and Deane, P. *Abstract of British Historical Statistics* (Cambridge University Press, Cambridge, 1962)
Mokyr, J. (ed.) *The Economics of The Industrial Revolution* (Allen and Unwin, London, 1985)
Morley, J. *The Life of Richard Cobden*, 2 vols (T. Fisher Unwin, London, 1881)
Morris, R. J. 'The Middle Class and British Towns and Cities of the Industrial Revolution', in Frazer, D. and Sutcliffe, A. (eds), *The Pursuit of Urban History* (Edward Arnold, London, 1983)
Moss, Scott *An Economic Theory of Business Strategy. An Essay in Dynamics Without Equilibrium* (Martin Robinson, Oxford, 1981)
Musson, A. E. *The Growth of British Industry* (B.T. Batsford, London, 1978)
——— and Robinson, E. *Science and Technology in the Industrial Revolution* (Manchester University Press, Manchester, 1969)
Myrdal, G. *Against the Stream: Critical Essays in Economics* (Vintage Books, New York, 1975)
North, D. C. and Thomas, R. T. *The Rise of the Western World: A New Economic History* (Cambridge University Press, Cambridge, 1973)
Penrose, E. *The Theory of the Growth of the Firm* (Basil Blackwell, Oxford, 1959)
Platt, D. C. M. *Finance, Trade and Politics in British Foreign Policy 1815 to 1914* (Oxford University Press, Oxford, 1968)
Pole, W. (edited and completed) *The Life of Sir William Fairbairn, Bart*, partly written by himself, with an introduction by Musson, A. E. (David and Charles, Newton Abbot, 1970 ed.)

Pollard, S. *The Genesis of Modern Management. A Study of the Industrial Revolution in Great Britain* (Edward Arnold, London, 1965)
—— 'Fixed Capital in the Industrial Revolution in Britain', in Crouzet, F. (ed.), *Capital Formation in the Industrial Revolution* (Methuen, London, 1972)
Prentice, A. *Historical Sketches and Personal Recollections of Manchester* (Charles Gilpin, London, 1851)
Radcliffe, W. *Origins of the New System of Manufacture* (James Lomax Advertiser Office, Stockport, 1828)
Redford, A. *Manchester Merchants and Foreign Trade*, vol. 1, 1794–1857 (Manchester University Press, Manchester, 1934)
—— *et al. The History of Local Government in Manchester*, vols 1 and 2 (Longmans, Green, London, 1939)
Ricardo, D. *The Principles of Political Economy and Taxation* (J. M. Dent, London, 1823 ed.)
Robinson, Joan *The Accumulation of Capital* (Macmillan, London, 1956)
—— *Economic Heresies: Some Old Fashioned Questions in Economic Theory* (Macmillan, London, 1971)
Rosenberg, N. *Perspectives on Technology* (Cambridge University Press, Cambridge, 1976)
—— *Inside the Black Box: Technology and Economics* (Cambridge University Press, Cambridge, 1982)
Rostow, W. W. *The Stages of Economic Growth. A Non-Communist Manifesto* (Cambridge University Press, Cambridge, 1971, 2nd ed.)
—— (ed.) *The Economics of Take-off into Self-Sustained Growth* (Macmillan, London, 1963)
Sargent Florence, P. *The Logic of Industrial Organisation* (Routledge and Kegan Paul, London, 1933)
Sawyer, M. C. *Theories of the Firm* (Weidenfeld and Nicolson, London, 1979)
von Schulze-Gaevenitz, G. *The Cotton Trade in England and on the Continent* (Simpkin, Marshall, Hamilton, Kent, London, 1895)
Shapiro, S. *Capital and the Cotton Industry in the Industrial Revolution* (Cornell University Press, Ithaca, New York, 1967)
Slugg, J. T. *Reminiscences of Manchester 50 years Ago* (Marshall, Simpkin, London, and J. E. Cornish, Manchester, 1881)
Smelser, N. J. *Social Change in the Industrial Revolution: An application of Theory to the Lancashire Cotton Industry, 1770 to 1840* (Routledge and Kegan Paul, London, 1959)
Smith, K. *The British Economic Crisis* (Penguin, Harmondsworth, 1984)
Steindle, J. Maturity and Stagnation in American Capitalism (Blackwell, Oxford, 1952)
Stigler, G. *The Organisation of Industry* (Richard D. Irwin, Homewood, Illinois, 1968)
Swindells, J. *Manchester Streets and Manchester Men* (Morton, Didsbury, Manchester, 1908)
Tann, J. *The Development of the Factory* (Cornmarket Press, London, 1970)

Thompson, W. H. *History of Manchester to 1852* (John Sherratt and Son, Altrincham, 1967)
Unwin, G., Hulme, A. and Taylor, G. *Samuel Oldknow and the Arkwrights* (Longman, Green, London, 1924)
Ure, A. *The Philosophy of Manufactures: Or an Exposition of the Scientific, Moral and Commercial Economy of the Factory System of Great Britain* (Frank Cass, London, 1967 ed.)
——— *The Cotton Manufacture of Great Britain*, vol. 1 (H. G. Bohn, London, 1861)
Utton, M. A. *Industrial Concentration* (Penguin, Harmondsworth, 1970)
Von Tunzleman, G. N. *Steam Power and British Industrialisation to 1860* (Oxford University Press, Oxford, 1978)
Wadsworth, A. P. and Mann, J. de Lacy *The Cotton Trade and Industrial Lancashire, 1600 to 1780* (Manchester University Press, Manchester, 1931)
Wallerstein, I. *The Capitalist World Economy* (Cambridge University Press, Cambridge, 1979)

B. Articles

Alford, B. W. E. 'Entrepreneurship, Business Performance and Industrial Development', *Business History*, vol. 19 (1977)
Blaug, M. 'Productivity of Capital in the Lancashire Cotton Industry During the 19th Centry', *Economic History Review*, vol. XIII, no. 3 (1960–1)
Bourne, A. M. 'Business History and Management Education', *Business History*, vol. XVII, no. 2 (1975)
Bruland, T. 'Industrial Conflict as a Source of Technical Innovation: Three Cases', *Economy and Society*, vol. 11, no. 2 (1982)
Cain, P. J. and Hopkins, A. G. 'The Political Economy of British Overseas Expansion', *Economic History Review*, vol. XXXIII, no. 4 (1980)
Catling, H. 'The Development of the Spinning Mule', *Textile History*, vol. 9 (1978)
Chapman, S. D. 'Fixed Capital Formation in the British Cotton Industry, 1770 to 1815', *Economic History Review*, vol. XXII, no. 2 (1970)
——— 'Financial Constraints on the Growth of Firms in the Cotton Industry, 1790 to 1850', *Economic History Review*, vol. XXXII, no. 1 (1979)
——— 'Quantity versus Quality in the British Industrial Revolution: The Case of Printed Textiles', *Northern History*, vol. XXI (1985)
Chevenix, R. 'History and Prospects of English Industry', *Quarterly Review*, vol. XXXIV (1826)
Church, R. 'Business History in Britain', *Journal of European Economic History*, vol. 5 (1976)
Clark, H. 'The Design and Designing of Lancashire Printed Calicoes

during the First Half of the 19th Century', *Textile History*, vol. 15, no. 1 (1984)

Clow, A. and Clow, N. L. 'Vitrol in the Industrial Revolution', *Economic History Review*, vol. XV (1945)

Crafts, N. F. R. 'Industrial Revolution in England and France: Some Thoughts on the question "Why was England First?" ', *Economic History Review*, vol. XXX, no. 3 (1977)

Daniels, G. W. 'Valuation of Manchester Cotton Factories in the early years of the Nineteenth Century' and 'The Early Records of a Great Manchester Cotton Spinning Firm', *Economic Journal*, vol. XXV (1915)

—— 'The Cotton Trade during the Revolutionary and Napoleonic Wars', *Transactions of the Manchester Statistical Society* (1915–16)

Delbeke, J. 'Recent Long Wave Theories: A Critical Survey', *Futures*, vol. 13 (1981)

Fores, M. 'The Myth of a British Industrial Revolution', *History*, vol. LXVI (1981)

Gatrell, V. A. C. 'Labour, Power, and the Size of Firms in Lancashire Cotton in the Second Quarter of the Nineteenth Century', *Economic History Review*, vol. XXX (1977)

Gerschenkron, A. 'Typologies of Industrialisation', *2nd International Conference of Economic History* (1962)

Henry, W. C. 'A Biographical Note of the Late Peter Ewart Esq.', *Memoirs of the Literary and Philosophical Society of Manchester*, second series, vol. VII (1846)

Holmes, G. and Ruff, H. 'The Perils of Entrepreneurial History', *Business History*, vol. XVII, no. 2 (1975)

Jeremy, D. 'Damming the Flood: British Government Efforts to Check the Outflow of Technicians and Machinery, 1780 to 1843', *Business History Review*, vol. 51, no. 1 (1977)

Landes, D. S. 'What Bosses Really Do', *Journal of Economic History*, vol. 46, no. 3 (1986)

Lazonick, W. 'Industrial Relations and Technical Change, the case of the Self-Acting Mule', *Cambridge Journal of Economics*, vol. iii (1979)

Lemire, B. 'Developing Consumerism and the Ready-made clothing Trade in Britain, 1750–1800', *Textile History*, vol. 15, no. 1 (1984)

Lloyd-Jones, R. and Le Roux, A. A. 'The Size of Firms in the Cotton Industry: Manchester 1815 to 1841', *Economic History Review*, vol. XXXIII, no. 1 (1980)

—— and Le Roux, A. A. 'Marshall and the Birth and Death of Firms: The Growth and Size Distribution of Firms in the Early Nineteenth Century Cotton Industry', *Business History*, vol. XXIV, no. 2 (1982)

—— and Le Roux, A. A. 'Factory Utilisation and the Firm: The Manchester Cotton Industry *c.* 1825 to 1840', *Textile History*, vol. 15, no. 1 (1984)

Lloyd-Jones, R. and Lewis, M. J. 'The Economic Structure of Cottonopolis: Manchester in 1815', *Textile History*, vol. 17, no. 1 (1986)

—— and Lewis, M. J. 'Ratebooks and Industrial Structure: A technique for Reconstructing the Local Economy', *Local Historian*, vol. 17, no. 5 (1987)

Loasby, B. 'Hypothesis and Paradigms in the Theory of the Firm', *Economic Journal*, vol. 81 (1971)
Lyons, J. 'Vertical Integration in the British Cotton Industry 1825 to 1850', *Journal of Economic History*, vol. 45, no. 2 (1985)
McCulloch, J. R. 'Distress of the Manufacturing Districts: Causes and Remedies', *Edinburgh Review*, vol. clv (1843)
Marglin, S. 'What Do Bosses Do! The Origin and Function of Hierarchy in Capitalist Production', *Review of Radical Political Economy*, vol 6, no. 2 (1974)
Marris, R. 'Why Economics needs a Theory of the Firm', *Economic Journal*, vol. 82 (1972)
Mathias, P. 'Business History and Management Education', *Business History*, vol. XVII, no. 2 (1975)
Mokyr, J. 'Demand and Supply in the Industrial Revolution', *Journal of Economic History*, vol. 37, no. 4 (1977)
Musson, A. E. 'Peel, Williams and Co., ironfounders and engineers of Manchester *c.* 1800–1887', *Transactions of the Lancashire and Cheshire Antiquarian Society*, vol. 69 (1959)
——— 'An Early Engineering Firm: Peel Williams and Co., Manchester', *Business History*, vol. 3 (1960)
——— 'Industrial Motive Power in the U.K. 1800–1870', *Economic History Review*, vol. XXIX, no. 3 (1976)
——— 'British Industrial Revolution', *History*, vol. LXVII (1982)
Nightingale, J. 'On the definition of Industry and Market', *Journal of Industrial Economics*, vol. XXVII (1978)
Redford, A. 'Some Problems of the Manchester Merchants After the Napoleonic Wars', *Transactions of the Manchester Statistical Society* (1930/31)
Rosenberg, N. and Frischtak, C. R. 'Technological Innovation and Long Waves', *Cambridge Journal of Economics*, vol. 18 (1984)
Samuel, R. 'The Workshop of the World: Steam Power and Hand Technology in mid-Victorian Britain', *History Workshop*, issue 3, no. 2 (1977)
Seed, J. 'Unitarianism, Political Economy and the Antinomies of Liberal Culture in Manchester', *Social History*, vol. 7, no. 1 (1982)
Shen, T. Y. 'Economies of Scale, Penrose Effect, Growth of Plant and Their Size Distribution', *Journal of Political Economy*, vol. 78 (1970)
Smith, R. 'Manchester as a Centre for Manufacturing and Merchanting of Cotton Goods, 1820 to 1830', *University of Birmingham Historical Journal*, vol. IV (1953–4)

Index

For Product Safety Concerns and Information please contact our EU representative GPSR@taylorandfrancis.com Taylor & Francis Verlag GmbH, Kaufingerstraße 24, 80331 München, Germany

Batch number: 10725802

Printed by Printforce, the Netherlands